PRAISE FOR BARRY NEWMAN

TONY HORWITZ (Pulitzer Prize winning former *Wall Street Journal* reporter whose books include *Confederates in the Attic* and *Baghdad Without A Map*)

❝ Barry Newman is better at 'getting the color' than any journalist I know. Now, in this album of his quirkiest hits—on pickled herring, foreskin restoration, guillotining bagels, and other scoops from around the globe—he gives us tips and color commentary on the craft he's honed over 40 years. Read, laugh, and learn from an unmatched pro. ❞

VAUHINI VARA (*The New Yorker*)

❝ Barry Newman is known as a legend among reporters at the *Wall Street Journal* and well beyond—one of the finest, and funniest, writers in modern American journalism. *News to Me* not only collects some of his most delightful stories but also offers rare and important insights into how he discovered, reported, and wrote them. It takes a lot of hard work to make storytelling look as effortless as Newman does. ❞

MATT MURRAY (Deputy Editor in Chief, *The Wall Street Journal*)

❝ Newman is a nonpareil, the master of micro-detail who can make any subject compelling, from the noble to the nitpicky. He is the writer whose stories we gobbled up first, the one we all aspired to be. Thank goodness he has decided to spill some of his secrets. ❞

CONOR DOUGHERTY (Reporter, *The New York Times*)

❝ There are generations of people, like me, whose idea of what a story could be—or even what journalism could be—was redefined by Barry's work. ❞ (*As told to Jim Romenesko*)

MIKE WILLIAMS (Reuters Global Enterprise Editor)

❝ Barry Newman, the best feature writer the *Wall Street Journal* ever had, has produced a book on writing. It isn't for everyone—just for journalists who, like him, insist on being unique. If you follow his advice, you will, like him, be a pain in the ass to your editors. That's their problem. Given how perishable routine stories are in the digital age, uniqueness is now more important for journalists than ever. ❞

BILL GRUESKIN (Professor, Columbia Journalism School; Executive Editor/Training, Bloomberg News)

" Barry Newman started off covering metals and mining for the *Wall Street Journal*, and thank heavens, he didn't last long on that beat. Instead, he headed off to write brilliantly composed and deeply reported features, on everything from the greasepots of Chinatown's restaurants in New York to the 3,488-mile fence that keeps out dingoes in Australia. Now he reveals how he comes up with and executes such brilliant ideas, to the great benefit of journalists, those who love them and those who want to be them. "

ALEX MARTIN (Page-One Editor, *The Wall Street Journal*)

" Barry Newman makes newspaper stories joyously offbeat events. And he makes them from so many different things: fish, Grape-Nuts, bicycles and lamps, just shelves and shelves of lamps. All the while, he has made it plain to editors that he knew just what he was doing, thank you very much. The stories, and now this revealing book, prove he indeed does. "

DOUGLAS A. BLACKMON (winner of the Pulitzer Prize for *Slavery by Another Name* and former *Wall Street Journal* bureau chief)

" Barry Newman is some kind of pen-in-hand superhero—endowed with a power unlike any other journalist to survive the apocalypse that wiped out almost everything that was ever enchanting in American newspapers. He has not only endured the editors, hacks, billionaires and web designers who spoiled the art of publishing newspapers, he is still writing, still charming every reader, and in *News to Me* showing everyone who cares about words the quiet magic that makes them sing. "

KEN WELLS (former *Wall Street Journal* Page One Editor, editor of *Floating Off the Page* and *Herd on the Street*)

" The first time I read a Barry Newman story on Page One of the *Wall Street Journal*, I was so jealous of its wit, clarity, vision and pace that I wanted to punch the guy. Who tells stories like that in under 1,500 words? Nobody. He's the master. "

News to Me

Finding and Writing
Colorful Feature Stories

BARRY NEWMAN

The City University of New York
CUNYJOURNALISM
PRESS

CUNY JOURNALISM PRESS IS THE ACADEMIC IMPRINT OF THE CUNY GRADUATE
SCHOOL OF JOURNALISM, PART OF THE CITY UNIVERSITY OF NEW YORK
219 WEST 40TH STREET, NEW YORK, NY 10018
WWW.PRESS.JOURNALISM.CUNY.EDU

First printing 2015

Cataloging-in-Publication data is available from the Library of Congress.
A catalog record for this book is available from the British Library.

ISBN 978-1-939293-83-1 paperback
ISBN 978-1-939293-84-8 e-book

Cover and text design by Bathcat Ltd. Typeset by CBIGS Group, Chennai, India.
Printed by BookMobile in the United States and CPI Books Ltd in the United
Kingdom.

Contents

For Isaac and Arkady

INTRODUCTION
by Barry Newman

I is a word I haven't used more than half a dozen times in the stories I've written in four-and-a-half decades as a reporter. In this book, I've used *I* five times so far and I'll use it a lot more. *You* is a word I haven't used much in my stories, either, and in this book I'll use *you* hardly at all. It's bossy: If you want to know how to write the way I write, here's how you do it. Bossy. You know what I mean?

I've never been an editor or a bureau chief, or a teacher or a critic. I'm a machine operator. I bang keys to make words. Here, I'm an exhibit. My stories are short enough to be reprinted in full. I've been re-reading them, rooting through my notes, interviewing myself. I turned out to be a fairly cooperative subject, and have put my answers into a set of non-bossy essays for journalists, journalism students, and anyone who might wonder how a reporter like me does the job, and how to produce the kind of feature that prompts readers to ask others, "Hey, did you see that story?" I hope some reporters and writers—including would-be journalists—will use the things I've learned about my work to make their own work better, and possibly fun.

When I got hired by the *Wall Street Journal* in 1970, the paper was running three stories a day on Page One. My editors told me that if I wanted to write Page One stories, I had to go out and get "the color." I wanted to write Page One stories, so I went out and got it. Later, stories like the ones I was doing acquired a label: "Literary Journalism." Now it's "Narrative Nonfiction," "Creative Nonfiction," "Narrative Journalism" and "Longform." Whatever. I try to describe places, get people talking to each other, cut from scene to scene, and explain what's happening in omniscient asides.

Novelists do that. So did the writers of the TV cowboy shows I watched when I was a kid. Before the *Journal* began running color pictures, it had an advertising slogan: "We save the color for the writing." Literature. Narrative. Longform. It's still about going out and getting the color.

The stories in this book are easier to define by what they're not: They're not news. They're news to me, I should say, but not to a lot of other reporters. Paul Steiger, the *Journal*'s long-serving managing editor, might call them "permanent scoops." Ten reporters covering a flood in Ohio ought to write ten similar stories. Ten reporters covering the pickled-herring caves of Kungshamn should write ten stories that are totally different. At the *Journal*, I was told to look for subjects that got me excited. If I got excited, I would excite my readers. That's my guiding principle in the hunt for story ideas that takes up the chapters in Part One of this book, and a big part of my life. I remember the story that first excited me about working for the *Journal*. It ran on Page One, four months before I started at the paper. The opening line: "Doris McCarley's wart went away the other day." The reporter was John E. Cooney. I can't say for sure, but I suspect Cooney had a wart.

Magazines still tell engrossing stories with the kind of tools I've sharpened, as do an expanding cluster of websites. Among newspapers, the *Journal* has been a rarity, especially in the fluff department. I'm not a humor columnist. I don't make fluff up. I'm a reporter, and though my inquiry into New Jersey's naming of a "state dirt" was meant to be funny, the paper held it to the standard of reportorial rigor it applies to the Fed's interest-rate projections. Part Two contains advice on reporting, such as: Pick up brochures at airports; use a pencil when it's freezing outside because ballpoint pens won't work; don't try to fool the CIA.

Reporting without thinking about writing is like going to the supermarket to buy food for dinner without thinking about the menu. If I plan to cook my special fried rice, I better buy the bean sprouts. If I plan to write about suburbanites who mow lawns with scythes, I better watch a suburbanite mow a lawn with a scythe. Part Three recounts some ways I shop at the reportorial super-market. Then comes Part Four—the hard part: sitting at a desk in a mess of notes, documents and hyperlinks, and writing a story worth reading.

Writers evolve their own habits and methodologies. I didn't go to journalism school and I'm no student of how-to manuals. I have dipped into the *Paris Review*'s "Writers at Work" series, where great novelists answer questions about how many words they write in a day, which Bible verses get them started, and whether doodling helps. My drawback in reading interviews with great novelists is that I haven't read enough of their great novels. My own stories might not be great, but they do slip snugly between my ruminations. So this book is a convenient twofer: stories and ruminations in one. The idea was tossed my way by Tim Harper, who runs CUNY Journalism Press, at a time when it's popular to worry that longform literary narrative—going out and getting the color—is on trial for its life. I'm pleased to submit myself as evidence for the defense.

PART ONE

IDEAS

Chapter 1
ESCAPE FROM HISTORY

The famous journalist Theodore H. White published a memoir in 1978 called *In Search of History*. If I ever write a memoir, I'll call it *Escape From History*. White wrote of himself (in third-person imperious), "If men made history, he would seek them out." Make mine read: "When he got a whiff of a history maker, he'd run like hell."

For a newspaper reporter, this isn't a positive attitude. News excited me from age 12 to 24. After that, we drifted apart. One reason was the beat I was assigned when the *Wall Street Journal* hired me: metals and mining. Steel and coal were off-limits—too important. My metals were nonferrous. Much as I enjoyed breathing smelter fumes in Arizona and standing at the edge of a big hole in Montana, my favorite nonferrous find was Merle Zweifel, an "old prospector" in Shawnee, Oklahoma.

Zweifel staked claims to the minerals under several hundred million acres of federal land. "I do have a lust for money, and I know that's a sin, and I hate myself for it," Zweifel said when I paid him a visit. He didn't plan to dig for anything, just to con mining companies into paying him off to get rid of him. The story ran with the flashline: "Never Mined."

Most of my days on the metals beat were spent soldered to a desk in New York, telling the world that the copper price had gone down or up, or the lead price had gone up or down. For relief, I did a story on a "resilient byproduct" of the goose trade, just for the chance to begin it with, "Down is up."

My escape hatch from zinc bulletins was to sneak out to do as many non-nonferrous stories as I could. Some colleagues at the coal face didn't appreciate that, but the higher-ups appeared to. One day in 1973, I was closeted in the *Journal*'s writing room when Glynn Mapes, the bureau chief, leaned in and said, "You're off metals." I asked what I'd be doing next. He said, "Whatever you want."

My "whatever" was anything other than daily news. I didn't lose my thirst for front-page bylines, but the *Journal* back then was a magazine wrapped around a bulletin board for business. Some Page One stories took weeks to do. They were more often about things that had been happening for ages, or might happen next year, than about things that happened yesterday. Office workers read their hometown papers at breakfast and didn't see the *Journal* until they got to work. By then, they already knew what happened yesterday. They scanned the business reports and read Page One at home after dinner.

Some might think, as I do, that those timelessly surprising stories would continue to thrive in the digital age, now that everybody knows what happened yesterday before yesterday is over.

When the *Journal* sent me to Singapore, I had a beat, too. It was less restrictive than nonferrous metals: South Asia, Southeast Asia, and Australasia (including the South Pacific). Nothing much happened: Vietnamese refugees, Cambodian genocide. I filed features, no news. Something made me want to stand clear of the journalistic pack. I couldn't win the daily race; the more I cared about writing, the more slowly I wrote. I found breathing room among the slow-lane stories that the pack raced past.

In the New Hebrides, a string of Pacific islands about to be freed from the "pandemonium" of British-French ownership, I learned a lesson in the hazards of interviewing prime ministers. The prime-ministerial interview was a trap I preferred to avoid, but those islands were so tiny, there was almost nobody else to talk to.

At the man's office, I was kept waiting. Imagine, a journalist from the United States of America comes to this little island and is made to sit for an hour? The minister of education appeared at last. "The PM is tied up with violence," he said. A small revolution had broken out on an outlying island. The PM had to go. How nice of the education minister to let me know. I folded the news into my story, which the *Journal* ran two months later.

By 1986, when I began covering Eastern Europe, I had come down with a deep aversion to big shots, a condition that responded poorly to the fall of communism. I did once interview a prime minister by mistake. On August 19, 1991, I woke up in Warsaw to hear on the radio that Soviet apparatchiks were overthrowing Mikhail Gorbachev. I figured I had to write something. I'd seen a poster for Double Delight, a Russian band playing the Hotel Victoria. What would they do now? Rush home? Seek asylum? I decided to profile the band.

My phone rang. It was a man from the office of the Polish prime minister. The prime minister wanted urgently to give an exclusive interview to the *Washington Post*, the man said. I hesitated. I wanted to meet Double Delight. But, dammit, I had to do the honorable thing. I went to interview the prime minister.

While he and George H.W. Bush yakked on the phone, I stirred my tea. When they hung up, the prime minister fed me the usual quotes. I gave him my *Wall Street Journal* card; he seemed not to notice that it didn't say *Washington Post*. I filed my news story, then knocked on Double Delight's dressing-room door.

"Gorbachev should have been removed a long time ago, but not by these people," the guitarist told me. If only the prime minister had said that. I worked quickly for a change, and the band's story ran on Page One a day later, in time for the Soviet coup's collapse.

This compulsion to escape politicians, other journalists, and news eventually resolved itself in a gusher of story ideas— or inverse story ideas. If the pack went after a story, I'd go after its opposite. During one year, back in the U.S., I only did stories about "lonely causes," on the theory that people who couldn't get anybody to write about them were worth writing about. If not for that series, I bet the *Wall Street Journal* never would have covered the foreskin-restoration movement.

The biggest pack of all runs at the Olympics. I went to four, sitting among the hounds as they typed about their national shot-put and pommel-horse heroes. I conceded sports to the sportswriters and spent a day with the Fair Play Committee, and another with the guy who drops a camera into the pool when divers go off the high board. For readers overdosed on London's Summer Games, my antidote was bobsledding (on concrete) in Lake Placid. For those unable to bear another TV spot on an Olympian with a tragic childhood, I hung out with Hammy McMillan, "skip" of the British curling team. Nothing bad ever happened to Hammy, except for that time his best player didn't show up at a championship because he had to go to a wedding.

Does this mean I'm not a team player? I guess so, but escaping from history—the first draft of it, anyhow—can expose larger truths. Home after 21 years abroad, I had a new beat: immigration. The pack stereotyped immigrants as wretched refuse in dirty jobs. I wanted to prove that the system didn't discriminate: It screwed rich immigrants, too. I profiled a Swiss couple banned from retiring to a cabin in Utah, and a German family at risk of deportation from the Texas bed-and-breakfast they owned. I interviewed a Russian doctor who was granted a Green Card in return for his collection of Central Asian stool samples. And when the pack converged on the Mexican border, I went the other way—to search for the one with Canada.

. . . .

Looking For America

BEEBE PLAIN, VERMONT

Kyle Hipsley, a chain-smoking 52-year-old Iowan, has spent 20 summers looking for America. More often than not, he has trouble finding it.

"The boundary's in those bushes," Hipsley said one morning, driving his rented Dodge along a line of scrub just to the south of the border with Canada. "That's got to be cleared." A mile later, he said, "The boundary's out there in that swamp. Monument's buried in the bog. Been that way for years."

From the Beaufort Sea in Alaska to Passamaquoddy Bay in Maine, Hipsley sees a lot of work to be done on the U.S.-Canadian border. Trained as a geodetic surveyor, he is deputy chief of an organization called the International Boundary Commission. In partnership with Canada, the commission is supposed to stake out the border and keep a 10-foot strip mowed on either side of it. The border is 5,525 miles long.

Aside from Hipsley, the commission's U.S. section has four full-time employees, an unpaid commissioner appointed by the president and a federal budget of $1.4 million. As its diplomats have pointed out to the State Department, Canada contributes nearly twice as much money, putting the U.S. in violation of the 1925 Treaty of Washington, which obliges each country to chip in the same amount. Mowing the grass between the U.S. and Canada, though, doesn't weigh heavily in the arena of border security. With the collapse of its immigration overhaul, the U.S. is promising to keep on spending billions for guards, fences, radar towers and robot airplanes. The focus is on the dry expanses of the Mexican border, where weed whacking isn't the main issue.

Meanwhile, the Boundary Commission—whose officials think it's probably the smallest and poorest independent agency in the federal government—is still working with the maps it drew up in 1937. It often has trouble finding the Canadian border, much less mowing it.

"They talk about securing the border; well, nobody ever came to talk to us," Hipsley said. He circled around Lake Memphremagog, just west of Beebe Plain, turned north up a dirt road and stopped at a border gate with a rusty padlock on it. "That's what we don't understand. What could be the most basic thing you'd think of? How can you protect it if you can't see it?"

Hipsley got out of the car and jumped the gate. "That'll shake 'em up," he said. "Border Patrol will be here in a minute."

He knew the roadway had sensors buried in it, products of heightened post-9/11 vigilance. There were cameras in the trees, too. But where the road fell off into a gully running down to the lake, the undergrowth was 10 feet high. "If the camera's up on a pole, nobody's going to see you," Hipsley said. "There's no way. You just walk on through."

Between 2001 and 2006, the Border Patrol caught 56,883 people sneaking into the U.S. from Canada. Most came from countries where a Canadian visa is easier to get than an American one. In this sector, a 295-mile stretch from New Hampshire to Ogdensburg, N.Y., the patrol caught 12,334. With instructions from a smuggler, the interlopers usually tramp through the brush to a waiting car. Once, Hipsley ran into a family of Russians at this very spot. They were looking for a bus ride to New York City.

He leaned against the gate and smoked until a patrol car pulled up. After Hipsley showed his diplomatic passport and explained the commission's treaty obligations, the Border Patrol officer said, "You going to hire little kids to get out here with lawn mowers?"

In another thicket—the political one—the job of explaining treaties passes to Hipsley's boss, Dennis Schornack. Schornack, 55, was Commissioner of Low-Level Radioactive Waste for John Engler, the former Michigan governor and friend of President Bush. After the 2000 election, he remembers, "Word came around—anybody interested in presidential appointments? I said, 'Yeah.'"

Schornack got a paying job monitoring U.S.-Canadian water disputes, which automatically elevated him to Boundary Commissioner as well. He has since made the Washington rounds, expounding on how the Treaties of Paris (1783) and Ghent (1814), the Ashburton-Webster Treaty (1842) and the treaty of 1925 all require the U.S. and Canada to shell out equally to cut the grass on the border.

"I'm not allowed to lobby, but I'm allowed to beg," the commissioner said. "I'm on my knees to everybody who'll listen. They make sympathetic sounds, lots of clucking, but nothing happens."

The Homeland Security Department confirms that Schornack has come calling. On the matter of cash, though, a spokeswoman will only say, "We fully support the president's budget." The Department of State, aware of Canada's protest, responded with a statement: "The U.S. agrees," it said, that the commission "could benefit from additional funds," and the department is "currently considering ways of assisting the commission in securing these."

It's enough to try Schornack's diplomatic skills. "If you're out hunting moose," he said, "you need to know where the boundary is, right? So you can say, uh-oh, I'm stepping into another country, right? Because it's different laws and all that stuff, right?"

That was the general idea 82 years ago when the U.S. and Canada agreed to cut "a clear vista to the sky" along their border and mark it with 8,600 monuments. But monuments get shot up by hunters. On the Alaskan tundra, they freeze and bust open. Prairie winds erode them and they fall over. In the Rockies, avalanches wipe them out.

The commission's contractors cleared the vista with herbicides at first, but during the Vietnam War a rumor got around that they were using Agent Orange. That was it for herbicides. Now the crews go in with bulldozers where they can. Where they can't, they go by helicopter and canoe, wielding chain saws and machetes alongside their lawn mowers and WeedWackers.

That costs. Even with Canada's $2.4 million, the Boundary Commission has dropped hundreds of miles behind in its work. On quite a few stretches, in fact, the border sometimes gets lost.

"By the looks of it, the stream's taken a turn into the U.S.," said Joseph Harrietha, Canada's head border surveyor. Toward the end of a long day's work, Harrietha, 44, was standing ankle-deep in water about 35 miles east of Beebe Plain, consulting a GPS navigator and squinting at a 70-year-old map. "Canada?" he said. "Well, it's over there. I have a feeling."

At Canada's expense, he and an 11-man crew are spending all summer on one of the Boundary Commission's priority projects: trying to locate the border between Quebec and New Hampshire.

In 1842, it was fixed for 20 miles along the center of Hall's Stream. In 1908, the commission set about marking it. But Hall's Stream hasn't stayed put. It has meandered—100 yards into Canada here, 200 yards into the U.S. there. The original stream bed is still the official border, but now it's dry, squiggling through dense woods.

The commission has never cleared it. Harrietha bets the Border Patrol hasn't put in any cameras, either.

Tromping through the brush, he came upon a cast-iron obelisk in an earth-crusted concrete base. Hours earlier, his crew had dug it out of the mud. Harrietha picked up a twig, scraped away some crust and exposed an inscription: "Renewed, 1916."

"This needs some attention," he said. Noting its coordinates, Harrietha rolled up his map and slogged on, looking for America in the overgrown old bed of Hall's Stream.

2007

Chapter 2
HUH?

Huh?

　Or, to put it another way: What the...? This can't be serious! Incredulity clangs the story bells. My "Huh?" reflex has normal adolescent roots nurtured by puddles of rubber vomit. My boyhood friends grew out of it. I grew into it, then on to man-bites-dog, which brought me to journalism. Reversals and contradictions make me laugh. When a man bites a dog, it's funny. The dog and the man may not think so, but readers might. At the urging of a philosopher I knew, I did a story about unemployed philosophers. One job hunter's qualification was his solution to the paradox of "the heap." He proved, as I wrote, "that if you have a bowl with 'a lot' of nuts in it and you take away one nut at a time, you will eventually arrive at a point where you no longer have 'a lot' of nuts." Readers, at least the ones who weren't philosophers, thought that was funny.

　My ignorance has never deserted me. Innocently abroad, I had no deeper knowledge of where I was than the typical subscriber I was told to write for: the dentist in Akron. When I met villagers living on the lip of a Javanese volcano, or societies of marching women in New Zealand, the dentist's undoubted dumbfoundedness was my own. I read a lot, talked to experts, but none of that diminished my shock on arriving at the huge nudist camp in Koversada, Croatia, to discover that a quarter of the naked city's population was "brazenly strutting about in a flagrant state of dress."

　The story bells don't clang for me when publicity pros pull the rope. No, I did not respond to the press release for "Psoriasis Awareness Month." I did write a profile of Todd Brabender, the public-relations man who sent me (and many others) a release about the Fish 'n Flush toilet fish tank. Brabender was a "Huh?" story in himself, but promoters of cute contests and Guinness-variety records leave me catatonic. I prefer people with reasonable reasons for doing cockeyed things, such as running a race track without horses in Kuala Lumpur because it's legal, or filming a Parisian mystery with English actors in Budapest because it's cheap.

In step with generations of returning expats, I came home to a nation littered with absurdities that seemed to be invisible to my fellow Americans. Fresh off the plane, working on a story about a new Dutch-built terminal at JFK, it hit me that the airport had an International Arrivals Building but none for departures. "America doesn't name buildings after quitters," I wrote. I'd been away a long time, and nothing set off my "Huh?" reflex more than the gravity of America's engagement with silliness.

As communism fell tumultuously in Poland, I asked a man in Warsaw for his views. "It's normal," he said dryly. Normal? How could a revolution be normal? "It's normal," the man said, "for a revolution." In the United States an answer that limp would insult the national character. When Americans feel something, they feel it strongly. Johns Hopkins University had an ineffably earnest professor of civility. A Savannah recluse wrote a book about his own unimpeachable cure for toenail fungus. "Huh?"

Like Ross Brodar, an outsider artist who sold pictures on the street because he couldn't get inside the Outsider Art Fair, outside is my favorite place. Outsiders don't play the game and don't care who wins. A reporter in the game—politics, art, business, science, sports, war, fashion—hesitates to report its folly. A diplomat once told me I had done a "disservice" to diplomacy by reporting that diplomats at a conference in Caracas were visiting a whorehouse. I told him I was serving people who buy a newspaper, not diplomacy.

The object of the game isn't ridicule. An idea born of my own ignorance, as most of my "Huh?" stories are, can unfold into understanding. When I heard that Dr. Subhas Mukerji was busy making test-tube babies in Calcutta, I raced to watch him bite that dog; when I learned that his hidden purpose was birth control, I felt enlightened. Kenyon Smith was an "Aquamaid," a male synchronized swimmer. The instant he hit the water, I knew he was a fine athlete, barred unfairly from the Olympics. My story didn't make a mockery of Kenyon; it made a mockery of the people who mocked him.

The *Journal* has a Web page where reporters post their beats. Not having a beat, I listed mine as "greeting cards," a joke that led me to the press releases of the Greeting Card Association. One of them announced that the Postal Service was charging an extra 17 cents to mail a square envelope. Huh? The greetings lobby condemned the square surcharge as shape-based bias. Touring a mail processing operation in Buffalo with a publisher of square greeting cards, I expected to hear him heap derision on the Postal Service. Yet something came over the man as he watched the "ballet of the mail" flowing around on the center's conveyor belts. He seemed to comprehend what it was that made square envelopes irregular, and why the square surcharge wasn't ridiculous after all. While I walked behind him, taking notes, he actually came to the belief that the post office was a beautiful place. I was incredulous.

. . . .

Square Envelopes

BUFFALO, NEW YORK

The square has four equal sides and four right angles. It is a regular shape. To the U.S. Postal Service, however, the square is "unusual." Its sorting machines, built for oblongs, can't find the address on a square envelope. People have to do it. That's why the post office imposes the square surcharge.

The square surcharge has been around since machine sorting began in 1979, yet even those who knew about it rarely knew how many stamps to put on a square letter. Postal clerks often didn't know, either, so square letters mostly got delivered anyway.

Then last May, the post office launched a "shape-based" initiative to discourage square-envelope abuse. Mailing a one-ounce oblong costs 41 cents. A one-ounce square costs 58 cents, including a 17-cent surcharge for squareness. At a Manhattan post office, a window clerk named Thomas Merritt took one look at a square envelope and said, "Nonmachinable. I would not use that shape, period."

Among square-envelope advocates, such sentiments elicit few best wishes. Alan Friedman, for one, is sending the post office no valentines. Friedman owns Great Arrow Graphics, a company housed in a former windshield-wiper factory here in Buffalo. Great Arrow makes greeting cards. Square greeting cards.

"Squares," Friedman said one rainy Tuesday, "are the most current and most exciting product in paper communications." He was on his shop floor, where printmakers were mixing inks, inking silk-screens and stacking racks of cards for Christmas. Several cards had drawings on them of round ornaments. "Look at the interplay between the circle and the square," said Friedman, holding one up. "It's the aesthetic, the balance. Such a compelling format."

Of the seven billion greeting cards Americans buy each year, squares are a disadvantaged minority, confined to remote corners at American Greetings and Hallmark Cards. Companies that rely on squares, like Friedman's, feel victimized by postal shapism. It's bad enough when grandma's birthday card comes back stamped "postage due." It's worse when grandma herself has to pay the extra 17 cents. Afraid of deflating card-customer cheeriness, some card shops are chucking their squares into the circular file.

"Square cards went over big right away," says Stacy Bock, a San Francisco sales rep for Great Arrow. "Then the post office cracked down and there was this spasm. People had bad experiences with square cards. If you put a stigma on something long enough, retailers aren't going to deal with it anymore." Bock adds: "The poor square. It's such a beautiful thing."

At Oblong Books & Music in the downstate village of Millerton, N.Y., the card rack held only one square birthday card on a recent Sunday. It was imported from the United Kingdom, where the Royal Mail still recognizes equilateral equality.

"Squares are nice, but they're too much trouble," said Oblong's manager, Lisa Wright. Millerton is situated in The Oblong, an oblong-shaped strip along the Connecticut border. "We've had to phase them out," Wright said. "It's really very obnoxious of the post office to charge extra for squares."

That was the emotion the Greeting Card Association tried to convey, cordially, at the Postal Regulatory Commission's hearings in Washington last year on the push for shape-based postage. It called on Andrea Sue Liss, founder of Hannah Handmade Cards in Evanston, Ill., who testified to "the novelty of the square" and its "basic appeal to people beyond what they might put into words."

Plato, Liss told the commission, "regarded the square as being absolutely beautiful in itself." The Romans, she noted, based many buildings "on the geometry of the square and its diagonal, the ad quadratum." She quoted Carl Jung, the founder of analytical psychology, who wrote: "The frequency with which the square and the circle appear must not be overlooked." Squares, said Liss, embody "traditional symbolic meanings," including honesty, stability, integrity, morality and solidarity.

At the Postal Service, however, squares embody extra handling. Its official philosophy, derived from decades of debate with mass mailers, is that envelopes needing extra handling need extra postage.

At Great Arrow Graphics, these tidings weren't glad. From 60 square cards for Christmas, Friedman's silk-screeners are down to nine this year. Other greeting-worthy occasions have been fully oblongated: for instance, death. "Nobody wants sympathy cards returned," says Friedman. "We don't mess with sympathy." In his sympathy line, only pet sympathy is still square.

Some square Great Arrow designs are being printed now on oblong cards. For those remaining, the shop has devised an oblong envelope with a middle pocket that squares slip neatly into. A 41-cent stamp is all they need. Friedman's sets of square Christmas cards with oblong envelopes are going on sale this season in oblong boxes.

"We're just trying to avoid the whole debacle," he says. Yet Friedman is a man of goodwill whose thoughts about the Postal Service are as kind as those expressed in his greeting cards—with an added twinkle of bemused curiosity. Which is why he was happy to leave his shop early this day for a drive across town and a visit to the USPS Buffalo Processing and Distribution Center.

"The post office is caring," Friedman said, walking up a ramp from the parking lot. "It embraces its neighbors. One of its quaint beauties is that you never quite know what's going to happen. If everything worked like clockwork, it wouldn't be enough fun." He passed through a set of doors into a 500,000-square-foot room and shook hands with Tony Mazurkiewicz, manager of in-plant support.

"I'm fascinated to see what makes square envelopes so hard for you," said Friedman. Handing him a shape-based-pricing template, Mazurkiewicz said, "It's the machines."

For an hour, he took Friedman down a trail of belts, bins and troughs, from the dual-pass rough cull, past the advanced facer cancelers to the delivery bar-code readers. Every step had reject pockets. Mazurkiewicz reached in and pulled out the squares.

"Wouldn't you think," Friedman asked, "that a machine could somehow know in an instant if a piece of mail needs to be rotated to read the address? Oops! Upside down. Turn it around. OK."

"In fact, they don't," said Mazurkiewicz. "A square is like an SUV turning a corner. It could be a rollover."

Rectangular envelopes are always knocked down by sorting machines onto one of two long, stable edges. Ink detectors find the stamps: front or back, upper right or lower left. It then takes only two steps—flip and turn—to line them up for a computer to read addresses and spray on bar codes.

But squares land on any one of four edges, not two. So for half of them, mathematically, finding addresses takes four steps. When the machines fail, humans get involved—at a cost, Mazurkiewicz explained, of $52-per-thousand envelopes instead of $4.

"Couldn't you absorb the cost?" Friedman asked, moving along to the manual-sorting area, where senior clerks were slipping non-machinable squares into old-time cubbyholes. As Mazurkiewicz began discussing postal pricing and aspect-ratio differentials, Friedman's focus seemed to drift from his shape-based worries. His eyes settled on the clerks and the cubbyholes.

"I love that letters are touched by people here," he said.

"It costs more money," said Mazurkiewicz, but his guest had wandered off to gaze at a procession of postal trays spiraling upward on a blue conveyor. "The ballet of the mail," Friedman said. He watched for a few more moments and then, with feeling, he added: "The post office really is a very beautiful organization."

2007

Chapter 3

RELATIVES ARE EVERYTHING

If novelists base stories on the lives of families and friends, why can't journalists? Essayists and memoirists do it. I do it, too, indirectly. Schmoozing with strangers at cocktail parties is a bore, but at Thanksgiving, Christmas and Passover, my private familial brain trust keeps the story ideas flowing.

Mom, Dad, girlfriend, ex-wife, daughter, wife, wife's sister, wife's friend's father, stepmother's son—they've all pitched in. My father's cousin Buddy, who was wounded in the Battle of the Bulge, had a brush cut, a sweet smile and a wooden leg. He said "swell" a lot. I sat across from Buddy at a Bronx Thanksgiving in 1971. He told me he was an engineer. What was he building? A vacuum chamber for freeze-drying, he said. For those strawberries in my cereal? No, Buddy said, the vacuum chamber was for a museum looking to cut its taxidermy costs by freeze-drying small animals. Freeze-dried animals! That made Page One. Since that Thanksgiving, I've put a pen and a little notebook into my shirt pocket when I'm invited to a family dinner at a cousin's house.

My friend Joe's friend Mike knew a guy named Milton, up in Maine, who didn't work for a living. I wrote a Page One story about Milton and ended up marrying Milton's girlfriend, Carol, who (through her ex-husband, Fred) knew Bert, an antiques dealer in New York, who introduced me to Jeff, who was searching for folk artists in backwoods North Carolina. Page One again. Dinah, my new wife, is English. She moved to New York and began wading into America's immigration system just as I was assigned to cover it. When a notice arrived informing Dinah that her fingerprints had "expired," the story bells pealed.

Such ideas come with an obligation: trust. I have never made anyone close to me into a main subject. Novelists risk relationships that way; journalists risk ethical lapses. But I'd sooner trust a friend of a friend than a spokesperson of a president. Gatekeepers stand aside when a reporter strolls by with a boss who is a husband of a wife's sister; I walked into an abortion clinic that way. Dinah's friend Teresa, an Italian new to New York, rented a room in a building where the tenants ate dinner together around a kitchen table—a rare, real boarding house. Teresa unlocked its front door, retreated to her room, and left me at the kitchen table with the other boarders, taking notes and eating spinach pie. The father of Dinah's friend Gillian worked for The Macallan distillery, in Scotland. He got the sack in a corporate shuffle and put me in touch with The Macallan's noser. The noser, who got the sack too, worried that the new noser wouldn't know how The Macallan was supposed to smell. He entrusted all his worries to me. Of course he did: I was the future husband of his friend's daughter's friend.

Conversations with strangers stir up stories often enough. A fellow guest at a Colorado dude ranch pulled out a Wisconsin fishing license and told me he was sorry it didn't have a painting of a fish on it anymore; soon I was visiting jobless Wisconsin fish painters. Doctors, barbers, plumbers, exterminators—they all moonlight in idea supply. On a flight from Sydney to Singapore I sat next to an Australian who let it slip that a multinational animal-gut suture maker was angling to enter the Malaysian market for Chinese-sausage casings. He was a highly-placed sausage source, and I would have lost that scoop if I buried myself in thick novels on long flights.

But accidental encounters in motel bars can't match the benefits of familiarity. In 1929, my mother, Emily, got a job as a stenographer at the Paramount New York studios, in Astoria. She was 24 years old and a looker. A paragraph she clipped from *Film Daily* in 1930 says my mom "is often mistaken for a star." She had her picture in *Photoplay Magazine* that year, sitting at a mirror while a man in a white coat painted her eyebrows. In 1931, *Picture Play* ran a photo of her on a set, not facing a camera but beside one, looking dreamy, with a script on her lap and a pen poised over a notepad.

The article's title was "Script Girl." Mom had been promoted out of the steno pool. Now she was a clerk on the sound stage, watching for "continuity errors." The article quotes her: "It's really fascinating work, although it is hard." It goes on, "And woe be to the script girl who gets sleepy and forgets to note down a bit of action. A mistake on her part may cost the company thousands of dollars in retaking scenes."

Forty years after she died, my mother gave me a story idea. Checking a movie listing on the Web, I came across the IMDb "goofs" pages and discovered that most of them were committed by sleepy "script supervisors." They were women now, not girls. Stories about failings don't make for warm interviews, but when Sharon Watt asked what fascinated me about her own failings, I told her that my mom once troubled over continuity, too. In a Brooklyn café, I showed her Emily's scrapbook and a wave of warmth seemed to overcome us both.

"It's a position where people will dislike you a lot," Sharon Watt told me. "I don't want to be the one everybody hates. I want to be the one everybody loves because I'm the one who saved them."

The story I wrote was about a sneezy overweight woman in St. Louis, lying on her living-room couch and playing snatches of CD movies over and over, hunting for goofs. I wish I could have written it about my mom but, as Joe E. Brown once said, nobody's perfect.

. . . .

Continuity

ST. LOUIS

Johnny Depp's fingernails are dirty when he gets drunk on rum and passes out in the movie "Pirates of the Caribbean: The Curse of the Black Pearl." When he wakes up and brings his hands to his face, the fingernails are clean.

Rikki Rosen caught that. She reported it to a website in Britain called Movie Mistakes, which does nothing but list mistakes in movies. While Depp inspects his pirate crew, the sun shines from different directions between cuts. Rosen also caught that mistake. When Depp bites into an apple, the bite mark changes shape from shot to shot. Rosen caught that one, too.

In all, she has reported 293 mistakes in the "Pirates" movie to Movie Mistakes. She has also reported 3,695 mistakes in 181 other movies—including the bit in "War of the Worlds" when Tom Cruise yells "We're under attack!" and it's obvious that the inspection sticker previously on his van's windshield is no longer there.

Rosen is an ample woman, 48 years old, with red hair and a bad cold. Her inner-suburban living room contains couches and cat baskets; an old Sony television with an Xbox under it; tea cups, a computer, and stacks of DVDs. At last count, she was Movie Mistake's No. 2 contributor, behind someone called "Hamster" with 4,413.

"Sure, a movie can have mistakes," she said, curled up under a quilt on her couch one morning. "People are imperfect. But sometimes it's just one after the other after the other. It smacks of not caring. These things should not be blatant on the screen." Rosen suppressed a cough. "So I look," she said. "I look at everything."

Every movie has a paid nitpicker on duty during filming. They were called "script girls," early on, then "continuity clerks," and now "script supervisors." Their role is to ward off the wobbles that make movies less believable. Now DVDs and the Internet have stirred up a nest of equally flub-obsessed volunteers. They nitpick the nitpickers.

Jon Sandys, 31, founder and sole employee of Movie Mistakes, posted a few gems on the Web in 1996 and asked people to send in more. He now lists 85,000 mistakes, among them the Cessna in "Terminator 3" marked "N3035C" on the ground and "N3973F" in the air. "How could they not fix it?" Sandys asks.

At IMDb, his huge rival, "goofs" rank among the top pages viewed by the site's 57 million monthly visitors. Keith Simanton, its editor, caught Julia Roberts eating a croissant in "Pretty Woman" that later turns into a pancake. Lots of others caught her, too. "It's smart people making connections," he says, "being outraged, making sure it's known." Clicking on the names of script supervisors on IMDb cast-and-crew rosters leads to lists of every mistake reported for every movie a script supervisor has ever worked on. It doesn't always enhance the supervisor's self-image.

"They think they see things nobody else sees—it makes them feel clever," says Sharon Watt, 32, an English script supervisor working in New York. "I can explain every one of my mistakes."

Like this one: In "Precious," a 2010 Oscar winner, Gabourey Sidibe steals some fried chicken and runs from a restaurant, leaving her notebook behind. In the next scene, she has a notebook again. In the script, someone gives her a new notebook. The moment was filmed exactly as written. "We shot it," says Watt. But disharmony arose in the production. Someone was fired. Watt left. Three script supervisors succeeded her. In the final cut, the moment when Precious gets a new notebook is gone. "The one person you don't want to change on a shoot is the script supervisor," Watt says. "A movie is like a jigsaw puzzle, and you're the only one who has the cover of the box."

A few supervisors use computers, but most still do the job on paper. They fill scripts with coded markings and keep thick logs of props, locations and costumes. Scenes are hardly ever shot in order. A bruise might have to look old on the set in the morning and fresh on the set in the afternoon. Actors are supposed to synchronize the same words with the same actions in each take and retake.

The idea is to give the film editor material that can be spliced into a coherent whole. Gigantic blunders usually land on the cutting-room floor. Yet if a collar button is missing in an actor's finest performance, an editor might forget about the button to preserve the performance. "If it makes a better story, the audience won't notice," says Michael Taylor, a New York script supervisor turned editor. "We're not assuming that people who watch DVDs will keep going back and forth and back and forth and back and forth."

Taylor obviously hasn't met Rikki Rosen—who was in her living room, feeding "Jaws" into her Xbox.

"That music," she said, watching the credits fade to a close-up of a boy at a beach party. Behind the boy is a guy in a long-sleeved shirt. But in the next wide shot, the sleeves are short.

Rosen hit the pause button and said, "See!"

"Jaws" looked scarily flawless when she first saw it as a teenager in Brooklyn. "I didn't go swimming all summer," Rosen says. Eleven years ago, she moved to St. Louis, where her husband is a salesman. She works at home, illustrating school materials. Her three growing sons got a copy of "Jaws" on DVD. They watched it over and over. So did Rosen.

The more she watched, the more mistakes jumped out—156 to be precise: A leg bitten off barefoot wears a shoe as it sinks to the seabed. A thumbtack changes places on a poster. And those yellow barrels the shark yanks off Quint's boat in the final petrifying sequence:

"Look—two barrels on deck," Rosen said, stopping the action and starting it and stopping it again. "But here—three. Now two! Two on the boat, three in water. Three on the boat, two in the water."

The more mistakes she saw, the less scary "Jaws" became. Rosen calls her insights "cathartic." Since 2007, Movie Mistakes has been her "great de-stresser." When she isn't watching horror movies, Rosen tries to keep her disbelief suspended, as most other moviegoers do, but she can't. Sloppy script supervisors, in her opinion, won't let her do it. "With their little clipboards, they need to stay exactly on top of what an actor is wearing, what is on a table," she said, sipping hot tea. "Certain people have to do a better job. One of my sons said to me, 'Ma, you should be one of these people. You have this eye.'"

To prove it, she teed up "Some Like It Hot," the all-time-great comedy with 51 IMDb goofs. Rosen had seen it once, years ago.

Instantly, she caught the broken (then unbroken) hearse window and the oddly leaky coffin. She saw that Tony Curtis and Jack Lemmon are in room 413 at first, then in 415. She got the rearranged beach chairs, and Marilyn Monroe's disappearing bra strap.

But when the girls in the band run across the sand for a swim, Rosen missed the mountainous backdrop—documented on IMDb—which reveals that the movie was shot in California and not, as the scenario claims, in Florida.

"I wasn't looking," she said, letting out a laugh. "I got carried away with the story."

Well, nobody's perfect.

2010

Chapter 4

NEIGHBORHOOD WATCH

News, all of which is local, begins in my bedroom, expands to my front door, and opens onto my walk to work.

I live in an apartment in Brooklyn, a nice apartment except for the sirens. The *dee-dah dee-dah* sirens of Paris say, "Don't Worry! We're Coming!" New York's sirens shriek: "Get Your Ass Out Of My Way!" When a siren passes under my window, my muscles knot until the wail trails away. I will never get used to sirens, but I had an antidote for what they do to me: Write a story about sirens.

After graduating from college, I got a job at the *New York Times* as a summer substitute night copyboy. A few days into it, when I was at home in Rockaway, my father sent me to buy pumpernickel onion rolls from the bakery on 116th Street. Down the block from the bakery, some guys with signs were walking around and around in front of the surf shop yelling, "We want surf!" I asked one what was going on. He said he and his buddies wanted the city to rope off a stretch of beach for surfboarding. I bought the rolls, went home, typed five paragraphs and phoned them in. The story ran the next day. I can still feel the euphoria. This was the *New York Times*, not the *Rockaway Wave*, and all I did was run into a "demonstration" down the block from the bakery.

The *Times*, in its way, was a local paper. The *Wall Street Journal* was national. Rockaway didn't make national news unless a crowded airplane crashed into it (2001) or a superstorm (2012) roared through it. But even if Rockaway wasn't making headlines, it made stories for me. I grew up watching jet fighters fly out of Floyd Bennett Field, across Jamaica Bay from my house, and then watched that air base collapse into buggy disuse. When the National Park Service opened a campground in Brooklyn, on a weedy Floyd Bennett runway no less, I made it my insider's scoop.

Rockaway has wings. It crosses bays and oceans. In Belle Harbor, my neighborhood, plastic slipcovers protected all couches. I thought they had been recycled into bad jokes long ago, but in Queens decades later I saw a sign on a telephone pole: "Plastic Slipcovers, Custom Made." I found a slipcover factory in Long Island City and visited its customers. One was a woman in a Manhattan apartment with plastic-covered dining-room chairs. I hadn't mentioned my origins when she volunteered: "My father calls it Belle Harbor, 1950s."

I learned to love pickled herring in Rockaway. The pickled herring against which all pickled herring must be measured comes from the Waldbaums on Beach Channel Drive. However, I have a confession: In Sweden, reporting on the international cultural importance of pickled herring, I called my father and asked him to check out the pickled herring in Brooklyn. "A trip to Sweden," my story said, "is the next best thing to standing in front of the appetizing counter at the Waldbaums supermarket on Ocean Avenue, in Brooklyn, breathing deeply."

I'm ashamed to admit it: Brooklyn plays better than Belle Harbor in a national newspaper. I resolved the issue by moving to Brooklyn. Listening to the siren serenade at my bedroom window one morning, I noticed a familiar silhouette in the distance: the Coney Island Parachute Jump—Brooklyn's answer to the Eiffel Tower. The Jump is a pretty thing, shaped like a dandelion. I got into the habit of picking it out on the horizon. One morning, five years later, it wasn't there. The Parachute Jump was gone! Temporarily, it developed, but I got a story, and all I did to get it was look out my bedroom window.

Something probably fell off my apartment house and landed on the sidewalk because, on another morning, a scaffold went up. I had to walk under it to get to the front door. A phenomenon I'd noticed all over New York had turned personal: Hundreds of buildings were being girdled by "sidewalk bridges." The city looked like East Berlin. Once installed, these bridges stayed and stayed. The one on my building was up for a year when I decided to find out why. My first paragraph: "What goes up must come down. But *when*?"

The walk from my front door to the subway takes me around Grand Army Plaza, Brooklyn's answer to l'Étoile. A bust of John F. Kennedy stood at the Plaza's north end. One morning, JFK was gone, like the Parachute Jump. I visited the sculptor to find out what happened to JFK, got a story, and in the process learned that a statue of Abraham Lincoln had also disappeared from the Plaza a century earlier. The city was planning to bring Abe back, but to make room for him, it would have to evict a bust of Alexander Skene, a Scottish gynecologist who moved to Brooklyn and discovered the G-spot. I knew about Skene because both my wife's sister and her husband are gynecologists in Scotland. My Lincoln-Skene story was family-neighborhood combo.

When an idea hits me where I live, physically and emotionally, it comes with background and context built in. A reporter from a foreign country, or from the next block, can only get that second hand. Staring out a window, walking a street, I notice things that trip memories and cohere into ideas. I haven't been free to write in the first person, but I think in it. When I was a kid, the seltzer-man delivered every week. I can hear his footfalls on our basement steps—a full crate carried in, the rattling empties carried out. Walking to the subway on a rainy Brooklyn morning, I caught sight of a seltzer truck, a vision of the ones that creaked to a stop in front of my house in Rockaway. Ronny Beberman was still delivering the glass.

· · · · · · · · · · · · · · · · · ·

The Spritz Mystique

BROOKLYN, NEW YORK

Spritzed by Flatbush Avenue traffic on a wet morning, the last known seltzer truck in New York City was a double-parked apparition, its tiers of lopsided racks holding a cockeyed pile of siphon bottles in cracked, wooden crates.

Arnold Brenner, a psychoanalyst walking to work, spotted the truck just as Ronny Beberman, the seltzerman, was wheeling a delivery toward an apartment-house door. Brenner yelled, "How much is a..." But Beberman was already inside.

Brenner stood unactualized on the sidewalk. "I was thinking I could get a case," he said. "It's the spritz that does it—that fizz—so soothing, so strong. Reminiscent of something, something romantic."

Ronny Beberman has his own analysis of the spritz mystique: Because nobody wants it anymore, seltzer has become desirable.

"People, they don't know what seltzer is," he says. "They moved from Iowa. They ask me, 'What's in those bottles?' I have people, they chase me in their cars. They're disenchanted. They're drinking out of plastic."

Beberman, 56 years old, has worked in the seltzer zone since 1971. The zone covers New York and parts of the northeast. Beyond the zone, seltzer sells as sparkling water. Club soda is seltzer with salt (unless the salt is left out). Water that bubbles out of the ground isn't called seltzer—it has swanky names and high prices. It's all basically water with gas.

True seltzer—seltzer that assaults the sinuses—comes in rare old siphon bottles. Outside Argentina, it's almost impossible to buy new ones. Beberman maintains a private reserve. So do the 10 or so other seltzermen left in New York City. The city once had hundreds, sometimes three to a block. Their ranks have been thinning for 40 years, ever since the beverage business started replacing bottles too expensive to throw out with bottles too flimsy to refill.

There is still one seltzer company in Pittsburgh, there's another in Florida and a couple in California. Connecticut has an operator called Castle Seltzer. All deliver out of ordinary vans. The seltzer truck belongs to Ronny Beberman.

"If he has the last real seltzer truck, he's the last real seltzerman," Ann McIver said while Beberman crouched in her kitchen, replacing empties. McIver comes from Texas. She gets seltzer delivered because "the bottles are beautiful."

Back behind the wheel, Beberman said: "People tell me, 'Why aren't you in the Yellow Pages?' I say, 'Because I get customers off the street.' The truck sells seltzer. I will never give up this truck."

He bought his first truck 32 years ago and changed the chassis three times before it all rotted away. He got this truck four years ago, when another seltzerman gave up his route. The first truck had four tiers of racks and side doors that opened out. This one has two tiers and side doors on tracks that are stuck open. A drive across the Brooklyn Bridge could risk a seltzer slide. Therefore, Beberman won't go to Manhattan.

Lucky for him, Brooklyn is the only place left in the city where you can get seltzer bottles refilled. Beberman shows up at Gomberg Seltzer Works in Canarsie five days a week, just as Kenny Gomberg is eating lunch. "He waits until I finish," says Gomberg, whose grandparents opened the works 50 years ago.

On the seltzer-room floor, New York's seltzermen stack their "glass." The bottles are thick, the seamless ones hand-blown, prewar, in Czechoslovakia. Metal heads and acid-etched bodies carry the names of seltzermen past. But bottles break. Heads get switched. So Cohen's head has Rubin's body, and Abramson's body has Dickstein's head. A few live seltzermen label their own glass. Beberman doesn't bother.

One Friday (after lunch), he stood watching as Gomberg and his seltzer master, Luis Machica, turned on the seltzer works.

Quality tap water from pristine upstate reservoirs began mixing with pure carbon dioxide. Then it hissed into "the Monitor," a bottling machine that "ensures a supremely perfect product," according to its British maker's 1937 catalog. Like a ball player about to bat, Machica quickly crossed himself and stepped up to the machine.

"Bottles blow," he said. "Blow like shotguns."

He threw a lever and a center column started to revolve. He set an empty into a passing cradle, a piston forced the nozzle up into a brass spigot, and after a few quick spritzes, the bottle was full. Then the Monitor sprang a leak. Seltzer squirted skyward. Gomberg rushed in.

"You got to adjust it," he said, working against the spray. Machica said, "No, you got to replace it."

In seltzer circles, it is agreed that two things finally murdered the seltzerman: working women and locked doors. Beberman takes cash only: $15 for a 10-bottle case of 26-ounce bottles. To catch spritz aficionados and their money before they leave for work, he and his truck have to hit the streets by 4:30 a.m. rain or shine. On this day it was rain.

Double-parked on a street of high-stooped brownstones, Beberman lugged a case to a basement door and rang the bell. He works a six-day week. He isn't big. He has a bad shoulder. A case weighs 75 pounds. He waited. No answer. He rang a bell two doors down and waited again. No answer. He got back in the truck, drove around the corner and rang Aldo Bianchi's bell. Bianchi opened up.

"A seltzer bottle on the table—always a point of comment," he said, letting Beberman in. Paying, Bianchi added: "I must say, there is some concern about the health issue. The bottling. The cleansing."

In the truck, Beberman said: "He's buying it all his life and he's worrying now?" His next loyalist knows no such fear, though his relationship with seltzer has been explosive.

"I ended up with 75 stitches," Marc Miller said as Beberman carried a case up his brownstone's steps. "Just imagine: It's summer. Seltzer is going hot. And then the bottom falls out of one of these cruddy cases—right on the steps. Those things were like bombs."

"And you're still getting seltzer?" said Beberman.

"You get hooked," Miller said. "It's good service."

"I carried you to the hospital," said Beberman.

The unscarred on his route win less recognition: Beberman doesn't count customers; he counts cases—about 150 a week. Business is good, but after filling his bottles and fixing his truck, he figures his take-home comes to the minimum wage. Many an ex-seltzerman today makes better money peddling bottles—for $75 apiece sometimes—on eBay.

Beberman says, "What for? I need glass to work with. I never have enough to work with." But as seltzer chic encroaches on spritzing, he is up against a moral dilemma. Now posers hog his bottles just to show off. When he delivers a fresh case, last week's case is sometimes still full. Seltzer snobs pay. They don't spritz.

"Ethically speaking, I should sell only to serious drinkers," Beberman said, driving back to the dingy cave in a Brownsville gas station where he parks his archetypical truck and stores his vintage reserve. Passing an apartment house on Prospect Park, he looked up and frowned.

"I used to have a customer in there," he said. "They weren't serious drinkers. I dropped them. They were tying up my glass."

2003

Chapter 5

IT'S ONE THING AFTER ANOTHER

The British bedroom, I learned on moving from Singapore to London, is not the coldest place on earth; the coldest place is the British bathroom. The bathroom in the house I rented in London had a fake marble counter, a bathtub with a fountain in the middle—and no radiator. I caught pneumonia in that house and was bashed on the back with such vigor in the hospital that I coughed myself into a hernia. After I stopped coughing, I did a story on Britain's aversion to indoor heat. To get the hernia fixed, I went to a nonviolent hospital that served caviar with every meal, and did a story on that, too.

One story begets another. It's a natural progression with sometimes unnatural consequences. At the Athens Olympics, I stumbled on a team of podiatrists who inspired me to approach a toenail-fungus guru in Savannah who piqued my interest in a man who gave elephants pedicures in Pittsburgh. Searching in Sioux Falls, Idaho, for a woman whose name appeared at the bottom of letters from a bank, I found a listing for a woman with a similar name whose husband was in business repairing pinball machines. That motivated me to spend a day with a pinball-machine repairman on Long Island.

To show how boring a Law of the Sea Conference was in Caracas, I mentioned in a story that a guy from New Jersey had gotten attention when he stood up in the middle of a dull meeting to plead for political asylum. That guy called me a few months later from a New York prison. He was John Tully, a thug who had helped commit four murders for a Newark Mafia family and then turned state's evidence. Tully kept calling me for months, recounting every hit. I handed in a two-part story: "A Job in the Mob." The editors thought one part would suffice. Shortly after I explained that to Tully, a rewrite man walked up to my desk, ashen-faced. Tully had called Page One to order the editors to run Newman's story as a two-parter, or else.

The story ran in one part. Tully called me after that. He was unhappy. In fact, Tully kept calling me for 30 years. We didn't buddy up again, but his wasn't my last story linked to the Law of the Sea. The seabed is sprinkled with lumps called manganese nodules that mining companies wanted to dredge up before any new laws got in their way. Manganese is nonferrous, so when Howard Hughes launched a nodule-mining ship, I had to write the story. It subsequently emerged that the Hughes ship was a front for a secret CIA attempt to raise a sunken Soviet submarine. I didn't like being fooled by Howard Hughes, and remained alert for nodule news in the hope that someday dredging would begin. I had been on alert for 34 years when I noticed that the Navy was selling the Hughes Mining Barge, a hulk the CIA had used in its sub-raising project. The barge had concealed the Navy's test runs of a secret stealth ship, the *Sea Shadow*. Having served her purpose, *Sea Shadow* was also on the auction block. Secret ships for sale wasn't the nodule story I'd been waiting for. It was better.

Some stories mate and spawn new stories. Apart from the miseries of poverty, two I wrote about people in Indonesia had nothing in common. One was about Hamim, a Javanese peasant who hoped to open a store. The other was about Tatang, a freed political prisoner who wanted a cigarette stand. A reader in Ohio sent me a $100 check for Hamim. I forwarded it to an Indonesian friend, who banked it and handed Hamim the cash. I sent a $250 check of my own to a church that helped released prisoners. The check cleared, and I assumed Tatang also got his cash. A year later, I paid Hamim a visit. His store was in business. Then I located Tatang. He was living in a hovel on a fetid Jakarta canal. My money hadn't arrived. At the church, the woman in charge dug around in her desk and found it—$250 in U.S. cash, stained by a rusty paper clip. "I decided I better keep that money," she said, "to prevent him from just buying things."

The two stories of Hamim and Tatang conceived one more: How aid agencies foul up, and why poor people might be better off if we'd hand them the cash and sideline the bureaucrats. I retrieved my dollars from the church, converted them into Indonesian currency and put them into Tatang's hands. That gave me a third story, with a gestation period of only two years.

I traveled around Eastern Europe for eleven years. Communism fell. Capitalism rose. In 1987, I went to Golden Sands, on Bulgaria's Black Sea coast, for a story on a tatty resort where East was supposed to meet West, but didn't. In 1991, I went to Golden Sands again and found that a luxurious resort, previously reserved for Communist Party apparatchiks, had been hidden away from me four years earlier "as cleverly as a missile base behind earthworks and shrubbery." Golden Sands earned a second visit and a second story.

Sticking around Eastern Europe for so long, I came to be surprised more by the things that hadn't changed since the end of communism—xenophobia, for example—than I was by the things that had. It was time to go home. In New York again, benefiting from the long view of a long absence, I put into practice an axiom of feature writing that jibes with this chapter's theme: A good story is worth doing every now and then. At a bathhouse on the Lower East Side that seemed doomed when I got a Russian rub there in 1974, I was struck, in 1997, by the enlivening changes in American society (and by a bucket of cold water). I corrected an old mistake.

....

Russian Rub

Caracalla it's not. But a better Russian rub it's hard to come by anymore. At a place called the Russian and Turkish Baths on the Lower East Side, they even use genuine oak leaves. Plus you can get kishke—the best—with chicken fat and grated black radish on top. (Kishke, in case anybody west of the Hudson is wondering, is stuffed cow's intestine.) Now *that* they never had at Emperor Caracalla's famous Roman baths.

Once the Lower East Side had lots of Russian rooms, where a wicked wet heat is thrown off by scorching boulders. There were Russian rooms on Rivington Street, on Allen Street, on Ludlow Street. There were plenty in central Brooklyn and at Coney Island, too. But the Russian Jews either died or moved out of the old neighborhoods, and most of the bathhouses went down the drain. Then came the health spas and the saunas, and now the rage for New York's trendy population is to be entertained by people like Bette Midler at flashy spots like the Continental Baths.

On East 10th Street, in the meantime, the Russian and Turkish Baths hangs on, a decrepit monument to the culture of the Jewish immigrants. Most of the men who go there (women on Wednesdays) have been going for decades or have fathers or uncles who have been going for decades. Not many are likely to walk in off the street, which now harbors an Italian social club, an Iglesia de Cristo, a Kung Fu academy, quite a few winos and a great deal of garbage. The baths, in a crumbling four-story brownstone, have been marinating in ethnicity here for about 80 years.

The first thing you see when you walk through the front door is Jake Levenberg, manager and chief cook. He doesn't have a shirt on, and his red-striped shorts are sticking out of his pants. On a chain around his neck is a medal with the Hebrew letter that stands for "life." Jake has been working at bathhouses, staying until they closed and then moving on, since he arrived in this country in 1946, a survivor of the concentration camps.

"I'm an old-time Jewish cook, specializing in kreplach, roast chicken, black radish, chopped liver with heavy chicken fat," he starts yelling after the barest introduction. "It's healthy for your stomach. Regular dinner every Friday night. Sunday morning, sturgeon, lox, whitefish, homemade schmaltz herring. We buy only fresh. All the politicians and the big businessmen come here," he goes on. "They love the baths, and they have the chopped liver with radish on top. This is the only baths on the East Side specializing in Russian rubs, where they rub you with oak leaves. Healthy for arthritis and any aches. Open six days for man and one day for woman."

The front room has a tin ceiling and fluorescent lights with pull strings. The walls are pale blue, decorated with girly pictures out of the 1950s. The floor is covered with strips of several odd patterns of linoleum. Sitting at the counter wrapped in a sheet and sipping a glass of tea is Willie Abrams, owner of a car wash in Yonkers, looking a little skeptical about Jake's spiel. "I've been coming here on and off 30 years," he says. "The place hasn't changed much."

"Improved! Improved! Improved!" Jake screams.

"Don't say 'improved,'" Willie says. "You kept your clients, but once a client dies, you don't improve another client. The young don't go for it. It's the last of the Mohicans."

The owner of the baths is Al Modlin, a man who looks like a friendly bullfrog with glasses. He comes in about 11 every morning. "I never knew what relaxed meant until I walked into a Russian room in Brooklyn 40 years ago," he says. That was the Belmont Baths on Belmont Avenue, and after going for a couple of decades, Al finally bought the place. Then the neighborhood changed, so he sold the Belmont and took a lease on the old Silver's Baths in Coney Island. But Silver's went under, too, so eight years ago, Al came to the Lower East Side, where he is sure there is a good future.

"It's catching on," he says. "it's catching on with the young people, and they enjoy it no end, thank God. We had all the Lindsay helpers in here. Lawyers. Doctors. We even had Timothy Leary. They come here to eat because we have a fine restaurant of food. But we don't encourage that. We want bathers. We don't want outside eaters."

The baths are down a steep flight of steps, in the basement. First there is a Turkish room with benches surrounded by hissing radiators, but it's empty. Then comes a large open area covered with tile, and a pool with the inscription above it in black letters, "James Siravato Marble and Tile Works." A man is lying on a marble pallet in one corner being given a soap rub by another man with a towel wrapped around his head. In another corner, several bodies are bunched up under two showers. A metal door in the center of the far wall leads to the Russian room.

You open the door and walk into a wall of heat. It is a small room, covered by rust-stained stucco and lined by a sort of three-tiered wooden grandstand. Cold-water pipes run all along the benches with spigots that empty into wooden buckets. When the heat starts to get to you (the temperature is at least 200 degrees), you're supposed to take a bucketful of ice-cold water and dump it all over yourself.

The furnace is a big stucco box built into one corner of the room. It is filled with boulders that are heated by gas jets. (They used to be heated by coal fires, but Al got tired of coal. "The aggravation, with those drunkards shoveling and taking out the ashes—it was terrible," he says.) After two or three years, the boulders start to crack and have to be replaced. Around New York, the only places where people dig holes and hit rocks the right size are cemeteries. So that's where Al gets his rocks, from cemeteries.

Just to the right of the furnace is a wooden tub filled with hot, soapy water used in the famed Russian rub. Brushes made of oak leaves tied in bunches float around in the tub. Once a year, Al and the bathhouse crew go out to collect leaves.

"We pick the leaves off oak trees in Monticello or Staten Island or New Jersey—all in wilderness," Al says. "We get up early in the morning and steal them. And the amazing thing is when we take these leaves and put them in hot water, they, like, come back to life."

On the top plank of the grandstand, right next to the furnace where the heat is most hellish, a man named Marty is lying face down, getting a Russian rub from Leibl Baker, who has been giving them for 30 years. Leibl is a round, smiling man wearing Bermuda shorts, an old rain hat, a handkerchief tied around his neck and wet cotton cloth wrapped around his forearms. As he swishes the soapy water around Marty's back with the oak-leaf brush, he fills bucket after bucket of cold water and splashes it over his own head.

"Marty, wanna flash?" Leibl asks. Marty grunts assent, and Leibl climbs down and opens the furnace door with an iron rod. Then he fills a bucket with hot water and heaves it onto the fiery boulders. Steam shoots out of the furnace. The metal door of the room flies open and then slams shut as the heat rises still more.

That's enough for Marty. He eases out of the room, his Russian rub complete. His body is crimson. His head is beet-red.

Upstairs, the men who are done with their baths are gathering around the counter while Jake cooks dinner behind it. They wear sheets and towels and are swathed in cigar smoke. Conversation is loud, obscene and punctuated by straight shots of whisky and vodka. "We're a tight-knit group, but a lot of us don't even know what the next guy does for a living," one man says. "It's one place you can unwind." Another man working his eyebrows authoritatively up and down says, "You got the guys who are millionaires and the guys who are broke. The greatest joint in the world."

1974

. . . .

Russian Rub Redux

NEW YORK

CORRECTION: The Russian and Turkish Baths on East 10th Street between First Avenue and Avenue A in Manhattan is still in business. A Page One article on May 3, 1974, erroneously suggested that the establishment was going down the drain.

Admittedly a boo-boo, but it's never too late to make amends. On the day after Spiro Agnew was disbarred, that 1974 paper said the "schvitz" on the Lower East Side (now everybody calls it the East Village) had been "marinating in ethnicity" for about 80 years. Well, the place is still marinating—and has been, to be exact, for 105 years. It's just the marinade that has changed.

The first thing you saw when you walked through the door 23 years ago was Jake Levenberg, concentration-camp survivor and chief cook, who yelled: "I'm an old-time Jewish cook, specializing in kreplach, roast chicken, black radish, chopped liver with heavy chicken fat. We buy only fresh."

The first thing you see when you walk in 23 years later is Artur Melukiants, former seaman from the Russian Black Sea port of Novorossiysk, who says: "Chicken fat? No. We have chicken breast. Chopped liver? Boris, what is chopped liver?"

Boris Smirnov rocks back on his stool behind the front desk; he's the manager. He explains chopped liver in Russian. "No, no chopped liver," says the cook.

Is Melukiants Jewish? "I'm sorry," he says. "I speak little English. Boris, what is Jewish?"

"No, you're not Jewish," says Smirnov, who is—but not of the Lower East Side variety. Before quitting Russia in 1989 (he took his wife's Russian last name) he belonged to the Soviet Union's judo squad. Chicken fat he doesn't go for.

In 1974, the front room of the bathhouse's brownstone had clashing strips of linoleum on the floor and girlie pictures left over from the 1950s on the walls. Gray-haired old men wrapped in white sheets sat around after getting their oak-leaf rubs in the Russian room downstairs. They blew cigar smoke and knocked back shots of vodka and yelled in Yiddish.

Terra-cotta tile covers the floor now. A "no smoking" sign hangs between two televisions, one showing sports and one stocks. Plastic fruit dangles above the food counter where a drink menu lists "Kidney Cleanser Juice" and "Heartbeat Juice" and a poster describes "the wonder of wheat grass." Men—and women!—sit around in green robes sipping watermelon-and-mango cocktails; some have gray hair, but they still look young. The yelling, when there is yelling, is mostly in Russian.

And covering the walls are glossy photos of famous customers—basketball players, rap stars, ballet dancers—and articles from sports and fashion magazines. "You've got the secret of youth," says an inscription on a cover of *Vogue*. A headline in another magazine reads: "Bathhouses Nineties Style."

When Jake Levenberg finished his spiel in 1974, a skeptical customer said the place hadn't changed much in 30 years. "Improved! Improved! Improved!" the cook screamed, but the customer said, "Don't say 'improved.' You kept your clients, but once a client dies, you don't improve another client."

Now Smirnov brings a bowl of cereal (Honey Bunches of Oats) over to a table and says, "This business is more bigger, more famous—maybe four, five times what it was maybe 23 years ago." He pours skim milk over the honey bunches. "If no Russians came to America," he adds, "there would be nobody left in this place."

Indeed, the Russian and Turkish Baths serves as a paradigm for an era when words like paradigm add weight to fluffy articles. The bathhouse has ridden the waves of communism's demise and the influx of Russian schvitzers, the antitobacco push, women's lib, the exercise craze, AIDS, the high birthrate of devout Jews, the litigation explosion. Plus glamour and glitz.

A young woman comes in. Smirnov gets up to greet her.

"I'm a producer," says Tricia Digirolamo, popping off pictures with a flash camera. She is scouting locations for an Italian women's magazine. "We're doing a fashion shoot on a Russian theme. Women in fabulous frocks." She goes downstairs to check out the Russian room; it's, like, hot. She comes back up and says, "I'm, like, shocked. My glasses almost melted."

The owner of the baths in 1974 was Al Modlin, a man who lived in hope of his place "catching on." He died around 1980, management passed to a relative, and the baths hit bottom. By 1985, the roof was falling in, water was leaking all over, there were rats and mice and hardly any clients. The bathhouse didn't exactly have a swinging scene, but with AIDS in full flame the city wanted to close it down. That's when two Russian immigrants, Boris Tuberman and Dave Shapiro, took over. Tending the front desk one Wednesday, Shapiro says, "Everybody thought we were stupid."

No sooner had the two bought the baths than they were hit with a suit; boiling water was eating through the wall into the house next door. "Money, lawyers," Shapiro says. The partners put in a new furnace and a new kitchen, then added a sun deck and an exercise room with fancy machines and mirrors.

Then came the fruit juice and the ladies. Wednesday has always been for women; now only Thursday and Sunday are men's days and the rest of the week is coed. "It's more straight," Shapiro says. "Bathing suits of course. For men, we got the shorts."

Business began to turn around, but a nonparadigmatic event followed: In 1992, Tuberman and Shapiro broke up. A notice appeared on the lockers. "The bath," it said, "is operated by separate owners on alternative weeks." No kidding. Every Monday morning, one complete Russian staff—around 15 people—replaces the other complete Russian staff, and the whole shebang changes hands.

"We don't have merchandise, only hot water and steam," reasons Shapiro. "We get the bills, we split them in half, down the middle." It works. The baths improve, improve, improve.

Don't get this wrong: The place is still a wreck, but in New York that's "ambiance." Clients pay $100 for a massage, a bath and a meal, and they keep on coming. A few real old-timers, like Heshie Eisenstein, show up on Sunday mornings. Sunday nights and Thursday nights, gay men; Sunday afternoons, fruitfully multiplying Hasidic Jews. Mixed days get politicians, flamenco dancers, Russians—and a Baptist sociology professor from Queens College, namely Steve Lang.

He's up on the sun deck reading a book called *Collective Behavior and Social Movements*. "This is the most interesting place I've ever stumbled on," the professor says. "Characters, characters. The ownership thing—nuts, so nuts. And very New Agey. Aromatherapy, hypnotherapy, yoga this, spirituality that…"

"I think we should all go naked," a customer called Janet interrupts; she's sunning herself (in a robe) on a plywood pallet. "It would be the hippest thing. All go naked together."

Down in the basement, even on a men's day, when nakedness is no crime, preferences are as mixed on that matter as they were in 1974. The baths aren't much different either. Black letters on the white tile over the cold-pool still spell out "James Stravato Marble and Tile Works." In the Russian room, gas jets still fire up rocks in the corner furnace. Nobody opens the furnace door anymore to fling a bucket of water on the rocks to produce a steam blast (it's done automatically; lawsuits again) but the genuine Russian rub lives on.

Dimitri Vinnik, a food technologist and sportsman two years out of St. Petersburg, is giving one to a man named Mikhail, who lies on a concrete shelf, his head inches from the furnace. Vinnik swishes two soapy oak-leaf brooms around Mikhail's back and dumps buckets of cold water over his head.

Ten minutes later, Mikhail walks out, glowing pink. "The best," he says in Russian, and in English, "Not good—excellent."

"It's exercise for the pores," says Daniel Young, a naked New Yorker who is looking on. Young hasn't tried a Russian rub yet, but he's thinking about getting one soon. "It's a dying art," he says. "Who knows how long this place will be around?"

1997

Chapter 6
WHY'S THE SKY BLUE?

At home, watching the Olympics in Sydney on television, I got hooked on the high dives. Divers stood on a platform and jumped off—head first, feet first, upside down. What fixed my attention wasn't their Olympian gyrations, but the way the TV picture dove with them. It sailed off the platform and plunged underwater in a fizz of bubbles at the precise instant the divers broke the surface themselves.

How could a TV camera do that?

In person at the Athens games, I sat in the stands at the high-dive pool. Cameras hung from the roof. More cameras were clamped to the railings. Cameras ran on tracks around the pool. Where was the camera that dove with the divers? I couldn't spot it. Later, studying my snapshots, I noticed a black line descending from roof to water. What was that? In one photo, a man wearing yellow gloves seemed to be pulling on a rope. Who was he?

Questions. That's what journalism is about. Isn't it?

Headlines, including some on my stories, often ask monumental questions: "Do Multinationals Really Create Jobs in the Third World?" Or raise micro-curiosities: "Who Needs a WeedWacker When You Can Use a Scythe?" But the questions that light my idea fuse are the ones with answers I can't guess. Had the dive-cam's secret been digitally dull, I'd have dropped it. But, no, its secret was gravity. My notes after a first phone call to the inventor read, in full: "Isaac Newton. Apple fall on head!" Back at the Olympics, this time in Beijing, I stood on the diving platform beside the man with the yellow gloves. He hauled the camera up on a rope. When the divers dove, he let go of the rope and the camera dove, too. Question answered.

On a visit to Turkey, I learned that a ban on coffee imports, imposed for economic reasons, had been lifted. I foolishly thought Turkish coffee came from Turkey. The news that it didn't (it came from Brazil) raised more questions: Why don't they serve New York cut steaks in New York? Do the English import English muffins? Where do Brussels sprouts sprout if not in Brussels? "Through journalistic oversight," I wrote, "these questions have gone unanswered in earlier dispatches. However, a trip to Turkey presents an opportunity to make amends, at least when it comes to things Turkish." Did the Young Turks come from Turkey? Yes. Do Thanksgiving turkeys come from Turkey? No. Turkish towels and Turkish baths? Yes to both (apologies to Russian rubbers). Turkish delight? Yes. Turkish Taffy? No: Turkish Taffy comes from Coney Island.

In Moura, a town in Portugal, I got the answer to a question I'd asked while staring into a martini: "The labor of 120 green-smocked, green-kerchiefed women in Fabrica de Conservas Patria," I wrote, "clarifies one of the earliest mysteries of condimentology: how the pimento got into the olive." In countries where oriental rugs proliferate, I came to want a rug myself. In Tunis, Tangier, Istanbul and Baku, merchants pulled me off streets and unrolled carpets, always sacrificially priced. I wondered: Why must rug merchants do business by going out of business? In Dallas, I met an Iranian doing business in a store called "Going Out of Business." He explained it. On a wet day in Warsaw, nobody was wearing galoshes. Wasn't *galosh* a Slavic word? Didn't the Russians have a guided missile called the Galosh? In New York, too, nobody but me and a few others were wearing galoshes. Why? I burned shoe leather. Driving through Rhode Island on a Sunday, I noticed that the auto dealerships were closed. Why? Driving through New Jersey, I couldn't pump my own gas. Why not?

I like questions raised by others because it shows I'm not the only one curious enough to want the answer or dumb enough not to know it. Jeff Grocott, a *Wall Street Journal* copy editor, came over to my desk with a form letter from Citibank. It was signed "S. Larson." Jeff told me he'd been getting letters from the same person at Citibank, signed in the same childish hand, for 20 years. He wanted to know: Is S. Larson for real? That was my story's first sentence.

In 1995, I spent a day in a scrap yard in Dąbrowa Górnicza, Poland, observing Poland's innovative low-cost method of demobilizing Warsaw Pact battle tanks. The objective of the Polish method, I reported, was "to turn something easily identified as a tank into something not easily identified." The method involved dropping a 17,637-pound steel ball onto the tank. The ball dropped. No more tank. Back in Warsaw, I described the Polish method to my colleague, Dan Michaels. Dan had been a consultant in the U.S. One of his clients was Post, the cereal company. After I filled him in on Poland's tank-smashing technology, Dan said, "That's how they make Grape-Nuts."

I wondered what he meant by that for the following 14 years. How *do* they make Grape-Nuts? I went to California and asked.

. . . .

No Grapes, No Nuts

CERES, CALIFORNIA

All the world's Grape-Nuts come from a dirty-white, six-story concrete building with steam rising out of the roof here in the San Joaquin Valley. The valley grows lots of grapes and lots of nuts, so the factory's location would make sense, if Grape-Nuts contained any local ingredients. Which it doesn't.

For 111 years, over breakfast, Americans have wondered: What's a "grape nut"? A grape nut looks like a kidney stone, but the name, unlike shredded wheat's, isn't self-descriptive. This raises many reasonable questions: Is it a grape that hasn't developed? What part of the grape do they use? For those who have read the box and learned what Grape-Nuts are made of (flour), a denser issue arises: How does a cereal with the mouthfeel of gravel get manufactured?

Teaser: On the factory's fourth floor, all day every day, objects with the proportions of hewn firewood and the heft of cinder blocks hurtle along a conveyor, dive into a steel chute, disappear down a black hole—and emit what sounds like a startled scream.

All the while, Fernando Vargas, who has operated the Grape-Nuts machine for 32 years, stands next to the chute in a hard hat yelling, "Dropping the bombs! Dropping the bombs!"

When soaked in milk, the final product is mildly sweet brown stuff. But if Grape-Nuts lovers don't know what the stuff is, Grape-Nuts sellers have no doubts. Carin Gendell, who was its senior brand manager in the 1980s, remembers how her staff described it. "Grape-Nuts," she says, "was people eating advertising."

Since people haven't been eating nearly as much of it as they used to, the latest Grape-Nuts ad campaign, running now on MSN's website, is trying a new tonic: It consists of skits in which male milquetoasts get droll advice on "looking cool while driving a minivan," or "letting your in-laws move into your house." The slogan—"That takes Grape-Nuts"—implies that the stuff enhances virility. C.W. Post might have written it himself.

The founder of Postum Cereals not only cooked up Grape-Nuts in Battle Creek, Mich., around 1898, but also concocted some of the earliest mass advertising to peddle it. A 1910 ad said Grape-Nuts had "phosphate of potash" for building "brain and nerves." It didn't. Another said the Panama Canal couldn't have been dug without Grape-Nuts because it "keeps almost indefinitely in any climate." Other ads claimed it prevented malaria and appendicitis. It doesn't.

By 1914, when Post apparently killed himself—shortly after an appendicitis attack—Grape-Nuts had cut its curative claims to one: constipation. Yet the ads kept coming: In the 1960s, a boy grabs a woman in a swimming pool; she's his girlfriend's mom. "Oh, no, Mrs. Burke!" he exclaims. "I thought you were Dale!" In the 1970s, woodsman Euell Gibbons asks, "Ever eat a pine tree?"

If Grape-Nuts were wood chips, nobody minded—the stuff was the seventh-biggest cold cereal in the land. But Gibbons died and the land became less earthy. Sales slid and never regained ground.

Grape-Nuts wandered in the wilderness as the Post operation passed from General Foods to Phillip Morris to Kraft—and wound up in 2008 as a division of Ralcorp, a maker of knockoff store brands. Cereals containing sugary objects like "Honey Bunches" dominated Post's line. In 2005, four Grape-Nuts ovens in Battle Creek were scrapped, leaving just the one here in California. With a share of the cereal market below 1 percent, the stuff was tilting toward crunchtime.

"We need to bring it back to life in a relevant way," says Kelley Peters, the "insights" director who charts Grape-Nuts psychographics for Ralcorp's $5 million resuscitation attempt. Her target: men 45 years old and up. "Men aspire to it," she says. "It's strong and stern, the father figure of cereals." Her marketing chief, Jennifer Marchant, points out: "It tends to break your teeth sometimes."

True, but Grape-Nuts loyalists don't all welcome the focus on maleness. Sylvie Dale, 38, an editor in New Jersey, and a woman, says: "The rhythmic crunching that reverberates around your skull could be ambient sound meditation. To have the patience to get through a bowl, you have to practice mindfulness." Dale adds: "I have a special place in my heart for this cereal."

David Smith does, too, though he says, "I don't want Grape-Nuts and testosterone in the same sentence, ever." As a teenager, he biked cross-country, eating the stuff out of a saddle bag. At 52, he sells flooring an hour's drive from Battle Creek. His devotion to Grape-Nuts remains constant. "It's a cereal that doesn't require much from me," he says. "I guess it isn't a real relationship."

When Peters conducted psychological interviews for the ad campaign, she was sometimes asked how Grape-Nuts are made. "I asked back," she says, "how do you think they're made?" Smith's guess: "Wheat, barley and nuclear fusion."

Fission is more like it.

On a hot day in the valley, a fruity scent hung over the Post plant. It was Apple Caramel Pecan Crunch, which is made here, too. The Grape-Nuts ingredients stood in silos outside: wheat (red and white) and barley, wet and malting. Maltose is the only sugar in Grape-Nuts. Post may have called it grape sugar, or thought Grape-Nuts looked like grape seeds, or that grape seeds looked like nuts, or that malted barley tasted nutty. Nobody seems to know.

The grain was tipping into mills that ground it into flour. Until five years ago, the mills spat out the husks for cattle feed.

Now they stay in, so Grape-Nuts can sell as "whole grain." That is one change in Post's formula. Another is a spray of vitamins and minerals. It qualifies Grape-Nuts for food-stamp programs, and adds an element—zinc—that enables Dana Johnson, in Arvada, Colo., to make home-brewed Grape-Nuts beer. ("Light and drinkable," he says.)

Mixed with yeast (one cup per 2,000 pounds) and water, the flour turns to dough, gets chopped into 10-pound loaves and sent into a huge oven—1,610 loaves at a time. "Now it gets interesting," Vargas said at his workstation, watching the loaves emerge from the oven and catapult into the darkness. An instant later, they hit the fan—a whirling high-speed shredder that rips them to smithereens.

In a nearby control room, Julius Larriva, who has overseen this process for 33 years, said: "Bake and destroy, bake and destroy."

The shreds dry for three hours. Then they're dumped onto rollers, crushed into crumbs, and poured through ducts down to the packaging floor—165,000 pounds a day, every day. Annual retail revenue: maybe $80 million. Not much, but Ralcorp has no plans just yet to sacrifice the brown stuff's identity for the sake of sales.

So what's a grape nut?

Arturo Palmerin paused on the boxing line, where he has worked for 18 years. "Whatever," he said. "A lot of things." Then he said, "I have no idea."

"It's bread," Vargas said, standing beside him.

"Bread?" Palmerin said.

"Bread," said Vargas.

2009

Chapter 7
SCISSORING

News stories—I'm a reliable source on this—are reliable sources of ideas. In 2006, the Texas papers reported the arrest of a bird lover for shooting a cat on a beach in Galveston. The *Los Angeles Times* covered the story. It was all over the Web. A year later, before the shooter stood trial, I went to Galveston and wrote it up for the *Wall Street Journal*. The *New York Times* covered the trial. The following month, the *New York Times Magazine* covered the whole thing again. Stray items like the cat shooter are breadcrumbs to the pigeons of the press. Murder, suicide, divorce—they all supply tidbits to peck at. Add the words "mass" or "celebrity" and the pigeons swoop. Cat killing is as far as I've gone in the cat-shock genre, but my clipping scissors are always at the ready. Bill Hartley, the *Journal* reporter I replaced in Singapore, bequeathed me a bamboo bookcase with the names of countries taped to the shelves. Bill subscribed to seven newspapers, clipped them, and made piles of clips for each country. Before a trip, he'd pull out a country's pile, sort the clips by subject, and have a set of stories to chase on arrival. I did what he did, following the story crumbs from mass hysteria in Malaysia to a monkey embargo in Bangladesh.

A reporter for a Russian newspaper in Brooklyn once clipped a story of mine, translated it into Russian and ran it under his own byline. I found out when the article was translated from Russian back to English by a clipping service. The plagiarist took a risk: My story might have been wrong. Translated articles and broadcasts buried me in Eastern Europe. I didn't recycle or regurgitate; I distrusted and reframed. Finished products by local reporters were my jumping-off points. I clipped a story from the *Warsaw*

Voice about a brand of vodka being certified as kosher by Poland's chief rabbi. A chief rabbi? In Poland? The Jews were nearly gone. Who could care if vodka was kosher or not? I learned that Poland had not one, but two rabbis claiming to be the chief. One was certifying vodka, the other insisted vodka was kosher by nature. But my story wasn't about vodka. It was about ghosts of prewar Poland fluttering to post-communist life.

The *Warsaw Voice*, in the 1990s, had no website. Its kosher-vodka coverage would have escaped U.S. readers, not to mention editors. If a paper I didn't read—the *Chicago Tribune*, say—beat me to kosher vodka, I never knew it. The *New York Times* had a heavenly morgue when I worked there. Its clippings came mostly from the *Times*. The *Wall Street Journal's* morgue was a set of loose-leaf binders and a librarian with a long memory. Back then, my clipping searches took me to Hotalings, a newsstand on 42nd Street stuffed with out-of-town papers. I'd harvest a sheaf, take it home and thrash it for ideas.

The Internet incapacitated Hotalings and gave birth to the worldwide morgue. As Google Bookmarks supplanted my clips pile, I came to realize that every story I had ever written had been written before, and every story I wanted to write had been written already. It doesn't matter. People not directly involved with runny cheese don't follow runny-cheese news on the Web, and when my runny-cheese story runs it will be different and, I hope, better than those that ran before. After White Castle put out a press release announcing an experimental wine list, the Associated Press picked it up. News sites picked up the AP story, appending reader comments, as in, "I wonder which wine goes well with explosive diarrhea?" But the news reports, with their Facebook and Twitter tails, stopped at the wisecracks. No reporter visited the White Castle in Lafayette, Indiana, to see how the experiment was going. So I did.

I heard an interview on NPR with a scientist in Florida who identified bugs by the splats they made on windshields. I gave that interview a five-year grace period, then spent a few buggy days with the man. A website (in Florida again) reported that Hillsborough County had named a "moral courage" award in honor of a deceased antitax campaigner. Moral courage in county government? I added the clip to my pile. Cruising the Web months later, I found a new and unrelated item on the courageous campaigner: His estate had received a $300 million bill for unpaid taxes. Two clips—moral courage plus tax evasion—added up to a story.

The deeper such treasures are buried the more I treasure them. The man in Savannah who self-published a book about toenail fungus peeked out at me from a classified ad on page 135 of the *Atlantic Monthly*. The Food and Drug Administration's decision to ban clove cigarettes was a wire-service report in the tobacco war. I'd been to Indonesia and knew it was wreathed in clove smoke. My story was about expatriates who remembered how sweetly Indonesia smelled.

When a Broadway star dies, a small item usually appears in the *New York Times*, announcing a memorial in a Broadway theater. I had no reason to attend, but one day I got curious. Why not take a look? I walked to the Majestic Theater for Kitty Carlisle Hart's memorial. A few thousand people were waiting to get in. Did other reporters over the decades have this story idea before me? Probably. I did it again.

. . . .

Regards To Broadway

NEW YORK

Francine Greene, 78 years old and the widow of a dentist, might be described as a cross between a groupie and a professional mourner. With hundreds of celebrity-struck theatergoers like her, usually including her bridge partner Carol Gutman, who is 73, she is a regular at a type of production that plays New York a lot: the big-name-cast sendoff for a star who has left town for heaven. Admission is free.

"Jerry Orbach was very, very good," Greene was saying as she waited in a line that extended from the Majestic Theater all the way to Times Square. "Everybody from 'Law & Order' came to

Jerry Orbach. Another good one was Fred Ebb. He wrote the lyrics to 'Cabaret.' Liza Minnelli stopped the show at Fred Ebb."

The goodbye show for the famed baritone Robert Merrill was Greene's first, in 2004, with Leontyne Price, Van Cliburn and Rudy Giuliani on stage. Then came Arthur Miller, Tony Randall, Spalding Gray, and restaurateur Vincent Sardi, not to mention Robert Altman and Peter Jennings. On this day, in a smart wool jacket with black slacks and seated on her portable stool, Greene was waiting for lyricist Betty Comden's final curtain.

"My father used to think I looked like her when I had bangs," Greene said. Standing beside her, Gutman said, "I saw 'Bells Are Ringing.' The original cast. Francine and I, we go to these things because we like the person. I mean…we *liked* the person."

Greene stood up, too. "People ask, 'Why go to a funeral?'" she said. "It's not a funeral. It's one of the best shows you'll ever see. Look at all these people waiting. Even though it's free, this takes a lot of your time. It's not just cheap—it's respect."

Hollywood, as a rule, doesn't put on public memorial services for departed greats. Yet for reasons cultural and actuarial, they are hits on Broadway. "It's about the postwar fantasy of optimism and love, a golden moment in the theater," says Lee Mindel, an architect who was a friend of Comden's and of her partner-in-song, Adolph Green. But for that era's headliners, it's time to call it a day.

Composer Cy Coleman spoke at Green's memorial service in 2002. In 2005, playwright Neil Simon spoke at Coleman's. Bandleader Skitch Henderson appeared at Merrill's show, and Kitty Carlisle Hart sang at Henderson's. Gerald Schoenfeld, chairman of the Shubert Organization, went on stage to honor Orbach for his musicals—"The Fantasticks," "42nd Street"—Sardi for his social skills and, this year, for being a New York grande dame, Mrs. Hart.

"Theaters have become a new kind of memorial chapel," Schoenfeld says. Having donated the Majestic to many farewells between performances of "The Phantom of the Opera," he knows what it takes to pack the house. "The public wants people of prominence, especially the entertainers, the stars," says Schoenfeld. "And the more popular the deceased the better."

A thousand fans were turned away from the 1,600-seat Majestic last spring at the finale for Kitty Carlisle Hart, who was in "A Night at the Opera" with Groucho Marx in 1935, married playwright Moss Hart, dressed elegantly as a TV panelist on "To Tell the Truth," and had a cabaret act in her 90s. She died in April at the age of 96. Greene, who lined up four hours in advance, got in to hear Tony-winner Kristin Chenoweth sing "I Like Him," and a string of speakers praise Hart's public service and her terrific legs.

"Wasn't it wonderful?" Greene said after the sing-along of "Always" at the end. "Even I didn't realize how much she did for the arts. Michael Bloomberg, Mario Cuomo, even Barbara Walters came."

All summer, Greene kept an eye on the obituaries for this season's potential playbill. "I watch, I listen," she says.

Her obit habit started 20 years ago, after she lost a job as a costume-jewelry buyer at Montgomery Ward. On the day of a dental appointment, she came across a death notice for another dentist's wife. Greene asked her dentist if he knew the bereaved. He did. They were introduced, and they got married.

"I found my husband in the obits," Greene says. Her third. The second, a tailor with Broadway clients, made her a stargazer. Her apartment is on Manhattan's Upper West Side where "there's a lot of showbiz living." She shares a bank with Lauren Bacall, a grocery store with violinist Itzhak Perlman. She writes down her sightings in a book.

Only once has Greene combined stargazing and obit reading with ritual: She walked in on comedian Alan King's funeral service at Riverside Memorial Chapel. "If you dress well and look like you belong, they don't stop you," she says. "Billy Crystal did the eulogy. Need I say more?" Still, a funeral home is no place for a big show, which is why Greene was pleased to learn that the Beverly Sills gala goodbye in September would take place at the Metropolitan Opera.

It was a bright Sunday, and 400 fans were lined up ahead of her. Thousands soon lined up behind her, the first being Rory Bernard, who is 72 and, it emerged after a long chat, was distantly acquainted with a cousin of one of Greene's bridge partners.

Bernard unfolded an article with a recent photo of Sills and said, "She looks wonderful for her age." Greene said, "We were both born in 1929," and not only that: "We went to the same grammar school in Brooklyn for two years. Beverly was my friend."

"You knew Beverly Sills?" said Bernard. "So what are we standing here for? Some friend."

When the lights dimmed, Greene had a good seat in the dress circle. But she didn't applaud after the Met's general manager, Peter Gelb, spoke, or Placido Domingo sang, or Carol Burnett almost cried. When Henry Kissinger, recounting a last hospital visit to Sills, said, "The nurse did not recognize me and thought I might be Walter Cronkite," Greene murmured, "Funny."

"I'm not a big clapper," she said afterward. "It takes a lot to make me clap."

At the Betty Comden sendoff, a lot was what Greene got. Outside the Majestic, showtime was near. Limousines unloaded invited celebs: Stanley Donen, Tommy Tune; someone shouted, "Celeste Holm!" and the crowd surged for a look. When the doors opened, Greene said, "Run!" She and Gutman landed in the mezzanine. In a minute, Lauren Bacall was on stage saying, "Welcome to the theater," and from then on, the Betty Comden tribute was all song and dance.

Greene whispered, "No speeches?"

That's how the producers wanted it. "Our goal was to do the shortest memorial in Broadway history," says Tony-winning lyricist David Zippel, who directed with Comden's friend, Lee Mindel. Comden's family and others chipped in $35,000 for expenses. After weeks of "dialing for divas," as Zippel puts it—the talent, all women, came free. To name a few: Leslie Uggams, Lucie Arnaz, Barbara Cook, Phyllis Newman, Lillias White and Elaine Stritch.

In just an hour, they wowed 'em with Comden-and-Green hits—"New York, New York," "Make Someone Happy" and a dozen more. When it was over, Greene stood up and clapped hard. Working her way out of the Majestic, a step behind Sidney Lumet, Gutman said, "That was a real Broadway show."

"Better," said Greene. "I wonder who's on next?"

2007

Chapter 8
ERRORS & TRIALS

A plastic box on the floor at my feet is filled with files for stories I didn't write. One is labeled "Cement Man."

John was his name. His wife was friendly with the ex-wife of the brother of a friend of mine. My friend told me about John. He dynamited concrete mixers for a living. If the drum on a mix truck stops turning, the concrete inside hardens. That ruins the drum. The mix truck's owner calls John. John puts on a blast suit, climbs into the drum, sets a charge, climbs out, blows up the concrete. The drum is repaired.

"I have no competitors," John said on the phone. I wanted to watch him work, but business was slow. "I haven't had a call in six weeks," he said. "You could wind up waiting months."

I waited, then emailed him. Could I tag along on a job? "Now that I'm going on 70," he wrote back, "I want to let go of blasting in cement trucks." I begged: "If you feel like taking on one more mix truck, I'd do a story about you...something for your children and grandchildren. It would only take one more job..."

John hasn't replied.

Three folders in the box are stuffed with random clips, press releases, Web printouts and notes to myself. The folders are labeled "Ideas," "Souvenir Ideas" (meaning they're old) and "Ideas—Losers."

A press release: "Citizens Union calls upon city elected leaders to stop the practice of placing their names on garbage cans." An article from the *Journal of Contemporary Ethnography*: "Corporate-logo tattoos and the commodification of the body." An invitation to a conference: "Repugnance as a Constraint on

Markets." Notes to myself: "Rubber band demand." "How nostalgia industry stays up to date—what's the next big thing in nostalgia." "Escape artist." "Is there a drug that stops hair from growing?"

I haven't made a call on those ideas yet. Or on this one: "Square Pegs—misfits working sidelines at serious organizations concerned with other things: clowns at football games, circus priests, writers of irrelevant stories at financial publications."

Many of my unwritten ideas have their own folders. Arrow signs: Stores roll out roadside signs with changeable black letters and flashing arrows. I'm collecting messages with wit and wordplay. That folder is still empty. Standing jobs: Workers forced to stand all day—chairless checkout clerks, museum guards, receptionists. When will they assert the right to sit down? That folder is also empty.

One idea in my file box came from an editor: Who watches quick-dry paint dry to make sure it dries quickly? Another sprang up with a new building outside my window: If views are valuable, where are the view appraisers? Another emerged from my ego: How does a nobody become a *the*? In *Vanity Fair*, Lily Rafii is "the" handbag designer. In the *New Yorker*, Greg Carr is "the" philanthropist. The *New York Times* announces that Tara Bray Smith, "a writer," has been betrothed to Thomas Struth, "the photographer." If I could find a *the* who studies the vocabulary of fame, or watches paint dry, or appraises views, I'd get these ideas into print, but I haven't found them.

I have, however, found people adept at evading reporters. To cite a case: Anyone who broke a leg tripping on a cracked sidewalk in New York used to be able to sue the city. The city wouldn't pay unless it had previously been told about the sidewalk crack. So New York's accident lawyers commissioned surveys of every crack on every sidewalk in New York, duly notified the city, and bound the crack maps into books and shelved the books in a library.

The law changed, but the library remained open for cases that were ancient yet active. I wanted to meet the library staff.

"It's just one person," the lawyer in charge said on the phone.

"Would I be able to meet that person?"

"You would not," said the lawyer.

"Well, how about letting me just…"

"We don't like employees being interviewed by journalists."

"Why not?"

"It's a command decision on my part," the lawyer said.

I'll try crack maps again after that lawyer gets a judgeship. On the other hand, many ideas in my folders are best left unwritten. I'm grateful to the editors who have declined to let me write them. I once approached a man who had bought the trademark of a bankrupt bank to reuse it as the name of his insurance firm. My proposal was rejected as unfunny. I sent a regretful note to the man, who replied: "I hope you rot and burn in hell. You and all your friends there at the *WSJ*…a colony of maggots and worms afflicting commerce and industry—we don't want to be in your stinking filthy rag."

That idea takes pride of place in my losers file. Others have died less gracefully. When a travel agency invited my father to the "Grand Reunion of the Newmans in Ireland," I thought it would be fun if a Jewish Newman attended. I went, but Page One killed my story. I have just sent it (again) to Glynn Mapes, the editor who issued the death sentence, and asked why. "It wanders," he replied. "And I wasn't surprised that there were Jewish Newmans in Ireland (or in the U.S. for that matter), so what's really the point of the story?"

I was so convinced of the idea's merit that I was blind to its fatal flaw. The Newman Clan was my "Bridge on the River Kwai." I submit it here on a note of caution, to show how easy it is to stumble into the abyss. Still, I had a grand time in Dublin.

. . . .

The Newman Clan

DUBLIN

"On behalf of the Ancient and Royal Clan Newman," said the letter on pale-green stationery, Halbert's Inc. of Bath, Ohio, was inviting my father, Milton B. Newman of Rockaway Beach, N.Y., to the "Grand Reunion of the Newmans in Ireland."

"You'll journey along the highways and byways of Ireland where Newman strongholds once held sway," the letter said. "You'll learn that the Newmans have always maintained their important clan status and that their roots are deeply imbedded in Ireland."

Rockaway Beach is a section of New York City where, I sometimes think, the zoning laws require each Irish family to be surrounded by three Jewish families, and vice versa. My great-grandfather, Herman Newman, stopped in England on his way to New York from points east. Maybe he stopped in Ireland, too. Who remembers? My father has never been big on royal reunions. I thought I'd go instead.

By the time I get to Dublin late on a Friday night, the clansmen have already been to Ashford Castle in Galway. ("Many a Newman made merry there!" the itinerary says.) They've seen Connemara, "this ancient land so rich with Newman heritage." And they've rolled through MacGillycuddy's Reeks to learn "why it was so difficult for earlier Newmans to leave this beautiful country."

Tonight, they slumber in Dublin's Gresham Hotel as their trip's final day approaches. On Saturday, they will meet the Chief Herald, Ireland's top genealogist, and rejoice in a gala Reunion Banquet. Before turning in, I check the Dublin phone book. It lists 3,120 Murphys and 56 Newmans. Perhaps Newman isn't the most common of Irish names. On the other hand, the book lists only nine O'Looneys.

"We've done all the big clans," Eithne Twomey says in the bus the next morning, heading for the Chief Herald's office.

She has guided Halbert's reunions since they began last year: busloads of O'Connells and Flynns and Brennans. Nineteen Americans have come this time. But the first four Twomey introduces me to aren't Newmans. They're Harpers. The next 13 aren't Newmans, either. They're all Hayeses. Halbert's invited every Newman it could find in the United States and Canada, and how many signed up?

Two. I make it three.

"You see the split in her teeth?" says William Franklin Newman, grinning at Nikki Newman Reece to show off the split in his own teeth. "I could tell she was in the family."

"If you say so," she says.

Reece, a widow from Fullerton, Calif., was born a Baptist. Now she's Episcopalian. She recalls her father saying his family was English, with beginnings in Germany or Holland. "He never mentioned any Irish connection," Reece says. "That's why I came on this tour."

Born a Baptist, too, Bill Newman's a Methodist now. He's 57, an electrician in Fort Wayne, Ind., and a cushion-shoe salesman on the side. He has a book with him that traces his ancestry all the way back to Walter Newman, who was born in England and spent 18 years in Dublin before moving to Perth Amboy, N.J., in 1683.

Walter's son, Walter Jr., founded Newmanstown, Pa. Down through the generations, Newmans fought in the Revolutionary War and the Civil War. There's a Benjamin Franklin Newman and an Alonzo de Lafayette Newman. Hester Newman had a sister named Emily. Emily was my mother's name and it's my daughter's name. The Milton Newman of Stark County, Ohio, born 1843, had the same color hair and was the same height as the Milton Newman, born 1906, of Rockaway Beach.

"Let's see those teeth," says Bill, grinning.

The bus pulls up to the Chief Herald's office, next door to the Alliance Française. Hayeses, Harpers and Newmans file into a meeting room where the Chief Herald awaits, pointer in hand, at a bulletin board with a map of Ireland pinned to it.

"You're Newman, are you?" Donal Begley says as Bill sits in the front row. "They're all over. We'll shake your family tree."

Nikki Newman Reece gets out a notebook. But first, Begley spends 20 minutes on the Hayeses. "Your name carries 2,000 years of Irish heritage," he tells them. All he tells the Harpers, who sailed over from England, is that their ancestors played harps. The Newmans were Normans, he discloses at last; the name means "new man."

"Their numbers were small, but their influence was enormous," Begley says. "We had John Henry Newman; he was English, of

course. We have Bishop Jeremiah Newman of Limerick. We have
a firm of auctioneers—Douglas, Newman and Good."

"My brother's an auctioneer," Bill Newman says.

"Sacred heart," says the Chief Herald. "I better stop."

Afterward, Bill is unhappy. Begley has handed him back
his family tree; Walter's Irish sojourn can't be traced. Reece is
unhappy. "He didn't mention Germany, did he?" she says. And I'm
unhappy. The Chief Herald never hinted at my Irish connections.
It looks as if this will require independent research.

"When one thinks of Ireland," wrote Carol Weinstock, a
young photographer from America, "Jewish is not what usually
comes to mind." This is true. Yet Weinstock was able to fill a whole
doctoral thesis with pictures of nothing but Jewish Irishmen. The
Jews, it turns out, have been wearing the green for ages.

Legend tells of two "God tribes" in Ireland that the Celts
believed to be two of the lost tribes of Israel. The tribes were dei-
fied, scholars say, and became the "shee"—Irish fairies. If this is
correct, it means leprechauns must be Jewish.

The Annals of Innisfallen, an ancient document, records a
visit by five Jews "from over the sea" to Turlough O'Brian, King
of Munster, in the year 1062. Yougal had a Jewish mayor in 1583.
Dublin had one in 1956 and again in 1961. That was Robert Briscoe.

Named after Robert Emmet, the Irish Patriot, Bobby Briscoe
fought for Irish freedom and then for Israeli freedom. He led New
York's St. Patrick's Day parade on March 17, 1956; Boston wanted
him so badly the city put off its parade until March 19. His visit
brought Irish coffee to the United States and gave rise to the story
about the old lady who says to her friend: "You'll never believe.
There's a Jewish mayor of Dublin." And the friend says: "How
wonderful. It could only happen in America."

Ireland's best-known literary characters are Jewish: Leopold
and Molly Bloom. In the imagination of James Joyce, Leopold
Bloom was born at 52 Clanbrassil St., Dublin, in 1866. Chaim
Hertzog, the highest-ranking Jewish Irishman, was born in Bel-
fast and moved to Dublin. Now he's president of Israel and the
only head of state in the world who speaks Hebrew with an Irish
accent.

President Herzog traveled to Dublin last June, and presided at the opening of a Jewish museum in a downstairs room of the old Walworth Road Synagogue. The museum contains an invitation to his Bar Mitzvah, dated October 17, 1931; Hyman Louis Mushatt's pill-making machine; and a chart showing that the number of Jews in Ireland declined from 3,907 in 1946 to 1,750 in 1984.

An old photograph hangs on the wall just past the museum's entrance. It shows a man in a wing collar laying the cornerstone of a Jewish school. He was a philanthropist, and his name was Arthur Newman. Behind him in the picture stands Abraham Newman, a distant cousin. In a semi-detached stucco house, a short taxi ride from Dublin, lives Abraham's son. His name is Cyril, Dr. Cyril Newman. He has a wife, Patricia; a mother-in-law, Daisy; two daughters named Ruth and Hayley; and a son, almost eight years old, who isn't home. There is a picture of him on the wall. His name is Barry, Barry Newman.

"My father came from Lithuania to Cork between 1890 and 1900," Cyril says at the dining-room table as Patricia and Daisy bring out tea and pound cake. "My uncle Philip came to Limerick. He was there for two weeks before he found out it wasn't New York."

He knows of no other relatives who did get to New York. In Ireland, his family started out selling holy pictures to Roman Catholics, then expanded into Dublin property. My great-grandfather Herman was in tobacco. Cyril Newman never heard of him.

In early evening, he drives me back to the Gresham Hotel, where the Newman clan's Reunion Banquet is about to begin. "Make sure you spell my name right," Cyril calls as I leave the car.

The private room is already packed, the bar open. Halbert's always invites local clansmen to join the fun. "You'll make merry with Newmans of every sort," it promised. Nearly everyone in the crowd is a Hayes or a Harper, of course. But John and Mary Newman have come to compare family trees with Bill Newman and Nikki Newman Reece. After a while, Elizabeth Neuman arrives.

The spelling may be wrong but the spirit is right. She is a psychologist, born here, whose parents fled to Ireland from Berlin in

1936. "This is great," she says, sitting with the rest of the clan at the banquet table. "This is the first time I've ever done the roots thing."

As our plates fill with beef stroganoff and the wine flows, we regale each other with tales from the ancient and royal clan's varied history. Then an accordionist gets up at the front of the room and the Hayeses, the Harpers, the Newmans and the Neuman all join in singing "There's a Hooley at Hannigan's House Tonight."

1985

PART TWO

REPORTING

Chapter 1
BLUNDERING

Story ideas are nothing. Anybody can get an idea. The ultimate journalistic challenge is gathering information to turn an idea into a story. Reporting a story, for a professional like myself, is a highly nuanced mélange of blundering and blind luck.

The best example of this universal truth is a story of mine. It is, in fact, the best story ever. It's better than anything Hemingway did. Or Plato. And if either of them sued me for telling a big lie, neither would stand a chance in an American court. Nobody could be so dumb as to believe a big lie. Big lies aren't untrue, in the eyes of the law, because they're unbelievable. They're just "puffery."

Puffery was the subject of my reportorial effort. The idea grew on me in years of exposure to the bluster of American advertising. Puffery irritated me no end, but how to transform the idea into print? The defining moment of that quest took place shortly after my plane landed on a rainy November night in Madison, Wisconsin. I was standing at the Hertz counter, waiting for the clerk to hand over my car keys. I noticed a rack with a pile of glossy brochures put out by the local convention bureau. I took one and put it into my shoulder bag. That was it, the defining moment.

I was in Madison to interview Ivan Preston, a professor emeritus at the University of Wisconsin. Preston, who taught advertising, was a renegade. He thought it was wrong for corporations to lie. He had written a book: *The Great American Blowup, Puffery in Advertising and Selling*. A cartoon on the cover showed a man blurbing in a quote bubble: "WOW!! This riveting page turner by American's most beloved author is sure to sell a million copies!" I read through the book before calling him. Wow!! Was it academic!

But Preston was my ally. If I could just inject some kind of color into a day with him, I'd have my ticket to a "Huh?" story about puffery.

On the phone, he'd said: "It really started as a matter of how you know what you know. Epistemology, we call it here on campus."

Epistemology wasn't a promising angle. When I proposed flying to Madison, Preston was welcoming. Maybe he thought we would continue discussing epistemology by the fireside in his study. He seemed less pleased when I asked him to dig up some local puffers, people we could go see and talk to about their appalling lies. I got on the plane with nothing but a file of court cases and notes from interviews with a few uncooperative lawyers. I was worried. Was Preston a dud?

He had invited me to his house—and his study—at midmorning the next day. I rose early, brewed a packet of "Superior Coffee" in my hotel room, sat with *USA Today*, then pulled out that airport brochure. As a regular reader of guidebooks and tourist handouts, I can attest that it was the greatest ever. Madison, said the first paragraph, offered "the best of all worlds," and the brochure's listings offered the best of all worlds for a story on puffery. International Crane Foundation: "Only place in the world to see fifteen crane species." St. Isaac of Syria Skete: "America's leading icon distributor." Happy Pastime: "Wisconsin's largest collection of Hummels." Three Dog Bakery: "World's best all-natural fresh-baked dog treats." Dry Bean Saloon: "Best Brewery in America." Paradise Gentlemen's Club: "America's only overhead glass stage."

Unbeatable! Instead of driving to his house, I phoned Preston and asked him to meet me instead at the Java EsCafe, "Madison's Premier Internet Cafe." He was at the counter when I got there. "Very thin," my notes say. "Soft-spoken, but excited and possessed." He got his coffee and was turning to look for a seat when I mentioned the café's "premier" status. "That's not true," Preston said, and his ensuing five-second exchange with the counterman was worth the flight to Wisconsin. It was a scene—and now I had a reporting plan.

We finished our coffee and went for a long walk and a few short drives, stopping along the way to visit Madison's principal puffers. Preston had a fine time annoying them in the extremely unique world beyond his study. By late afternoon, scenes filled my notebook. I could have left it at that and headed for the airport, but Preston wanted to tell me about the only genuine victory of his antipuffery struggle. He asked me home. We stood in his kitchen, drinking beer.

It was 1979. Preston had a job at the Federal Trade Commission, in Washington. "If a possible puff came along," he said, "they'd pass it to me. They passed me Miracle Eraser. If you rubbed it on the wall, it crumbled and gave off a smell." Preston sent the manufacturer a "demand letter," stating that the eraser wasn't miraculous and ordering an end to miraculous claims. The eraser disappeared forever. "It was the one little thing in the direction of puffery I was ever able to accomplish," Preston said.

My day in Madison was an unparalleled success. Lacking Ivan Preston's jousting with the town's shopkeepers, I'd have had nothing to write about—just an obscure legalism that bothered me. As it turned out, my beer in Preston's kitchen gave me a final scene. There was no room in my story for his Miracle Eraser boast, though. Preston didn't complain. He wasn't expecting a puff piece.

. . . .

Puffery

MADISON, WISCONSIN

Ivan Preston, the world's greatest expert on "pure baloney" in advertising, stopped in one morning at the Java EsCafe, honored by Madison's official visitor's guide as the town's "premier (and only) Internet Cafe."

"As far as I know," the counterman replied when Preston asked whether he was sure of that. Carrying his coffee to a table, the professor muttered, "I'm wondering."

What occupies Preston's mind is "puffery." He has been wondering about it since 1970 when he read in a law book that a puff is legal even if it's a lie. A company accused of false advertising when it claims to be "the best" can say it was merely boasting. If a judge agrees, the company is absolved.

"Lying," Preston said. He is 71-years old and not given to overstatement, but he added, "Lying is bad!"

Once an ad man himself—he was in ketchup—the professor has taught advertising at the University of Wisconsin for 35 years. For 33 of them, in two books and many papers, he has huffed against puffs. Few heeded him until 1995, when scholars revising the Uniform Commercial Code—a model that most states incorporate into their laws—proposed a requirement that companies put facts where their hypes are. That was Preston's most dazzling triumph.

The code is now due for final approval by the American Law Institute—but with the rules likely to remain intact. It will be Preston's most crushing defeat.

"It's cultural," he said. "You can't change it."

The puff law lets puffery float free in America, from Illinois (World's Largest Barber Shop), to Texas (World's Greatest Plumber), to Coney Island (World's Smallest Horse). In their whitest whites, Americans can hop into their ultimate driving machines, and, of course, take in the Greatest Show on Earth.

While the Federal Trade Commission stalks phony diets, and the Supreme Court decides the limits of Nike's "commercial speech," bombast lives on as advertising's safest haven. *Prosser and Keaton on Torts* calls the puffer rule "a seller's privilege to lie his head off." Why? Because the law assumes that nobody with any sense would ever mistake a puff for the truth.

"Consumers understand it for what it's worth," says Jeffrey Edelstein, a lawyer who rallied the ad industry against the change in the commercial code. When the American Law Institute, as expected, agrees to leave the puff clause alone, puffery's immunity from candor will be preserved.

The testimonials Edelstein got from creative directors at advertising agencies made the industry's best case: "People like to buy from a company that claims it is the best, the biggest, or whatever," wrote Martin Pottle of Thomas Martin Inc. A truth-in-puffery law would "insult the intelligence of the American people," wrote Linda Kaplan Thaler, now of the Kaplan Thaler Group. It would, predicted James Paddock of Fitzgerald & Co., "literally destroy the advertising business as we know it."

"Preston's an interesting guy," says Edelstein. "But this is a battle he's going to lose."

After his coffee, Preston strolled down State Street to the Fanny Garver Gallery. According to the Madison visitor's guide, it is "the most interesting gallery in the world."

"I made that up," said Jack Garver, the owner's 51-year-old son, when Preston walked in. "I firmly believe it."

He stood among vases, jewelry and glass elephants. On the walls hung paintings priced between $100 and $10,000.

"People come in here and go, 'Wow, this place is fantastic,'" Garver said. "We get people from around the world who have the same comment."

"Some galleries are more famous," Preston said.

"We're not claiming to be the most famous," said Garver.

Outside, the professor said in disbelief, "He said that with conviction." And then he headed for lunch at the State Bar & Grill, Madison's "most unique bistro," as the visitor's guide asserts.

"Bistro?" said Preston, having noted, while finding a table, that there can be no degrees of uniqueness. "I've been to Paris and I still don't know exactly what a bistro is, but it sure isn't this place." Waiting for a BLT, he said:

"Advertising people are smart. If puffery means nothing to consumers, why do they bother with it? If advertisers had the facts, they might use the facts and forget the puffs."

Puffs and facts, in fact, can be hard to tell apart. Puffery comes up often at the FTC, in the courts, and before the advertising division of the Council of Better Business Bureaus. In dozens of cases a year, judges separate puffs from lies.

Thus Bayer was freed to be "the world's best aspirin," Hush Puppies "the earth's most comfortable shoes," and Firestone (before recalling 6.5 million tires) could promise "quality you can trust."

Only puffs open to measurement lose their invisible shields. Yet when Pizza Hut ("Best Pizza Under One Roof") sued Papa

John's over its slogan ("Better Ingredients. Better Pizza") a federal court ruled that Papa John's could puff away—if it quit claiming that it had better dough and better tomato sauce.

"If Papa John's says it has better dough, you can attack it," Preston said driving toward home. "But if Papa John's says it's better overall, OK. The bigger the lie, the bigger the protection. That's amazing. Isn't that amazing?"

Passing Jeff Stanley's house, Preston stopped in for a chat. Stanley, who is 61, owns Dotty Dumpling's Dowry, a restaurant the professor frequents. Between locations at the moment, its slogan was and will be: "World Hamburger Headquarters."

"You feel pretty sincere about that?" asked Preston.

Stanley said, "Oh, absolutely. I hand-cut the onions."

"But it shouldn't be what Jeff believes," said Preston. "It's what the customer believes. You've got to see what people think."

"I have to admit there's a little BS there," Stanley said. "I guess I've been brainwashed into it. I fall for everything myself. I mean, the average Joe is getting sucker punched."

Ivan Preston's solution is to ask average Joes, in consumer surveys, if they believe a puff to be true. "I'd say you can fool 20 percent of the people all the time," he said when he got home. As the professor poured a beer in his kitchen, his wife, Robbie, brought out a snapshot.

It showed Preston standing in front of a sign that read, "The Best Hamburger You'll Ever Eat." Mrs. Preston took the picture on a trip to Carrizozo, N.M. A friend had told them that a place in Carrizozo had "the best green-chili cheeseburger in the world."

"It was excellent," said Preston.

Mrs. Preston said, "It may actually have been the best."

"In our experience," said Preston. "We've never seen any other green-chili cheeseburgers with which to compare it."

2003

Chapter 2
TIPS & TRICKS

The *Journal's* managing editor, Fred Taylor, sent me to Singapore in 1976 with two pieces of advice:

1. Always take a leak when you get a chance.
2. Don't miss anything.

I have never grasped the meaning of No. 2. (Could it concern the news?) I have, however, unfailingly followed No. 1.

From colleagues, I've picked up many such tips on the job's mechanics and evolved some of my own. In 1968, running copy at the *New York Times*, I noticed that Steven V. Roberts, a reporter, used a notebook that fit into his sport coat's side pocket: the National 1 Subject, Narrow Ruled Eye-Ease® Paper, 80 sheets. I have since used no other notebook. It opens like a regular book and lines up well on shelves. (I have 737 so far, and haven't lost one yet.) Peeking from my sport-coat pocket, the notebook marks me as a reporter.

If I'm wearing a sport coat. Climbing a slimy wooden ladder in a dark, wet goldmine in Yellowknife, Northwest Territory, I jammed it between belt and belly. Climbing a dangling rope ladder to an oil tanker's deck on the Bosporus, I jammed it between belt and bum. Many reporters use the so-called "reporter's notebook," which slides into the back pocket of their pants. But the National 1 Subject has major structural advantages that come later, when I start writing. Anyway, what good is a reporter's notebook when the reporter is naked?

With my National 1 Subject in hand, in 1974, I pulled open the door to the Russian room of the Russian and Turkish Baths and took a steam blast full in the face. My glasses fogged up (they were all I had on) and the notebook wilted. I scribbled illegibly and wrote from memory. In 1997, on my second visit, I placed my glasses and notebook on a ledge outside the Russian room, and took my notes by shuttling in and out. Such is the value of experience. I'll leave where I kept my pen (BIC® Cristal Easy Glide Bold 1.6mm) to the imagination, but the corollary lesson—where to put the pen when outside during a hard freeze—is this: Leave it home and take a pencil. And a sharpener. I came at that revelation standing on Lake Winnebago, frozen ballpoint in hand, waiting for an ice-boat race to begin. I waited two days, during which I also learned that the stretchy-plastic ice grippers I bought don't stretch over snow boots when the mercury drops below zero; they snap like icicles.

Wardrobe tip: Match the wallpaper. At public events, I stay on the crowd side of crowd barriers and out of the press pen. Approached by a flying wedge of riot police at the Yip-In at Grand Central Terminal when I was 21, I feigned disinterest, checking my watch as if wondering why the train to Brewster was running late. The flying wedge flew right past me. When I wanted to board a container ship in Port Elizabeth, New Jersey, the Seamen's Church Institute provided a name tag identifying me as a chaplain. It worked. However, I didn't enjoy my conversion. Pretending to be something I'm not makes me nervous. In Alice Springs, Australia, at the main gate to the "Space Base," where the CIA collected satellite pictures of Russia, I told a guard that I was a teacher and wanted to inspect the base's picnic ground for a possible school trip. My reward for that pathetic deception was getting tailed for the rest of my stay in the Alice by a Yank in an obscene T-shirt and carrying a two-way radio.

Arrest is best avoided. Two "hunters" with rifles invited me to leave a cemetery in Budapest, where I was visiting a revolutionary's unmarked grave. They requested my notes. I tore out a random page from my National 1 Subject, surrendered it and ran. In Haiti, another man with a rifle offered to let me leave another gravesite (Papa Doc's) in return for $5. I paid. The police in Turkey like to point a gun at your nose during passport checks. I memorized a Turkish phrase that I recommend learning in any number of languages: "*Ateş etme. Ben yabancı gazeteci.*" It means, "Don't shoot. I'm a foreign journalist."

Logistics should conform to reporting plans. When moving between countries, for instance, it's wise to look at a map. On a train from Poland to Lithuania, I didn't know that the rail line crossed a corner of the Soviet Union. I had no Soviet visa. The Soviet guards kicked me off the train. When press credentials are required, it's wise to get them. In a charity's rice truck, I was en route to a refugee camp on the Thai-Cambodian border. I didn't know I needed a military pass. A Thai soldier kicked me off the truck.

Money: Take cash. The Chanthaburi Travel Lodge, where I landed after being kicked off the rice truck, didn't take credit cards. I had $60 in baht. The hotel bill was $70. The town had many banks. None of them took credit cards, either. I borrowed baht from an aid worker, caught a bus to Bangkok, and always carried plenty of cash from then on, which brings me to security: I built a cardboard false bottom inside my shoulder bag, hid $3,000 in U.S. currency under it, and placed a device on top of it that emitted hysterical laughter when exposed to light. At the Grand Hotel in East Berlin, the $3,000 was stolen by someone who must have laughed all the way to the hard-currency shop.

Hotels: Expense account permitting, stay in international-class hotels when in big cities. Don't trust the water. If the phones work, assume they're bugged. When interviewing dissidents or buying black-market money in the room, play loud music on a radio. Carry tea bags, dry soup, a mug, an immersion coil and prunes. Restaurant lunches take too long. The reportorial objective is efficiency and security. Note: The International Dateline Hotel in Tonga is not an international-class hotel; it's located on the International Date Line.

In the United States, international hotels lose cachet; their standardized interiors match the standardized exteriors of everything else. I prefer old motels. I still carry cash (ATMs swallow credit cards), but to improve digestion of old-motel breakfasts, I've swapped granola for the dry soup. Reporting in America beats the Third World for efficiency; so much can be organized on the phone in advance. Yet of all the countries I've worked in, Australia possibly excepted, only the United States makes reporting impossible without wheels.

There were no taxis at the station when the Union Pacific train I'd been riding dropped me in Bald Knob, Arkansas. I got a lift to a motel in Searcy, a town with a car-rental place. I had a car booked for the next morning so I could drive to the Little Rock airport. In the morning, the rental place was out of cars. No buses stopped in Searcy. Malaysia, Morocco, Turkey, Poland, India—they all had long-distance taxis. Not Arkansas. The motel clerk called some friends. A guy came in a car that smelled of dog, and drove me to the airport for $85, complaining all the way about the marijuana laws.

One last reporting tip: The basics take longer than forty years to learn.

. . . .

Off The Rails

ON THE LITTLE ROCK EXPRESS

If corporate jets are your idea of sky's-the-limit business travel, try riding a corporate train.

Every big American railroad has one for its bosses: a string of sleepers, dining cars, theater cars, gym cars and—bringing up the rear—a private "office car." They date to streamliner days when the freight lines still hauled passengers. Now they haul executives.

The railroads don't brag about these trains. "It might be seen as a luxury," says an official at one. A Norfolk Southern spokesman: "We're not interested in making it public." Tom Lange, spokesman for the Union Pacific: "It's not mysterious—just not accessible."

Which made it all the more incredible to Jim O'Connor that he was in one. He was seated on the green plush couch of the Feather River, a Union Pacific private office car—one of eight the railroad owns—at the end of this special express heading west past Dexter, Mo., and on toward Poplar Bluff.

It's a fair bet that Jay Gould passed this way 130-odd years ago, when he owned the Missouri Pacific, nibbling ladyfingers baked by his French chef. O'Connor had a coffee in a paper cup.

"A lot of high-level business is conducted here," he said, watching the tracks recede. "You can sit out there on the platform and smoke your cigar so the ladies with you won't complain."

His teenage son, Mike, stuck his head into the living room and said, "Dad, I'm taking a shower."

O'Connor, 55 years old, fixes radiators at O'Hare Airport in Chicago. In his other life, he's a railroad romantic. Not long ago, he competed in a Union Pacific social-media contest and won a five-day ride from St. Louis to Little Rock behind a steam locomotive. He didn't know that the UP had decided, at long last, to let a few humble rail fans make the run in a car with a permanent "private" sign on its door.

Neither did Skip Waters, who was sitting on a Chippendale chair at the Feather River's dining-room table. Waters, 48, gives toy-train rides to kids in Dallas. A trip on this train got him down on one knee to propose to Cindy Collins, his guest and girlfriend.

"He popped the question," she said, holding up a ring. Said Waters, "This here's a mansion on wheels. Pullman treatment!"

George Pullman laid out his "palace cars" of the 1890s exactly like this one: galley, dining room, staterooms with full beds and baths, living room and porch. All gilt, crystal and inlaid mahogany, a private Pullman was the "grandest property to which any American could aspire," as rail historian Lucius Beebe put it in 1961.

Rail barons, and presidents, had to have one. Franklin Roosevelt logged 243,827 train miles, mostly aboard the armor-plated U.S. No. 1. Harry Truman washed out his socks on it.

Campaign rules have since turned whistle stops into photo ops, though Barack Obama did travel to his inauguration aboard the Georgia 300, a palace car given new life by Jack Heard, a Florida mortician.

Barbara Bush horrified fans when she called her husband's 1992 campaign car a "caboose." But "palace" didn't sit well with politicians or executives, so the railroads settled for "business car" or "office car," terms Beebe, the historian, classified under "evasive euphemism."

Business does get done on office cars. In 1989, Mike Haverty, then president of the Atchison, Topeka & Santa Fe, took J.B. Hunt, the trucking magnate, for a friendly ride out of Chicago.

"We paralleled I-55, and it was plugged with traffic," Haverty says. "Before long, we hit 70 miles an hour. By the time we got to Galesburg, Ill., we shook hands and had a deal."

Hunt had agreed to ship truck trailers on flatbed cars—one of the biggest railroading coups since the Golden Spike.

Every so often, Union Pacific executives go on a town-by-town tour to meet and greet politicians. In Eugene, Ore., councilwoman Andrea Ortiz had this to tell them: "Can't you be better neighbors and clean your yard?" The executives said they could be, and have since tidied up. They also gave Ortiz a peek inside chief executive James Young's single-stateroom office car, the St. Louis. "Wood-paneled walls," she recalls. "Not ostentatious. Old money."

Freight executives rarely use their cars to just go someplace, not even to the office. (Amtrak's chief does use his, a spokesman says, to set a rail-travel example.) Office trains do stop at such business venues as the Kentucky Derby. The stated purpose is hospitality, not leisure, though not all railroaders have seen it that way.

"People used them to go to golf courses," says Hays Watkins, 85, who mothballed most of the Chessie System's office cars when he was its president back in the 1970s. "They'd entertain their friends and their wives' bridge clubs," he says. "I'm no fan of office cars."

On the Little Rock Express, lingering at Poplar Bluff to let the locals gawk, the office car's fans entertained themselves.

"In Pullman Palace days, porters served meals right here," Skip Waters was saying. He had a ham sandwich in a box, provided by Union Pacific. Mike O'Connor said, "But they had tablecloths." He found the service bell and pushed it. Nobody came.

They retired to the living room for fruit salad and power bars. The train swung south, into Arkansas, pausing on Front Street in Walnut Ridge. Jim O'Connor went out onto the porch in the afternoon heat.

"What's it cost to ride that thing?" a man in the crowd yelled. O'Connor said, "Can't pay. Got to be invited." The man held up a camera and took a picture. "Guess I never will be," he said.

The train moved on, along the White River. Pickup trucks chased it. A crop duster buzzed it. Mike stretched out for a nap, but gave up. "It's like trying to fall asleep on Christmas Eve," he said.

Bald Knob was the day's last stop. Union Pacific wouldn't let its rail fans spend the night, dreaming of Pullman treatment, in the Feather River's staterooms. The four of them slept in a Hampton Inn. A day later, they were rolling into Little Rock, grabbing taxis to the airport, and catching their flights home.

2011

Chapter 3
JUST GO

The rain was steady the evening two friends and I were due to meet at Citi Field to see the Mets and Yankees play. Ball clubs don't call rainouts easily. I went. I was at the gate, waiting and soaking, when one friend phoned: Both were thinking of skipping the game.

I texted them: "If you don't go, you'll never know."

They showed up. The rain stopped, and we watched Mariano Rivera blow a save in the bottom of the ninth. Rivera never needed lessons in humility. I got mine early: Stay for the last out. Nothing is predictable, scores or rainstorms. When in doubt about going or not going—to ballgames or revolutions—don't think. Go.

Speaking of baseball, a *Journal* reporter once stopped at my desk to talk about his idea for a story on a semi-pro team in New Jersey that had no home field and, consequently, no hometown fans. Terrific, I told him, just wander for a few days with the homeless baseball team. First, though, the reporter was told to submit a story proposal. He telephoned the coach and asked for funny anecdotes. But a homeless ball club did not amuse its coach, and the reporter's proposal didn't amuse his editors. His idea struck out phoning.

During my first 30 years at the *Journal*, I didn't submit story proposals. In 1975, I read *Wait Till I Make the Show*, a book by Bob Ryan. It described Appleton, Wisconsin, as a great baseball town. I told my bureau chief about Appleton. He said, "Sounds good." So I flew to Appleton. Ryan was right, but before I got there, I didn't know that Appleton's home team, the Foxes, stank, or that the hometown fans were sick of them. That turned into my story's theme, a quiet comment on the weevils eating away at white-bread America.

My most vivid image of Appleton couldn't have come from a phone call: The Foxes' manager flinging a folding chair onto a dimly lit field after a night game and screaming, "We can't bunt!"

The "just go" precept conforms with another one: A story about something can't just be "about" something. Encyclopedia articles are "about" things. Stories are about things that happen to things. How can anybody propose a story if it ain't over 'til it's over?

Abroad, I sent editors lists: I'm going to check out the descendants of *Bounty* mutineers on Norfolk Island; I'm going to visit the troglodytes in Cappadocia. My lists closed with a caveat: I'll tell you if I got a story when I get home. I rented a car in Ljubljana and drove to the naked city of Koversada unaware that its nudists were dressing up. In a helicopter over the Ord River in Australia, I had no idea that I was flying with a poacher, not a prospector, or that my day (and story) would end in a helicopter chase.

An editor once praised me for taking "risks." Risks? War correspondents take risks, and I'm no war correspondent. My one combat experience took place in New Guinea while I was profiling a Bible translator from New Zealand. I didn't know until we were in his Land Cruiser on a boggy track that his village was in a war zone—"enemy territory," my notes say. "A woman in a grass skirt comes up at us with a rock, screaming," I scribbled. She heaved the rock. It bounced off the hood. The woman advanced and heaved another rock. Then three mostly naked guys with bows and arrows came tearing out of the forest and tackled the woman. We gave them 40 kina and they left. The "risk" that editor praised me for, in fact, was the willingness to leave the office to report a story before knowing there was a story to report.

That's why "just go" reporting is such nerve-wracking fun. In the Tangier souk, I met Soulaiman Madini, whose family perfume stall was full of Calvin Klein knockoffs. I assumed he was an everyday crook. We talked for hours before I realized that Madini was less a crook than a victim of Western mass marketing; there was a story in that. I went to Amsterdam to meet Ferry Schwartz, whose job was to fish bicycles out of the canals. I assumed he'd know how bicycles got into the canals. He didn't, and that was a story.

Reporting can be like lab work. During the Soviet Union's "openness" period, I went to the Katyn forest with an official Intourist guide to run an experiment in how open he'd be about Stalin's massacre of Poland's officer corps there in 1940. I couldn't know what my story would say until the chemical (vodka) had reacted with the guide and the results were in. I did talk over that lab test in advance with an editor in New York. He said, "Sounds good."

The real risk in "just going" is coming back empty. At the Bulgarian Interior Ministry in 1991, a detective let me in on plans to catch the killer of Georgi Markov, the dissident stabbed by a poison-tipped umbrella on London's Waterloo Bridge in 1978. I wrote a long story. But the case wasn't (and still isn't) solved, a sizeable hole in a murder mystery. The story was remanded to the foreign page.

Fear of empty-handed returns can breed hesitancy in editors. In my youth, at least, I thought it best to ignore them. When I sent a note to New York announcing my need to rent an airplane to visit a long Australian fence, the reply was frugally skeptical.

I just went.

. . . .

The Dingo Fence

WOMPAH GATE, AUSTRALIA

The Great Wall of China is about 3,889 miles long. What's so great about that? Australia has a wall, too. It runs for 3,488 miles. It's a fence, actually. The Dingo Fence.

Heads of state who visit Australia don't usually come out to walk along the Dingo Fence. It isn't a whole lot to look at. But it's impressive enough to get pilot Kerry Provis to put down the novel he's reading and circle his Piper Cherokee around for a better view.

From a few thousand feet, the land looks like brown bread overgrown with pale-green mold. It also looks as though someone has taken a knife edge and drawn a sharp line across it. That's the fence.

It starts way down south near the Great Australian Bight, works its way across the Great Victorian Desert, turns north through the Great Artesian Basin, then swings south again along the Great Dividing Range and ends up in the South Pacific near a place called Surfers' Paradise. It should be called the Great Dingo Fence, but Australians are modest.

Dingoes are wild dogs that kill sheep. The purpose of the Dingo Fence is to separate the sheep from the dogs. It cordons off the southeastern third of the continent for the sheep. The dingoes get the rest.

Kerry Provis puts the Cherokee down with a crunch and rolls up to Wompah Gate. That's all it is. Just a gate in the Dingo Fence. A sign says anybody who leaves it open will wind up in the clink. On the ground is an empty bottle of Duke's Own Very Fine Scotch Whisky. The gate is conveniently located just under a thousand miles from most of Australia's major cities, in the middle of nowhere. From horizon to horizon, the land is silent and empty, except for a mob of kangaroos relaxing under a lone shade tree.

A wisp of dust rising in the distance heralds Geoff Smith in his Land Cruiser. Geoff is an overseer for something called the Wild Dog Destruction Board, which was good enough to send a telegram through the Royal Flying Doctor Service alerting him to a visit. With nine "boundary riders," Geoff tends a 217-mile stretch of fence here on the border between the states of New South Wales and Queensland. The riders and their families live in cottages along the fence, spaced 25 miles apart. Their assignment: Watch for holes.

Geoff rolls a cigarette and clamps it firmly in his front teeth. He pushes the cowboy hat off his forehead, rubs the back of his neck and explains the fence: "It's six-foot high, on the average, and a foot in the ground. You got a plastic netting one foot in the ground and one out. Then two foot of rabbit netting and three foot of marsupial netting. You got a top running wire, a belly wire and two down below, gauge 1.6 mils…"

A horn honks. There's a truck trying to get through the gate, and Geoff's car is blocking it. "Sit here for a week and nobody passes," Geoff says. "Just get here today and we got a traffic jam."

He moves his car and the truck rumbles through with a dog howling in the back. "G'day mate," Geoff yells to the man in the truck, and he secures the gate.

A few feet on the other side of the Dingo Fence is a line of cracked, sun-bleached posts with a few rusty wires clinging to them. That is (or was) the Rabbit Fence. Back in the 1880s, when Australia was first fencing itself off, the menace was rabbits. Millions of them would swoop down and eat every blade of grass in sight. So thousands of miles of rabbit fence were strung. But that didn't bother the rabbits. "There's nothing you can do to stop a rabbit," Geoff says. "They just hop over it or dig under it." So the government gave up on the Rabbit Fence and converted it to the Dingo Fence.

The Dingo Fence works fine against dingoes, as long as there aren't any holes in it. That's a problem. The fence is forever under assault. Kangaroos go walloping into it at full tilt, punching big gaps. Emus—goofy-looking birds with long legs and no wings— do the same. "They'll hit the fence at 30 miles an hour, bounce off, pick themselves up and away they'll go again," Geoff says. Wild pigs are worse. "They just tear up the bloody fence. You know what pigs are like, I guess. Nothing's pigproof."

Something there is that doesn't love this fence. In the desert, where it undulates over high dunes, a big blow will bury the fence in sand. Or the wind will burrow underneath and the fence will fall down. Here, in what they call "stony clay country," bush fires during droughts burn through the fence, leaving it charred and weak. When there aren't droughts, there are floods. In 1974, heavy rains brought the usually trickling Bulloo River raging into the normally dry Bullagree Swamp. Wompah Gate was inundated. Geoff Smith's house, with Geoff and his family on the roof, was washed away. The fence was mangled for miles.

Almost four years later, the water, starting just east of here, is still 20 miles across. Geoff drives toward it and stops when the earth goes doughy. This is where the boundary riders have to get out, load fencing onto their backs, and trek through the muck to rebuild the fence as it emerges from the receding swamp. If they didn't, everything south of here would be dingo country.

That would mean more work for Geoff Gash, the "dogger" on this stretch of fence. He hunts dingoes for a regular salary plus $10 a "scalp." In 1976, he came in with only 17 dogs; the fence must be doing its job. It would be nice to meet Gash, who is 64 years old and has been hunting dingoes all his life, but nobody knows where he is. "He pretty much lives in his car," Geoff Smith says. "Wherever there's dogs, he camps. You can't keep track of him."

There used to be two doggers here. The other one, Billy Baldwin, called it a day a couple of years ago at age 72. After Geoff Gash, there isn't likely to be anybody. Finding boundary riders isn't as hard, but it's hard enough. Not everyone is suited to the life; people go crazy out here. "The odd ones never go anyplace for months on end," Geoff Smith says, driving along the fence to Laurie Murphy's house. "We've had 'em shoot 'emselves and do all sorts of things. They stay at it too long. They're usually mad as hatters."

Laurie Murphy, who is in his 60s, has been riding the fence for 16 years. He has a beer belly, a cracked, sweat-stained leather hat, a fine white stubble on his chin, and all his marbles. In the early days, boundary riders were presented with two tents and two camels and sent their way. Today they have all the amenities: radios, electricity generators, windmills that pump water, trucked-in food. "Oh, no, we're not isolated or anything like that," Laurie says.

When the thirst moves him, Laurie goes to Tibooburra, a town an hour-and-a-half's drive from here on bush tracks. Tibooburra is so small it's nearly invisible from the air, but it has two bars. "I like a beer," Laurie says.

Most of the time, he and his wife, May, are happy to stay at home, a little place with a corrugated iron roof and an accumulation of sheds, gas cans and old tires around it. Inside, the floors are covered by several kinds of linoleum. There are folding tables and chairs in the living room. On the walls are pictures of race horses and cows, a picture postcard of Elvis Presley and one of the Queen. In the freezer is a whole pig.

"I love the bush," May says.

Laurie nods. "We never worry about getting around much," he says.

Driving back to the airplane at Wompah Gate, Geoff Smith and Kerry Provis, the pilot, get into a discussion. There is a difference of opinion in Australia about the dingo. To some, it's savage. To others, it's sort of cuddly. Sheep farmers say dingoes eat sheep, but scientists wonder if they aren't partial to wombats and wallabies. In the big cities, there are a few people who want to breed dingoes and keep them around the house.

"Come across any pups lately?" Kerry asks.

"Oh yeah," Geoff says.

"I want a couple. Pay good money."

"Not allowed to keep 'em, you know," Geoff says. "A dingo is a wild animal. Some will go through 30 or 40 sheep at a time. Just tear 'em to pieces."

Kerry sighs, "Ah, well..."

Geoff drives on in silence. He has been on the fence nine years, keeping the dingo out. It's a good fence. And, when you come to think about it, maybe the dingoes have been pretty good neighbors. At the gate, Geoff watches Kerry climb into the cockpit. He waves goodbye and starts to drive off.

Then he stops again and calls out, "How big you want those pups?"

1978

Chapter 4
DON'T JUST GO

I take it back. Story proposals are good. They have the same calming power over editors that arrival-time clocks have over subway passengers. Editors like to know when a story is due at the station, and that the station is Times Square, not Kookamunga. Proposals also benefit reporters who prefer uneventful journeys over derailments.

It would be nice to describe the way a proposal is supposed to look. No doubt samples abound on the Web, like college application essays. I haven't consulted any. Once, I overheard a *Wall Street Journal* editor tell a reporter that a proposal should have a summary at the top, followed by the story's main point, its socio-historical context, a catchy news angle, and a "why we should care" sentence. Something like that.

To show editors why they should care about a "remote encoding center" run by the post office, I boiled the activity of its clerks down to four words: "They read rotten handwriting." I learned of the remote encoders in Buffalo while investigating the square-envelope surcharge, and added that curiosity to my ideas folder. Four years later, the post office ran into a budget crisis, a catchy enough angle for a story about remote encoding.

Americans talk on the phone sooner than people in many other countries, making it easier to write story proposals in America and harder to report stories. My first remote-encoding call was to the National Postal Museum's historian, who designated the clerks who read bad handwriting as a "last vestige of human intelligence." I downloaded a government report on the threatened postal bankruptcy, and a 107-page paper entitled "A History

of Mail Classification and its Underlying Policies and Purposes."
It was very socio-historical. I phoned the Postal Service spokeswoman in Washington, who told me that the country's two remote
encoding centers would survive any budget cuts because people
still addressed envelopes in scribbles machines couldn't read.
There was my main point.

I wrote the proposal, sent it to my editor, and it was approved.
I emailed the Postal Service spokeswoman to say I was all set to
meet the remote encoders of Salt Lake City. She wrote back: "We
haven't been letting media into any of our facilities, so when you
find out if this is going forward let me know and we might be able
to make an exception." My shocked reply: "I'm a feature writer, so
I have to get out of the office and meet people and see stuff. If I
can't go and watch the job being done, I'll probably have to aban-
don the proposal."

Derailed! For editors, knowing in advance what a story will
say sometimes seems a greater concern than knowing how it will
be told. I was so fixated on getting my remote-encoders proposal
approved for its newsy, socio-historic relevance that I neglected
to get permission to set foot in the giant box where the remote
encoders work. Pushing relevance too hard can also send light-
hearted proposals to the junkyard. Riding through New Jersey in
my Buick, asking myself why I couldn't pump my own gas in that
state, I decided to propose a story on pump jockeys. In groping for
a "why do we care" sentence, my proposal became so mired in gas
taxes and highway trust funds that Page One nearly sent it to the
editorial page. Then an editor wisecracked that full-service gas
stations were probably New Jersey's chief cultural advantage—and
it became the story's theme.

For all my misgivings, I admit that proposals make the trains
run on time. Working the phones in my own language from an
American office, amassing background and narrowing focus, I
can submit a proposal that insures me against the unexpected and
still frees me to take risks. A proposal for a story of 1,000 words
can run 500. I'm halfway there before I'm out the door. Which is
why, once out the door with an approved proposal, I never give
the thing a second look. I have my go-ahead. Now I might come

up with something I didn't get on the phone—something better. An editor could only object if I came back with something worse.

It happened on a story about a Los Angeles comedy writer who moved to Nebraska to open an online gong store. My proposal hit the gongs hard: "Andrew Borakove didn't know it seven years ago when he started an Internet gong store, but gongs are economic indicators." In Nebraska, I was so taken with Borakove that I swiveled the spotlight away from the gong biz and onto his escape from writing for "Hankey, the Christmas Poo" in Hollywood. An editor balked. "This wasn't your proposal," she said. No, and for once the proposal was better. I cut out the first few paragraphs of my story, and pasted the proposal's in their place. As for the remote encoders, after some begging I did visit them in Salt Lake. The story ran pretty much as I wrote it. I didn't look at the proposal again until just now.

....

Poor Penmanship: The Proposal

As long as hand-addressed letters stick around, one set of postal clerks will stay employed: They read rotten handwriting.

With the Postal Service in financial turmoil, there's angst in the air about the future of mail. Saturday deliveries could end, cherished small-town post offices could close. Meantime, the service praises itself for cost-cutting, high-tech innovations that will save the old stamped, first-class letter from death-by-email.

Nothing makes the Postal Service prouder than its world leadership in building machines that can read addresses. When they went online in the early '90s, the Post Office was sure that those high-speed computers would soon be able to read every single envelope fed through them. For letters with addresses that the machines couldn't decipher, the service created offices filled with clerks trained to specialize in reading the machine-unreadable.

At first, the service had 55 of these centers. They were the only post office buildings that never saw a real piece of mail—they were filled with clerks who stared at images of envelopes sent to their computer screens from mail-processing operations all over the country. The clerks unscrambled the scribbles, and then keyed in the right codes. Now, after more advances, only two "remote encoding centers" are left, one in Wichita and one in Salt Lake City.

In the lists of cutbacks now on the Postal Service chopping block, the two remaining remote centers are not to be found. It seems the machines, for now, have met their match: the last 2 percent of scrawled envelopes that real humans have to squint at.

The 2,000 clerks in these places have a hectic, brutal job. A good number of them can't hack it. Of course, even they can't read every envelope. When they give up, a letter is eyeballed physically by a clerk back in a real processing center. When that clerk can't read an address, it's shipped to the dead-letter office.

Two dead-letter offices are left, in Atlanta and St. Paul. Clerks there comb through envelopes and parcels that look like they contain something valuable. What happens to a stamped hand-addressed letter that lands in a dead-letter office today? It gets shredded.

Story will hang out at remote center in Salt Lake, a blank box on an anonymous plain, and maybe also take a quick peek into the dead letter office in St. Paul. Art: possibly unreadable addresses (if permitted) and pix of clerks at work.

. . . .

Poor Penmanship: The Story

SALT LAKE CITY

A man in Emden, Mo., recently mailed a letter that he had addressed, in a scribble, to somebody in "Shelhjreille, Mo." That's the way his handwriting made it look, anyhow.

The letter was delivered the next day. Gary Oliver, a postal clerk 1,200 miles away, got it there. Oliver works in the Salt Lake

City "Remote Encoding Center" of the U.S. Postal Service—a room where hundreds of clerks sit in silence, day and night, staring at America's worst-addressed envelopes.

Just hours after the man in Emden mailed his first-class letter, a picture of it showed up on Oliver's computer. He is 64 years old and has worked in the Salt Lake REC (pronounced "wreck") since 1994.

Oliver said, "I can read the first three letters—S H E." He typed them. A list appeared of every Missouri town starting with "She." Oliver eyeballed the envelope. "Not Shelbina," he said. "Not Sheldon. Not Sheridan. Not Sherman." He punched Shelbyville.

On his screen, the envelope disappeared—the computer's way of telling Oliver he was right.

The Postal Service has money troubles. It's closing post offices, axing staff. One-day delivery may end. Saturday delivery may end.

Email is the prime culprit: 104 billion first-class letters were mailed in 2001, 78 billion in 2010. Still, the service is obliged to complete its appointed rounds. If the handwriting is atrocious, no matter. Postal inspectors don't police penmanship.

Which is why Oliver can look at an envelope hand-addressed to "GALLERY303FIFTH-AVESUITE1603NYNY" and see in it: "Job security." The National Postal Museum's curator, Nancy Pope, calls his scribble-disentangling responsibility "the last vestige of human intelligence versus machine intelligence in the sorting race."

The race—to modernity—began with a hand-cranked canceler in 1875, and then another device known as the "hamper-dumper." After World War II, thought was given to sending mail by missile. Postmaster General Arthur Summerfield said at the time that he would try anything, "Yes, even ballpoint pens." But machines could barely read print in 1965. By the '80s, they were able to detect handwriting—and then give up.

"Peek-and-poke" clerks in postal plants were still sliding envelopes into pigeonholes when, in 1994, the Postal Service hired Siemens and Lockheed Martin to teach machines to read scribbling.

At Salt Lake's regional plant, five miles from the REC, the newest version of the reading machine—a welter of belts and rollers—was showing its stuff one Tuesday. Letters—36,000 an hour—shot past a camera. A computer speed-read the addresses, and the machine sprayed on their bar codes. Except for the envelopes that boggled its digital brain.

Like the one whose address was annotated: "Hello Big daddy Its your Sexymama! I love you & always will!!" An image of that envelope was flashed to the REC for its encoders to elucidate.

In the '90s, computers needed remedial reading, stumped as they were by nine addresses in ten. The Postal Service hired 32,000 clerks at 55 RECs to make sense of them. Computers have since learned to see words in scrawls and squiggles the way voice-recognition software hears them in hemming and hawing. The Postal Service says their reading score today is 95 percent.

What's left over is the handwriting from hell. It pours into just two remaining RECs—here and in Wichita, Kan. Their 1,900 clerks cope with machine-unreadable mail from the whole country. Last year, that included 714,085,866 chicken-scratch first-class letters.

In late afternoon, when volume peaks at the Salt Lake center, a blinking panel showed 67,000 letters awaiting attention—from San Juan, Paducah, Los Angeles, Kokomo. A clerk wearing a headset had hit a patch of pen-pal letters from pupils in Memphis. She was decrypting them at a rate of 800 per hour, down from the desired 1,100.

"We ought to teach kids how to address letters," said Bruce Rhoades, a manager looking over her shoulder. His boss, Karen Heath, stood watching beside him and sighed, "A lost art."

If a clerk broods over an envelope for 30 seconds, it gets snatched away for another clerk. Scribble-reading isn't everyone's gift: Up to 20 percent of new hires quit within five weeks. After 17 years and maybe 30 million letters, Oliver can't explain how he does it.

"A lot of immigrants cross their sevens," he was saying as a blur appeared on his screen that seemed to read: "Rham Emanuel (Leader), 121N LaSalle St., Chayo, I.L. Rm 502, 60602." He hit a few buttons and said, "Foreign handwriting. I sent it to the mayor."

But then came an image too faint for him. "Red envelope," said Oliver. He hit his "reject" button. The address inside a window envelope was hidden from view. Another reject. A letter to "Brighton Park Apartment" in Indianapolis lacked a street. Rejected again.

Oliver and his fellow clerks, in fact, couldn't unscramble 27 percent of the addresses—or return addresses, if any—bounced at them last year by baffled computers. As long as the computers are semiliterate, the clerks will have jobs. But what about the 195,479,866 envelopes neither could read?

Ben Franklin, who began sorting mail in 1753, would know. In the plants, after computers fish them out of the mail stream, those letters are placed in the knowing hands of the few surviving peek-and-poke clerks.

In Salt Lake's plant this night, Jim Herlin was on duty at his pigeonholes. He tapped a window envelope to nudge its address into view. He slid a letter to "College Park Plaza, Salt Lake City" into a slot for Ogden, Utah, because "I know that's in Ogden."

When he picked up a letter to someone in "October, Utah," he stopped. "No such place," Herlin said. "That's a nixie."

A *nixie* (it's in the dictionary) is a letter with an illegible or incorrect address. Salt Lake's nixies land on a table where nixie clerks take a last stab at divining where they're supposed to go.

Debbie Holender was there at the end of her shift, looking at black blots on an envelope while searching for anything similar in a pocket street guide. "What penmanship!" she said.

That nixie's next stop would be a hamper marked "dead letter office." There's one left: the "Mail Recovery Center" in Atlanta. Its clerks will open nixies that show signs of harboring documents or cash. What happens to a letter of no obvious interest to anybody but some illegible addressee?

It's hand-delivered to the shredder.

2011

Chapter 5

MISINTERPRETATION

Every reporter, I was advised early on, ought to go abroad. I went, stayed a couple of decades, and filed stories from 65 or so countries. (Some were countries when I visited, but aren't now; some weren't countries when I visited, but now are.) Home or abroad, the reporting job was the same: Ask questions. A difference, though, was that not as many foreigners understood a word I was saying.

And the other way around. On my first trip to Indonesia, I embarked on a story about shadow plays. In Javanese, the word for shadow is *wayang*. I looked it up. I'd read that shadow plays mirrored Indonesia's shadowy society. It seemed like a fine first subject. At the U.S. Embassy in Jakarta, I got the name of an Indonesian *wayang* expert, who gave me an interview in English. "The *gara gara* is the climactic section of the *wayang* in which the order and tranquility of the cosmos is disturbed," my notes read. I was in luck. A play was scheduled for that night in a pavilion outside the city. It would start at eight and end at eight the next morning. I took a taxi, and sat through it all, increasingly aghast that the whole show was in Javanese. I waited for the *gara gara*, but it must have shot right past me. Outside at sunup, there weren't any taxis. I got into the back of a pickup truck, and rode to Jakarta with a pile of cabbages.

The last page of my notebook—right after the observation, "place covered with peanut shells"—contains a list of Indonesian phrases I assigned myself to learn: "I'm looking for ____. Do you know where I can find ____? I need____." But one word would fill in all those blanks, and many more, in any language. The word is *interpreter*.

Interpreters aren't translators. Translators sit at desks turning the written words of one language into the written words of another. Interpreters translate spoken words. They walk alongside reporters, whispering in their ears. They arrange interviews, make phone calls, hail taxis, buy train tickets, order dinner, do the laundry. The best interpreters interpret more than words; they interpret cultures.

In Warsaw, Agnieszka Mitraszewska was my interpreter for ten years. She was a young mother when we met, a graduate with a degree in English who had lived in England. I rarely spent more than a couple of months a year in Poland, but the *Journal* kept Agnieszka on call. The money helped buy her a car and build her family a house. When her parents moved into the house, I moved into their apartment. Agnieszka knew what stories I liked. She was my private clipping service. She had connections to politicians. If stories needed everyday human beings, she trucked out neighbors, cousins, friends.

At sit-down interviews, Agnieszka sat just behind me, gently siphoning English into my ear. She made people pause in midsentence, passing me one clause at a time. She didn't paraphrase. Agnieszka was on autopilot, processing every odd sliver of conversation, whether it seemed relevant to the story or not. That's what I wanted. Agnieszka was so good that at times, when she wasn't with me, I forgot I didn't speak Polish. In an Old Town shop, I filled a basket with tea, rye bread, honey and pickles, and was at the cash register, fully intending to communicate with the checkout clerk, before I realized that I didn't know the Polish for "plastic bag please."

I'd been going to Poland for a year before a friend sent Agnieszka my way. In places I visited less often (or once), I fished for recommendations from teachers, diplomats and other reporters. Professional interpreters, who sit at conference tables between men in suits, were the worst. In New Caledonia, a woman who interpreted for mining engineers broke down and ran out on me during an interview with a man who was trying to incite a rebellion. (That was when I decided to study French.) A robotic business interpreter in Trieste charged three times my meager norm

for a day's work; when I suggested lunch, she said, "Is it required?"
A Serb who evidently missed her Anglo-Saxon class put words
like "parameters" into the mouths of metal workers. An American
Peace Corps volunteer, fluent in Malay, insisted that a peasant had
said, "You can't cry over spilt milk." I told him I preferred a literal
meaning which, in this case, was "The rice has gotten wet and
turned to gruel."

Local journalists (sometimes, even, the ones who work for
local dictatorships) make the best interpreters. In Turkey, for
me, that was Metin Demirsar. Metin was blond. Until he started
talking, people thought he was the foreigner and I was the Turk.
Metin organized an interview with Chever Ozden, a loan shark.
We sat across the desk in Ozden's opulent office down a dusty
hallway of Istanbul's bourse. I asked questions. Metin interpreted.
Between questions, the loan shark worked his phones. A sample
from my story:

> *Ozden dials a number. "It is a matter of organization," he says,*
> *waiting for his call to be answered. "I take advantage of certain*
> *funds." Someone picks up at the other end and Ozden starts*
> *screaming: "Postpone until Thursday? Why a week's delay?*
> *This is going to cost me my life! I can't stand it!"…Suddenly, he*
> *is livid and bellowing into the phone: "I'll screw you! I'll screw*
> *you!" He smashes the receiver down so hard, the phone falls off*
> *the table.*

Ozden alternated screams into the phone with screams at
Metin, who translated them: "Don't translate this! I said I don't
want you to translate this! Stop translating!" Metin translated.
Turkey, at the time, was under martial law. In Fatsa, a leftist
enclave on the Black Sea, 300 men had been arrested and put on
trial for their lives. Fatsa was off-limits to journalists, but Metin
said, "Let's go." We got there after 13 hours on a bus. "Driving
sleet," my notes say. "Smell of anchovies. Sidewalks buried in mud.
Big sacks of hazelnuts." Warmed by hazelnut shells in an iron
stove, Metin translated as I talked to a leftist who had avoided
arrest. Metin didn't drink. The leftist and I emptied three bottles

of Dutch gin. The leftist grew less coherent. My notes grew more illegible. Metin translated. "Go talk to the chief of police," my interviewee suggested, according to Metin. "He's a modern man." We went, and the modern police chief arrested us.

He had us driven to an army camp (where an officer questioned us), driven to a hotel, guarded all night, put on a bus, and sent back to Ankara. Herein lies the lesson: Turkish journalists were being put in prison back then. Some were tortured. One had died. Metin Demirsar wanted to do his best for me. At worst, I might have been deported. The worst for Metin would have been much worse than that. Fatsa was a good story, but when he said, "Let's go," I should have said, "Let's not."

I must attach a warning about employing journalists as interpreters. In Tunisia my interpreter was spying on me, writing reports; I had to sneak out to interviews without him. Even when not spying, journalist-interpreters ask their own questions. They can't help it. At times, my presence has slipped their minds. Touring the kitchen of the Stockholm opera house with a chef and an interpreting journalist, I stopped for a moment of quiet note taking: "Kitchen crowded with assistants. Great smell of pickled fish. Blonde girls in white hats..." I looked up. The interpreter was gone. He had walked on, deep in his own interview with the chef. Catching up, I had to remind him: This Rockaway-inspired pickled-herring scoop was mine.

. . . .

Pickled Herring

STOCKHOLM

In Sweden, as in other Northern European countries and certain sections of metropolitan New York, cultural identity is closely tied to pickled herring.

The Swedes eat pickled herring in midsummer. They eat it on Christmas. They eat it for breakfast. A Swedish father, in the course of consuming pieces of pickled herring for an appetizer one evening, recounts his son's coming of age in pickled-herring terms: The boy loved it; the adolescent rejected it; the law-school graduate can't stop eating it.

Some people probably aren't in love with pickled herring. But they probably aren't Swedish. On the other hand, you don't have to be Swedish to love pickled herring. For someone whose mouth waters at the very thought of the stuff, a trip to Sweden is the next best thing to standing in front of the appetizing counter at the Waldbaums supermarket on Ocean Avenue in Brooklyn, breathing deeply.

From a pickled-herring perspective, Sweden's premier place to eat is Operakallaren. It is a restaurant in the opera house, amid the domes and steeples of Stockholm's waterfront. A guest who walks up on a cold afternoon can look through its windows at ladies in fur turbans choosing discreetly small portions from a discreetly elegant smorgasbord. It doesn't seem much like Waldbaums to me. At Operakallaren, pickled herring is obviously haute cuisine.

Chef Werner Vogeli, all in white, waits in the lobby. He exudes the aloof confidence of a man accustomed to accomplishment. Chef Vogeli prepares banquets at the royal palace. Once, he served 350 cheese soufflés at a single sitting. And can he ever pickle a herring! In Brooklyn, they would call him a herring maven.

The chef leads the way down a narrow staircase and into the wine cellar, where 40,000 bottles repose in darkness. Behind a small bar, he breaks out a bottle of champagne.

"Some newspaper in Norway just claimed that I said Norwegians don't know how to slice herring," he says, setting out the glasses. The chef is piqued at the pickled-herring press. "All I said was the pieces were too big. If you're trying 30 kinds of pickled herring, you don't want pieces six inches long. Now I can never go back to Norway."

He pours, toasts, sips, then pauses in deep thought. "There are better champagnes," Chef Vogeli decides, and suggests lunch.

Upstairs, in the main dining room, chandeliers glitter beneath a coffered ceiling. Forest nymphs cavort on the walls. Fluted oak columns descend to a red carpet. And, in the room's center, the smorgasbord rests like an imperial launch in dry dock, all polished brass and lacquered wood. The pickled herring is on a bed of ice in the bow.

Laid enticingly on shallow platters are matjes-herring fillets, matjes herring in Rhode Island sauce, marinated smoked herring, herring in mustard sauce, herring with caviar, spiced herring, pickled salt herring, plain pickled herring, and herring first fried and then pickled.

Chef Vogeli selects a gold-rimmed plate and places two tiny pieces of plain pickled herring on it, along with a small boiled potato. "It's not right to put too much on your plate," he instructs. "You must go back and forth many times."

Four trips, one beer and two glasses of aquavit later, the chef returns to check on his guest. I have a question: Where are the chopped herring and the herring in cream sauce with tons of onions, like they have at Waldbaums?

Chef Vogeli is puzzled. He is unfamiliar with the gastronomy of Flatbush. Only one kind of herring is deliberately excluded from his smorgasbord: the infamous *surstromming*.

"It is something you must learn to appreciate," he says. "I have not had the opportunity to do so yet. It cannot be served in a restaurant. All the guests would leave."

After lunch, I discover a cache of *surstromming* in the back of a stall at Stockholm's old fish market. The clerk, sniggering, hands a bloated tin over the counter. "Open it in a bucket of water," he says. "Otherwise, it will shoot up in your face. And I wouldn't do it inside."

Duly warned, I do the deed alone, in a deserted parking lot. The controlled explosion and ensuing aroma bring to mind a Southeast Asian fruit called a durian. Durians have creamy pulps but smell awful. Eating one has been likened to eating vanilla custard out of an oil drum. By comparison, a bite of *surstromming*—which is herring partly pickled and mostly rotten—is like eating tuna fish out of a grease monkey's boot.

A few Swedes allegedly like *surstromming*, but all great causes attract extremists, and pickled herring does, too. It has dissenters, however. They are based in the Waxholm, a turreted hotel on an island near Stockholm. Fishing boats tie up opposite the Waxholm's entrance. The chef, a stout German named Rolf Durr, crosses the road each day to buy his herring fresh. It is the specialty of the house.

"People come here just to eat this," the chef says, jiggling a frying pan at the kitchen's stove while an assistant chops dill behind him. Chef Durr puts some dill between two herring fillets, dusts them with flour and slides them into hot butter. They're ready in a minute. "That's your dish," he says. "So fresh."

The chef strides out into the dining room with the herring on a plate. He sets it on a table. I sit. He sits in the next chair. I taste. He leans in to witness the reaction.

Very good.

"Everybody prefers it fresh," Chef Durr declares. "Herring had to be pickled in the old days to preserve it. After they invented the refrigerator, pickled herring just hung on. Every kind of food is better fresh."

What heresy. A pickled-herring believer must be cleansed of such thoughts. Total immersion is the answer. This calls for a pilgrimage to the pickled-herring caves of Kungshamn.

A quick flight west and an icy, three-hour drive north from Gothenburg bring Kungshamn into view. Its wooden houses cling like lichen to the treeless granite at the tip of a fiord. On the edge of the sea, a sheet-steel building rises from the rock: the headquarters of Abba.

No, not ABBA the pop group, Abba the pickled-herring company. Abba is Sweden's biggest pickled-herring company. It is owned by Volvo, Sweden's biggest car company. Volvo makes 270,000 cars a year and 5,000 tons of pickled herring. That works out to roughly 180 million bites, on crackers. The man in charge is Thorsten Thornblad. He is the chief of the pickled-herring division.

"Today, in Sweden, matjes herring has been supplanted by herring in mustard sauce," Thornblad says in his corner office. "It's a modern taste." We put on white coats and paper hats and walk out, through a pair of swinging doors, onto the factory floor. "Cream sauce?" Thornblad says. "Sweden isn't ready for that. Cream sauce is the next step."

But on the near end of the floor, women at long counters feverishly shove pickled herring into jars half-filled with that same ambrosial nectar. "Milk and fish," one says, making a face.

Abba, Thornblad explains, is about to invade New York. For years, Vita Food Products has been the kingfish in New York's pickled-herring game. Vita's radio spots star "the herring maven," who sounds like an old man in a rumpled suit, size 48 short. But Abba's advertisements will feature a tall, Swedish blonde in a slinky dress. Thornblad expects her to set off a pickled-herring war in the Big Apple.

"Incidentally," he says on the way to the parking lot, "this word 'maven'—what does it mean?"

The winter sun grazes the horizon. Thornblad adjusts the windshield's visor and steers his Volvo along the seafront, toward the caves that hold Abba's subterranean treasury.

"The state blasted them out in 1956," he says. "They were for storing oil in case of war. But they were perfect for us, and the state agreed. Even in war, Sweden will need pickled herring."

He swings the Volvo onto an asphalted wharf, built against a granite bluff. At the far end, like the entrance to the Brooklyn-Battery Tunnel, is the cave mouth.

"So this is our pickled-herring shelter," Thornblad says, hailing a dark-haired man in a quilted jacket. "And this is the real maven." Nils Olsson buys Abba's herring from the fishermen of the North Atlantic and the North Sea and keeps vigil as it marinates in the caves. "I eat pickled herring every day," he says as we walk into the dripping tunnel. "I've eaten pickled herring every day of my life."

A man in hip boots hoses down the concrete floor. Another drives by in a forklift truck. The tunnel curves. We arrive at a large, metal door in its outer face. Olsson throws a switch and the door rises slowly, like a theater curtain. He throws another and carbon lamps begin to glow, revealing a cavern with a vaulted ceiling of rough-hewn rock.

Receding more than 400 feet into the semi-darkness, the chamber is filled to the gills with wooden barrels, stacked on their sides, six high and 35 across—11,000 in all, each packed with 220 pounds of herring steeped in marinade. The air is briny, vinegary—and sweet.

"It amazes me every time," says Olsson, taking in the sight. And the granite conceals three more chambers, just as big. Periodically, each barrel must be rotated, so that the brine flows evenly. A crew of three turns 1,200 barrels a day, year round. "It's like champagne," Olsson says.

Walking out, he stops at an upright barrel of matjes herring and breaks it open. He lifts out a fish, colored maroon by sandalwood in the brine, and fillets it with his thumbnail. "Try it," he says, and watches as I chew.

Valhalla.

"You realize," Olsson says as we surface, "that if the government wanted to store something more important here, they could still chase us out."

But what's more important than pickled herring?

"I don't know," Olsson says.

Neither do I.

1984

Chapter 6
ABROAD AT HOME

Living abroad was an education. I learned that the weirdest country of all was my own. I came home to cover immigration feeling like an immigrant. America's "them" was my "us." Immigration law defined the outside world as a prison; to provisionally reenter the land of the free after a trip overseas, green-card candidates had to apply for "parole." The official penalty for renouncing American citizenship was to be forever barred from buying a gun.

Because I'd been to Bangladesh, I could discuss the Awami League with a Bangladeshi handing out fliers for a Democratic City Council candidate in Ozone Park, Queens. Because I'd been to North Africa, I could walk into a hookah café in Astoria, smoke a hubble-bubble with an Algerian and talk about the city's hubble-bubble ban.

The good-hearted people I interviewed usually didn't see the oddity that I saw in their doings. Hussein Hussein, an Egyptian who worked in an Italian restaurant, had a Polish girlfriend. When he got a job running a Greek diner, he dropped the Greek food and introduced a Polish-Italian menu. Why is that funny? Everyone in Britain kids Morris dancers, men who dress in white and skip about to village tunes with bells on their ankles. Morris dancers were an old joke in Britain, but in America they were funnier, for me, when they danced on a Cooperstown sidewalk in baseball season. Boys heading to the ball field laughed at the men in silly suits. The boys saw no joke in their own silly suits, known as baseball uniforms.

Among the joys of coming home (bagels, the Rockies, my Buick), the unmediated tunes of America's language pleased me most. I'd hummed to India's, Australia's and Scotland's Englishes, but America buzzed with words that didn't travel. "These green splats are lacewings," said the Florida bug-splat scientist, naming the gunk on the window of a Greyhound bus. "Those little guys are leaf hoppers. This is just a really gross flying cockroach." I celebrated the millennium with Americans who spelled it millenneum, malanium and millionian. Where besides America would a podiatrist say: "Our goal is to put their feet in a better mindset."

Being abroad at home, though, still required interpreters. I needed them to get me past barriers, linguistic and cultural, Mexican to Bosnian. The Bowery was a street of Jewish lamp merchants before I left New York, and still was—except that now a few shops had Chinese letters on their awnings and Chinese salesmen inside. I wanted to know: Were new Chinese lamp sellers displacing the old Jews?

My cultural connections in New York were as good as Agnieszka Mitraszewska's in Warsaw: My cousin Bobby's wife's father, who was in electrical supply, cleared my way into the chandelier jungles of the Bowery's Jewish lamp peddlers. But in the Chinese lamp stores, I was met with vacant looks of indifference. A guy with a notebook? He doesn't want to buy a lamp? An interview? Not interested!

Mandarin Dynasty was a lamp store dense with crystal and rosewood furniture. Sandy Yu, my notes read, "sits in a little back office behind plywood door reading Chinese newspaper and shouting on phone. She's young, nice smile, unacculturated. Language barrier too high here." That's when I hired Ka-Kam Chui, whose business card identified him as "linguistic specialist." Chui was no journalist; he spent his days interpreting in hospitals. When we spoke on the phone, I explained my linguistic frustrations. He named his price and told me to meet him in two days at 62 Mott Street. Why Mott Street? The story was about the Bowery. Just meet me, Chui said.

The address was the headquarters of the Chinese Consolidated Benevolent Association of New York. Chui—middle-aged, black attaché case—steered me into the elevator and up to a glassed-in office where the Benevolent Association's president, Ting Din Ng, sat behind a desk. Several other people sat around him. Chui told me to ask questions while he translated. Fine. What could the president tell me about the lighting business on the Bowery?

"Immigrants need to make a living," Ng said. "They will start anywhere." He was bald and smiling. He talked about the jewelry trade, restaurant supply, tourism, real estate. "There's a six-story limit. We are out of space." A man in the corner, I noticed, had a camera on his lap. Did Ng have any friends in the lighting business? He didn't. "I worked for Weiss Hardware 30 years ago," he said.

We left. I still didn't know what I'd been doing there. Chui told me we'd visit Mandarin Dynasty the next morning. We met on the corner of Bowery and Grand, and walked. Chui stopped at a candy store to buy a Chinese newspaper, the *World Journal*. He opened the paper, and there it was—a picture of me and Ng. The caption, as Chui translated: "*Wall Street Journal* seeks views of Chinatown leader."

Mandarin Dynasty was deserted, except for a woman at a table, stringing crystal beads. A crew-cut man in a crew-neck sweater came out of the office. Chui learned his name, Guo Sheng Huang, had a quiet word with him, and took the *World Journal* from under his arm. He opened it to the picture. Suddenly, Huang was beaming.

"You Jewish?" he said. His English was broken, but I pieced it together with Chui's help. "I born Shanghai. My neighbors all Jewish. Now, Jewish neighbors again." Sandy Yu, his wife, joined us, sending the young woman to fetch tea. We sat around a table with a Chinese scene carved into it while the couple told us their life stories. My notes fill thirteen pages. If I had known the value of interpreters on that night at the Javanese shadow play in Jakarta, I might have come away with a few good quotes then, too.

. . . .

Lampland

NEW YORK

For two blocks along the Bowery, the Main Street of New York's Lower East Side, storefront after storefront opens into dim, air-cooled caves where ceilings drip with crystal, alabaster and Tiffany glass. To its regulars, this promenade between Grand Street and Delancey Street is the Lighting District. In the new, high-rent lofts above the stores, tenants call it Lampland.

Lampland isn't large—29 stores—but the forces working to change it have been. It has survived a century of transitions: from gaslight to electricity, from metalworking shops in Brooklyn to the riptides of global production, from the era of urban souks to suburban megastores, and now from a zone of teeming tenements to a real-estate bonanza. This unkempt row of retailers has held on.

Lampland generates energy from immigration—four generations so far: Jews from Eastern Europe and then Israel; Chinese from Guangdong province and now from Fujian. The crowds have thinned, but customers still come to shop for a deal from store to store. The owners battle to keep Lampland alive mostly by battling each other.

Gary Fitterman, a third-generation Jewish New Yorker, has never met Li Chun Hu, a recent immigrant from China. Their stores face each other across the Bowery, at opposite ends of the immigrant stream that has sustained Lampland's timeline.

Hu, 36 years old, is from Fujian's capital, Fuzhou, source of much of the Chinese exodus that has popped the demographic seams of New York's Chinatown. All day all week, Hu works in a swirl of chandeliers and track lights, speaking not a word of English but gripped by ambition. "After days of struggle in my mind, finally I decided," he says, with an interpreter's help, describing his determination to open a lighting store. Two years ago, he did. "After I decide," says Hu, "no one can stop me." Fitterman, 43, born on Long Island, started out working for one of Lampland's Israeli-immigrant innovators. Now he owns four stores to Hu's one, and intends to expand. "I want to be the biggest and the best," he says. "Either I get bigger, or I go home."

The single-commodity district is part of urban nature. Furs, antiques, flowers: Whatever the goods, density draws shoppers. And ethnic businesses are part of American nature. Indian motels, Korean nail salons, Greek diners: When immigrants stick together, commerce is often the glue. Lampland and districts like it combine it all: one nationality, one product, one place.

Like old neighborhoods where newcomers find space to live, these commercial enclaves pass from group to group. New York's jewelry districts have been reinvigorated by Indians and Chinese, its garment districts by Koreans and Hispanics. The transfer rarely takes place neatly. In Lampland, where Chinese newcomers are groping for a toehold on a street where Jews still dominate, it's taking place now: Chinese ideograms decorate five of the Bowery's cleaner awnings.

In 1907, when an Eastern European immigrant named Isidore Eisner opened New York Gas Lighting on the ground floor of the Pioneer Hotel, the lettering was Hebrew. The Bowery had already lost its theaters and mansions. It was mired in flophouses, brothels and saloons. Gaslight hardware wasn't a big seller, but by the 1920s every gas mantle in New York was being converted to electricity and lightbulbs needed fixtures. Factories bloomed in Brooklyn. Eisner's business took off. Competitors moved in, immigrants like him, and Lampland was born.

As Herb Shiner says, "It was an old Jewish community of stores." Shiner, 73 and retired, went to work as a manufacturer's rep in 1952, filling orders on the street. Apart from the Eisner family, Lampland's biggest operators in those days were Joe, Julie and Abe Lichtfield of Paris Lighting, and the Kupferberg brothers, Sam and Dave, who had rival stores and never spoke to each other. Their designs lured buyers from Europe, but for New Yorkers, discounts took precedence and a price tag was just an opening bid. Lampland was—and is—a war zone. Some business districts form associations, run promotions, share suppliers, agree on hours. In Lampland? Not a chance.

As the Bowery began to look less sordid in the 1970s, early Jewish immigrants made way for a second set, from Israel. David Cohen started out making lampshades in Tel Aviv. He moved to New York in 1960 and made lamps in Brooklyn. Ten years later, he opened a store on the Bowery. Soon, he had half a dozen. In a small way, Cohen was a pioneer: He got rid of the boxes, the wires all over, and put carpet on the floors. He gave his showrooms class. And he was a pioneer in a big way: For merchandise, he looked beyond Brooklyn.

"I imported cast bronze from Spain," he says. "My cost was less." Labor costs and pollution rules started chasing lamp makers out of Manhattan, out of Brooklyn, out of the country. Cohen had designs executed by factories in South Korea and Taiwan. In 1982, he hired 22-year-old Gary Fitterman as a stock clerk. The son of an aeronautical engineer, Fitterman was the first member of Lampland's first American-born generation.

But the good times didn't last after Fitterman went to work. Lampland's suburban customers lost the urge to drive across broken bridges into downtown traffic. Home Depot and others like it sprang up, stores founded on the belief that people buying lamps will buy other things, too. "If someone wants to visit 20 retailers to find a lamp," a Home Depot spokeswoman says, "perhaps they should—if they've got a full day to spend on that."

Fitterman remembers his heart sinking as he unpacked closeouts from Brooklyn suppliers going into liquidation. "Everybody thought it was the end of the Bowery," he says. The Asian knockoffs were worst of all. "You'd have a new item, and in a month you'd see a cheap copy from Taiwan. On prices, there was no bottom."

Following Lampland form, Fitterman eventually broke with his bosses and opened a store of his own. His line was "traditional," lamps and fixtures in the shape of elephants, dogs, horses, frogs and monkeys. Soon he had four stores—and was planning a trip to China, the world's newest source of cheap labor. As Lampland turned toward China, however, New York's Chinatown turned toward Lampland.

It is only a geographical coincidence that Lampland stands on the frontier of Chinatown's push north, up the Bowery into Little Italy, the Lower East Side and SoHo. The old First National City Bank became a Chinese wedding palace. Moishe's Deli turned into a noodle shop. In the early '90s, Fitterman watched from his window as two new showrooms appeared across the street. Their awnings read: "European Crystal Chandelier" and "Mandarin Dynasty."

Sandy Yu and her husband, Guo Sheng Huang, own both. They immigrated to Chinatown from Hong Kong in 1991, sponsored by relatives whose U.S. roots date back to railroad days.

Huang, a designer of porcelain vases, planned to import and sell them to New York's Chinese. He knew the storefronts he rented were close to Chinatown. He hardly noticed the Lighting District. "In 1991, American economy is no good," Huang says, sitting on a rosewood bench in Mandarin Dynasty. "A lot of Jewish stores, they close up." Yet he quickly discovered that not even Chinese people came to the Bowery shopping for Chinese porcelain. "Chandeliers were better business here," says Yu. "We noticed. All customers knew this block before they came. Knew before!" Huang says, "Our ceiling was empty."

Now it is a canopy of crystal. The frames come from Hong Kong, the beads from Egypt. The chandelier suspended above his head, Huang says, would sell for $24,000 across the street. His price is $8,900, but he'll let it go $3,000. "Market changed," he says. "That's why Jewish people get out."

Gary Fitterman got in deeper. As imports from Taiwan receded, big American lighting manufacturers rode the Chinese current. Traveling to China in search of factories to make his own designs was risky for a low-volume operator, but to survive in Lampland—and for Lampland's survival—Fitterman saw no other option. "The goal for me," he says, "is to cut out the middle guy, take him out, bring the stuff in myself."

In Guzhen town, a section of the Guangdong city of Zhongshan, a corridor of lighting stores three miles long borders 700 private fixture factories—China's Lampland, writ large. Fitterman's early trips there were "disasters," but he went back until he made the right connections and struck deals with a dozen manufacturers. He started importing by the container load. "We'd literally sit in their factory and take the arms and the glass and change things around," Fitterman says. "China affects everything."

But will it also affect Chinatown's incursion into Lampland? "They have to know who the customer is," Fitterman says of the stores beneath his window. "They can't outdo me, I hope."

Li Chun Hu believes he can. Hu is Fujianese, part of New York's new Chinese influx, and he didn't open a store in Lampland by accident. "I went to school and studied electricity," he says from behind an invoice-blanketed desk. "In 1985, I was assigned to Fuzhou Light Bulb Factory, 2,400 workers." He was 18, struck by a "vision to bring to the world great lighting from China." He ran away in 1990, when Fujianese were being smuggled out by the thousands. He wound up tending a Chinese medicine shop near the Bowery.

"So many lighting stores," Hu says. "I noticed the prices. So high!" He made up his mind: "I will do business between the U.S. and China. To use the technology I found here—the structure, the glass. So beautiful!" Seed money—$100,000—came "through friends." Thus did America Golt Lighting Fixture, a name coined by his accountant, open its doors. Hu has a factory in Fuzhou, with 150 workers making chairs and lighting frames. He has plans for a second in Guangdong province. "I will export 100 percent to the U.S.," he says. "My principle is: Less profit, more business."

Is he aware that Gary Fitterman, his rival across the street, is competing with him in China, too? "I knew that," Hu says. "He is free to do business in China. Competition brings progress."

Fitterman's flagship storefront is New York Lighting. His strategy against high-end mass marketers is to give expert advice—and to aim higher. The ideal customer, he says, is "white middle-class American, building a house in the suburbs." On a warm Sunday, the ideal walks into his store: Anthony Solazzo, a urologist in Watchung, N.J., and his wife, Gina. "We come here for the lights and the choice and the price," Solazzo says. "You get a decent deal on the Bowery. Probably. The stores out in Jersey— the selection isn't as good."

Fitterman's top salesman, Tommy Palmeri, steers the couple onto a silk settee. "Just bought a house, 7,000 square feet," Solazzo says. "We have a foyer with a 25-foot ceiling. We're looking for three, four chandeliers. I like crystal, my wife doesn't." Mrs. Solazzo says, "You want your house to look like a catering hall?"

Above them dangles a chandelier with 20 arms, each culminating in an alabaster bowl. Price tag: $7,199. Palmeri says, "It's the last one." "Hold it for a month," says the doctor. "We'll be back." And the ideal customers drift out onto the Bowery—as Lampland customers almost always will—to keep on shopping.

Across the street, Hu's sales tactic also is to provide expert advice—but he aims low. On another Sunday, he is on his knees in a blue suit, unpacking frames from China. It's 6 p.m., closing time at New York Lighting, not at America Golt.

"Maybe customers are late—we lose business," says Stanley Tang, one of Hu's English-speaking salesmen. At 7 p.m., Golt's closing time, Parag Paul and his wife, Subrita, who moved to New Jersey from Calcutta, stand stonily under a frosted-glass chandelier as salesman Jay Huang says, "I give you 10 percent off. Lowest price I can give you." The couple fold their arms. Huang says, "OK, $207—more than 20 percent off!"

Carrying the box into the street, Paul says, "In Jersey they discount 5 percent only." Hu's staff leaves too, heading home, but as the grate comes down on America Golt, Hu stays inside, still working.

Some Jewish owners have an answer to the likes of Li Chun Hu: Surrender, and get rich on the way out. As Chinatown encroaches on high-rent SoHo, they're betting that real-estate has got to give. David Cohen, pioneer of the offshore factory, has closed all but one of his crystal emporiums. He expects bistros and boutiques to be moving in. And then there's New York Gas Lighting, the Bowery's first Jewish lighting store. It has been in the hands of the Eisner family since 1907, but with luxury apartments rising next door, Isidore Eisner's descendants have put a "For Sale" sign on their grime-caked tenement. Price tag: $4.75 million. In Lampland, that's a steal.

2002

Chapter 7
GATHERING STRING

Displeased with the frying pan in the kitchen of my apartment in Warsaw, I went out to buy a new one and wound up gathering string for six years. String gathering is behavior common to hoarders, junk dealers and journalists who collect "found objects," intending to "use" them someday. It can be conscious, semiconscious or compulsive. In this case, the motivator was a frying pan made of communist-grade aluminum that bonded chemically with kielbasa.

This was 1986. On the first day of my visits, Mrs. Marczyniak, the landlady of an apartment I sporadically occupied, would ring the doorbell wearing a black negligee and bearing a platter of duck with prunes. The rest of the time, I cooked kielbasa, slowly poisoning myself with that pan of hers. At Sezam, Warsaw's department store, the housewares department was a bauxite mine. But outside on the sidewalk, I came across a lone hawker, Wladyslaw Misiel. A Romani (a Gypsy back then), he had three heavy-steel pans at his feet. I bought one for $2.50. It was (and is) a very good frying pan.

Misiel didn't rate a story, but I didn't forget him. By 1990, after communism's collapse, Warsaw's sidewalks were jammed with hawkers selling jeans, sneakers, cheap perfume—all trucked in from the West. The hawkers had metalwork stands that opened like steamer trunks. Moving with the crowd, interpreter in tow, on a November night, I came to the front door of Sezam—and there was Misiel, at his old spot, with a stack of pans on a folding table. Now he was one among thousands. No story in that, either. I asked about his business. He said it was good. I took a note and moved on. Two years went by. Private stores had opened all over. Warsaw had cleared hawkers from the sidewalks. In front of Sezam on an October afternoon, I saw Misiel. He was alone again, banging a pan as pedestrians marched by. I had been a customer before communism ended, had watched him stand his ground in the scrum of revolution, and now he was upright in its aftermath. That did rate a story. "Things around here change," was Misiel's opening quote. "I don't change. I've been here all the time, and I'm still here."

Change, or lack of it, is string gathering's reward. I had no need to grill Misiel about his pre-capitalist pan peddling in Warsaw. I was there. He was part of my memory, a repository of context that cuts down on library research. Returning to a familiar field after an absence combines the comfort of a homecoming with the elbowroom of the long view. Religion, sailing, immigration, baseball, mining, liquor—those are fields I've grazed in a few times. Folk art is another.

Folk art is easy to look at, and folk artists are nice folk. That's how I thought about it in the early 1970s, when I bought one old painting of the Hudson River and, from a store in Brooklyn, a couple of new ones of a village in Haiti. My interest led me to do a story about Jeff Camp, a dealer in Richmond, Virginia, who tore around back roads in North Carolina looking for root sculptures and whirligigs. I stayed mildly interested in folk art after that.

By the 2000s, it had its own critics, curators and magazines. In a nostalgic moment, I Googled Jeff Camp. An exhibit catalog mentioned him, and my 1974 story: "Newman alerted a new generation of collectors to the adventures and acquisitions awaiting them if they traveled the South's country roads." Curious again, I picked up a few books on the subject. Folk art had acquired a new name: "outsider art." Each January, an Outsider Art Fair came to New York. I started going. In 2005, I noticed a truck parked on the street in front of the show's entrance between a snow pile and a generator powering floodlights. People were riding the truck's tailgate to a curbside gallery. Paintings of boxy faces and stick-figure bicycles hung on the walls. The artist, Ross Brodar, was stationed beside them in a fur coat and earflaps. I rode up to meet him and got out my notebook. "That's the insider art fair, OK?" he said. Brodar was angry and cold, stomping his feet. "They're inside and I'm outside and I can't get inside."

An outsider who couldn't get inside the Outsider Art Fair? That was a story, and my folk-art self-education allowed me to tell it. I looked Brodar up again before the next fair and hung out with him as he readied his exhibit. His profile appeared the morning he pulled his truck to the curb on opening day. The story ran only 1,300 words, but its ball of string was 30 years long.

Getting out of the office makes string gathering painless, not only over time, but space. Traveling from country to country in Eastern Europe, I stopped at ad agencies to collect information on the advance of post-Communist hucksterism, and conducted a cross-border pizza survey to measure economic progress by choice of toppings. Gathering string about the way foreigners speak in English to each other, I visited England, Denmark and Poland, did a lot of reading, and made a lot of long-distance phone calls. In Prague—to work on a story about freight trains, and another about the rise of plastic surgery—I tied up the loose ends.

. . . .

Chatter

PRAGUE

Let's talk ballpark figures: A billion babes and dudes under the sun have what it takes to chew the fat in English.

Or, to discuss the matter in approximate terms: A billion women and men in the world are able to speak English.

Many talk among themselves; they chin wag one-to-one. Do they communicate effectively or just shoot off their mouths? Do they speak grammatically or make a hash of it? Large numbers receive information electronically. Zillions are up to their necks in dope from the net. But do they understand? Do they, like, get it?

Prague has 20 cable-television stations and satellite dishes by the thousand. Czechs can watch every episode of *Miss Marple* and 10 Barbara Stanwyck movies in a row. But does the drift get caught? More people in the world now speak English as a foreign language than as a native one. Millions bank and trade in it every day. They must have gotten the hang of it by now.

"I am getting hang?" asks Satoshi Nishide, managing director of Daihatsu Auto in Prague.

Nishide studied English for 10 years and has done business in it for nine. He and his Czech staff sit at a table in their office behind the showroom, groping for the hang of it.

"Means...I depend on it?" wonders technical manager Vladimir Moravec. Spare-parts manager Milan Jandak: "I'd like to have it?" Sales manager Arnost Barna: "I'd like to stop it?"

"I know this phrase," Nishide says. "But I don't know."

At Daihatsu in Prague, English is the only common language. The staff communicates with Nishide in no other way.

"We discuss technical matter," says Moravec. "If I don't understand very well, so I can expect what my boss want to say. We have special vocabulary." But Barbara Stanwyck highballs right past him. As Jandak puts it, "If you hear two English person, they discussing their problem, it's other language than we use."

So what language does Prague Daihatsu use? Purists would call it broken English, or "foreigner talk." Czechlish-Japlish may come close, "Autolish" closer. "Daihat-Praglish" hits the nail on the head.

The global chatter explosion has blown the language to smithereens. English no longer divides itself into regionally rooted dialects—or distinct "Englishes"—but into a rabble of nonnative registers, purpose-built (the English would say) for specific purposes. "Duolects" are dialects only two people speak; oil-talk and commodity-talk have enough speakers to justify textbooks. Here is a conversation lesson in textbook swine-talk:

Farmer: "Can the gilts be bred any earlier?"

Adviser: "No. They are bred to farrow at one year of age."

Farmer: "It sounds too good to be true."

Sure, but swine-talkers may not know that gilts are British government securities, anymore than bond traders will know that a gilt is a virgin sow. As English atomizes beyond its mother countries, words take longer etymological leaps. Quite a few are disappearing into cyberspace.

"Trapdoor?" Jiri Valenta says, running a finger down a list of terms culled from *The New Hacker's Dictionary*. "It is a secret way how to get into a system." The original meaning? "I know what is trap. I know what is door. Trapdoor? It's very strange."

Valenta is an administrator in the computer lab at Charles University, where students sit batting out English emails. Manuals stacked around him have titles like *Review of Ultrix Subsystem Resource Usage*. As he reads them, Valenta picks up new words. To him, "tar and feather" means "to create a transportable archive." "Lint" is a lexical program, "peek" a memory-access command. What else does it mean? "Something like touch," Valenta says.

He does know the derivation of "defenestration." It is something Czechs have historically had a habit of doing to politicians; in cybertalk, it means "to exit Windows."

While native linguists busy themselves defending the Queen's English against alien defilement, words in cyberspace take leave of their senses, foreigners slap together English norms of their own, and the global hubbub builds. There is a pattern to it: English follows markets. As China dipped into capitalism, its masses ran to English class. The cracked East Bloc ran, too. Malaysia quit suppressing English. Vietnam snubbed French for it. Only 20 percent of people over 55 in the European Union get by in English, but 83 percent of teenagers study it. In Denmark, a Danish minister has said, English used to be the first second language; now it's the second mother tongue.

Job applicants at Sony Corp. who list English as their foreign language are told that English isn't foreign at Sony. Much as it beefs, even France can't duck English. The operator at Alcatel-CIT in Paris answers in it. Agence France-Presse writes news in it. Singer Johnny Hallyday, officer of the Ordre des Arts et des Lettres, has come out with "Rough Road," an album in it.

As more people struggle with English, they have more English to struggle with. But ask the mills that churn out English for a worldwide audience if the meaning comes across on the receiving end, and the answer is: We can't tell. The strategy is strictly seat-of-the-pants. "We keep it simple," says Peter Vesey, CNN's international vice president. "We tell the story in a way that viewers who do not have a sophisticated knowledge of the language can benefit from."

Pulling that off, however, is no piece of cake.

Any American can belt baseball metaphors out of the park; it takes a natural to clarify phrasal verbs. Foreigners who don't know what a sentence is "getting at" might know what it "implies." They may "accept" one word, but not "go along" with several. As Samuel Johnson noted, the phrasal verb is a quirk of English "from which arises to foreigners the greatest difficulty."

A study for Britain's Industrial Language Training Service records talk between immigrants and job interviewers. One man sits mute while an interviewer urges: "Fire away." An interviewer trying to learn whether a man has a wife asks for his "domestic circumstances." Another exclaims, "Really?" when a man says he can fix cars; the man thinks he is being accused of lying. The English of gatekeepers, the study says, is among the "least understood aspects of discrimination."

From the mouths of "air-speakers," it can kill. Just before two jets collided in Tenerife, the tower radioed: "Clipper 1736 report clear of runway." The pilot thought he was cleared for takeoff; he wasn't, and 600 people died. Edward Johnson, a professor at Cambridge University, has tried to count the number of people killed by airborne ambiguities. "I stopped at 3,000," he says. Johnson, striving for clarity, is a builder of "operational languages." His version of "sea-speak" has won the blessing of the United Nations, and he has lately come up with "police-speak," to help *flics* at one end of the Channel Tunnel decode what bobbies say at the other end. Police-speak outlaws slang, jargon and ad-libbing. No longer can "seven-one to control" be taken for "seven-one-two control," or the phonetic "Alfa Romeo Golf" get mixed up with automobile brand names.

Of all the android Englishes, only the Voice of America's has soul. It...is...called...Spe...cial...Eng...lish...and...it...sounds... some...thing...like...this.

VOA delivers Special English at nine lines a minute. It started with 1,500 words, using "bird clothes" for "feathers," and "temporary cloth homes" for "tents." Words on the latest blacklist: undermine, strongman, caretaker and kingpin. "It's not so slow that it will put you to sleep," says Christine Johnson, who heads the service. She pauses. "Well, after a big lunch." Why don't other broadcasters try it? "Because they don't speak to foreigners, I think," Johnson says.

Other broadcasters think otherwise. "It sounds insulting," says Tom Sattizahn, an adviser to global televisors. Rather than slow down, some play with dubbing and subtitles. Those who stick to English have another theory: Let foreigners do the talking.

"All you can do is reach out and hope that something will get to the other hand," Bettina Luscher says on the line from Atlanta. Straight from German television, she is CNN International's first nonnative anchor. But Luscher still reads what natives write. Someone once handed her an item about a bankrupt company holding a "garage sale." "People might think they were selling garages," Luscher says. "It's the same with the British phrase, 'trunk sale.' Is that an elephant thing?" It is mentioned that the British would actually say, "car boot sale." "Car boot?" Luscher says. "I wouldn't get that."

A boot is also something that belongs on a foot, of course, and it is, to boot, a way to boot up computers. Yet it turns out that such infuriating confusions would cause fewer problems if native speakers would just butt out. When foreigners speak English to foreigners, their vocabulary may be deficient and grammar defective, but they do communicate. Alan Firth, a telephone-tapping linguist, is trying to understand how they do it. Firth, who hails from Yorkshire, works at the University of Aalborg, in Denmark. A local dairy lets him tape its overseas calls. He knows all about "cheese-talk."

A classic recorded example:

> "So I told him," says an importer in Cairo, "not to send the cheese after the, the blowing in customs."
> The Danish exporter says, "I see, yes."

"So I don't know what we can do with the order now."
"I'm not, er, blowing, er, what, er, what is this, er, too big or what?"
"No, the cheese is bad. It is, like, fermenting in the customs' cool rooms."
"Ah! It's gone off!"
"Yes, it's gone off."

Both importer and exporter knew what "bad" meant. Now the Egyptian knows what "gone off" means to the Dane, and the Dane what "blowing" means to the Egyptian. They have traded cheese and synonyms. But what interests Firth is the semantic two-step: First, the Dane acts as if he understands "blowing." Only when his sale seems at risk does he demand a definition. Then he provides a definition of his own, and the Egyptian acts as if he knew what "gone off" meant all along.

After dissecting this dialogue and many others, Firth has an idea of what makes foreigners so good at getting points across in English. They don't joke. They ignore gaffes. They pay no attention to grammar. They don't mind pauses. They don't care if two people speak at once. They aim for normality, and live with confusion.

"They're brusque," he says. "They're bombastic. They're direct to the point of threatening. The lexical weirdness of it all! Once you clear things up, you get the contract—and 5,000 tons of cheese are on their way to Egypt."

At the Czech factories of Asea Brown Boveri, English operates pretty much that way, though turbines replace the cheese. ABB has 200,000 workers; 20,000 speak English. It has 7,000 workers in the Czech Republic; nearly 1,400 need to speak English, and 800 are studying it. Otherwise, no one could stand up for ABB Prague when ABB Paris faxes: "We are very stonished of you new scheduled deliveries for casing and we cannot accept such a slippage!"

Erik Fougner, the country manager, says, "One thing we have in common at ABB is we all speak poor English. We get by with what we have." Fougner comes from Norway. He speaks German, and his English isn't poor at all. But Fougner has a problem with CNN.

"This Bettina Luscher," he says. "She has like a potato in her mouth. I suppose this is some very highbrow American English. Where does she come from? East Coast?"

Not exactly. She comes from Germany.

"German! I would never have thought that she is a German. She doesn't have a German accent. She must have a very good ear for the language. She's German? Oh, God. That is amazing."

Fougner pulls a face. He doesn't know what to make of it. He can't take it in. His goat has been gotten. He's flummoxed.

1995

Chapter 8

GATEKEEPERS

A man in a black-leather trench coat sat on a sofa against the wall of an office in East Berlin while an economist I was interviewing said, "You can't change suddenly. Countries are not run like that, even in the socialist world..." The man on the sofa chewed a toothpick. His trench coat creaked. Less than a year before the Berlin Wall came down, he was in that office, I guessed, to keep the economist chained to the party line. In the United States—even then, but much more so now—there would be no mystery about the identity of such a chilling presence: a public relations professional.

Macaroni factory, potash mine, dermatology office, sewer—no matter where I go to report a story, a PR person will be trailing me, hovering, guarding the gate. The Bureau of Labor Statistics counts 58,000 journalists and 229,000 public relations specialists in the U.S. PR people have two functions: to beg for publicity, or to insist on privacy. Reporters cope. Since I don't have a beat, I rarely call gatekeepers twice and don't much care if a story offends them. But because I'm never a good old buddy, it's harder to get past them.

Propaganda science peaked under communism, I once thought. At a failing collective farm in southern Russia, reporting a story on the possibility of famine shortly after the Soviet collapse, I was served fried pork, fish, stew and spaghetti for breakfast. Following a drive around the feedlots came lunch: steak and sausage. I was then taken to the home of a private farmer whose wife had laid a table of grapes and chocolate, two bottles of cognac and two of vodka. My interpreter and my shadowy PR minder clinked glasses to the farm chairman's toast: "As long as we have workers like our

host, there will be no hunger here!" Woozily, I pleaded to continue my farm tour and famine reporting. We drove a while, and
veered into a green valley, at the base of which a dozen farm workers were enjoying a drunken barbeque. Dinner that evening was
at the chairman's house: shasklik, potato salad, jellied chicken and
vodka, vodka, vodka. I boarded the Moscow train in the morning
with a headache and a notebook full of deceptions.

As a young reporter, I could call the PR department of the
Environmental Protection Agency, ask for a sulphur expert, get
the expert's number and dial it myself. I could call New York's City
Hall press office, say I was doing a story on the mayor, and soon be
in Abe Beame's office, alone with Abe. Then a shadow fell across
America's realm of light. I first sensed it in Ankara, in 1982. I'd
called the U.S. Embassy and asked for the ambassador, who picked
up his own phone. Robert Strauz-Hupé, 79 years old, invited me
in for a *"tour d'horizon."* He was moving from terrorism to trade
when his door flung open and a public-affairs officer barged in. He
informed the ambassador that he was not to give reporters tours of
horizons, or of anything else, without a PR presence in the room.

By the time I returned to America, the darkness had descended.
Communism's propagandists were outclassed. Could I call the
immigration service to ask for an expert's number? No way. Only
spokespeople spoke. Could I watch Agriculture Department agents
shoot seagulls at JFK? "It's airside," said the PR person. "We don't
allow press airside." After taking months to let me cross New York
Harbor on an old rail barge, my Port Authority minder ordered
me not to talk to the deck hands. No railroad in America would
give me a ride on a train's office car while its officers were in it.
At my four Olympics, reporters were herded into press pens to lap
up canned treacle spouted by autonomic athletes. New York's sub-
ways couldn't have had a better publicist than Carmine Dargenio,
a clerk I fell in love with the day I saw him straighten a commuter's
collar, but after I phoned to tell a spokeswoman what a wonderful
person he was, she sent this note:

"Barry, Let me make this clear to you. You must go through
our office in order to interview our employees. If agents appear in
the *WSJ* without having been cleared by the Press Office and their

supervisors, they can be subject to disciplinary action. We will be perfectly happy to facilitate these interviews for you...."

Carmine didn't care (and neither did his union). People like him still resist public-relations representation. They are my refuge, throwbacks that survive even in crevices of the federal government: International Boundary Commission (mows grass on Canadian border); Domestic Names Committee of the Board of Geographic Names (erases apostrophes from maps); Federal Duck Stamp Office (administers federal duck stamp program). At the Olympics in Beijing, feeling obligated to write about an athlete, I found Aishath Reesha leaning against a wall with an ice pack on her neck at a track on the city fringe. She was from the Maldives, limbering up for an 800-meter run in which she would place 40th in a field of 40. I didn't go through Maldivian PR to speak with her.

For asylum from big, silent corporations, I go to their small, chatty competitors. IMDb was the first stop on my story about mistakes in movies; it kept an enormous cache of goofs. I wanted the names and numbers of its top goof spotters. Amazon owns IMDb, and Amazon PR did put me on the phone with IMDb's editor. However, its goof spotters were off-limits; Amazon, as we know, is committed to protecting privacy. But at Movie Mistakes, IMDb's pipsqueak rival, the boss sent notes on my behalf to his champs, who rejoiced in the attention.

The rejoicing sometimes ends when a story comes out. The Bagel Guillotine's maker wasn't happy with my views on his breakthrough. Nor was the inventor of Shuella, the umbrella for shoes. When press agents promote products that aren't yet off the drawing board, I repeat the warning I was ordered to issue on the mining beat when someone called to announce that they'd struck copper in Panama: "Call back when you start taking it out of the ground."

Press releases have one thing in their favor: They may look like announcements, but they can also be invitations. White Castle's announcement that it was serving wine with its sliders was an invitation to report a story mocking the slobs who eat at the place and the snobs who never would. White Castle was happy. Zippo brags that it repairs any broken lighter, free of charge; my story said its repair shop had a hard time telling the difference between genuine Zippos and Chinese Zippo rip-offs. Zippo was happy.

Then there was Jack Daniel's. A PR man from Brown-Forman, the Kentucky leviathan that owns the homely old Tennessee distillery, offered the *Journal* an exclusive on an announcement of "refinements" it was making to the whiskey's label. I looked into it, and discovered that the new label refined away some items on the old label that were short on the truth. I had a fine time in Lynchburg. I went on a tour of the distillery and had lunch at Miss Mary Bobo's Boarding House. I hope Brown-Forman appreciated the publicity.

. . . .

Gentleman Jack

LYNCHBURG, TENNESSEE

The Jack Daniel Distillery, located here, is removing a few words from its label, which currently reads:

> *Jack Daniel's Old Time, Old No. 7 Brand, Quality Tennessee Sour Mash Whiskey, Distilled and Bottled by Jack Daniel Distillery, Lem Motlow, Proprietor, Lynchburg (Pop. 361), Tenn. U.S.A., Est. & Reg. in 1866.*

"We hope you understand why our label is a good deal wordier than most," a video tells the 250,000 visitors who come every year to the source of what stakes claim to being the world's single biggest-selling whiskey. "It's because we have more to say."

Jack will have less to say now.

From a bar's-width away, the changes won't leap out: The letters will stay white-on-black, just be crisper. The distillery is calling the label a "refinement," even if refinement isn't an idea easily associated with a favorite snort of bikers and rock stars.

But for the population of Lynchburg, what's off the label is a real eye-opener—starting with the population. "Pop. 361" is gone.

Hollie Embling moved here 30 years ago, married a Jack Daniel barrel roller and had four kids. "That made it 366," she joshed one day. Jack Daniel's label stuck to 361, regardless.

The 1920 census came close to that: 365. But back in 1988, Lynchburg and its county consolidated into Metropolitan Lynchburg, Moore County. The population as of 2010 is 6,362, and it isn't "naturally separated from the outside world," as a Jack Daniel's calendar put it a couple of years ago.

Some folks in Lynchburg might still sit on the porch and whittle. A good few have jobs at the distillery. (Ask anybody how many people work there, and the answer will likely be, "About half.")

But some folks also live in million-dollar houses on Tims Ford Lake, or work nearby at Arnold Air Force Base, simulating space flight.

True, Lynchburg has no big-box stores. The closest mall is 20 minutes away. That's because Lynchburg is full up. Nestled in every hollow are the warehouses and packing plants of its biggest taxpayer. They ship 119 million bottles of Jack a year, worldwide.

"People come in wanting to know, is the population 361?" said Sloan Stewart, Lynchburg's Metropolitan Executive, from behind his courthouse desk. "No, we're not staged. We're a working town."

Almost every store on the courthouse square works at selling Jack Daniel's souvenirs. Besides the cafés and the bank, the ones that don't are Lynchburg Ladies Handiwork and the Harley-Davidson shop. Packs of bikers grumble through the square, day in, day out.

One thing they can't buy is a shot of Jack—and for that, Stewart said gratefully, "We're blessed."

Lynchburg is dry. That's not news: It has been dry since 1909. You can make whiskey here. You just can't sell it. Lynchburg doesn't have a bar or a liquor store. Of course, Jack Daniel himself built his still and registered it long before 1909.

Exactly when? In 1866, the label has said. A side panel added: "The Oldest Registered Distillery in the United States."

Registered, that is, with the Internal Revenue. After the Civil War, federal revenuers descended on the South to collect excise taxes on tobacco and alcohol. Southerners generally did their best to avoid them. Why would a still in Lynchburg rush to pay federal taxes? Peter Krass wondered as much while working on a Jack Daniel biography, *Blood & Whiskey*. Digging into the records, he couldn't find any business under Jack Daniel's name until 1875.

After his book appeared in 2004, Krass says he got a letter from the distillery saying, "they weren't changing anything." On Jack's new label, "since 1866" survives on a side panel—but the "oldest" assertion is gone, along with "Est. & Reg."

So is "Lem Motlow, Proprietor."

Over iced tea at the Bar-B-Que Caboose Cafe on Lynchburg's square, Joel Pitts said, "I can understand taking that 1866 off—and the population, too. Because they're wrong." He took a sip. "But taking the Motlow name off the bottle? I disagree."

Pitts is 48 years old and belongs to the International Society of Jack Daniel's Collectors. His great-grandfather, Spoon Motlow, was Lem Motlow's brother. Lem inherited the distillery when his Uncle Jack died in 1911. His name went on the bottle.

Through prohibition, Lem Motlow kept Jack's whiskey alive, if not flowing—even after he shot a man on a train while drunk in 1924. (He was tried for murder and acquitted.) Lem died in 1947, and his four sons took over the management.

"If it wasn't for Lem, there'd be no Jack Daniel's," said Pitts, as Candy Richards approached his booth with a tea pitcher.

"Lem off the bottle?" she said, pouring his refill. "You never know what the corporate's going to do."

Pitts thanked her and said, "As long as we remember him, I guess that's all that matters. You can't change big corporate."

Why did big corporate mess with Jack's label?

"I'd call it refined," said Nelson Eddy. He is Jack Daniel's official historian, and a director of its ad agency in Nashville, 70 miles north.

Nursing a coffee at the Iron Kettle on the square, Eddy explained that foreigners—half the market—don't care about obscure Americana. "Lem's important, but some things had to go," he said. The man is dead, after all.

The registration claim has been dropped from the label, too, though Eddy insists Jack Daniel was first in line to sign up when the revenuers came. "I can't tell you what Jack was thinking," he said. "I don't think anyone can." As documentary proof, he has one old photograph showing "Est. 1866" scrawled in runny paint on Jack's office wall, since painted over.

Asked why "Pop. 361" is being erased, Eddy said, "Truthfulness."

In the interest of accuracy, the new label also adds one forthright amendment: Below a portrait on the side panel of Jack in his full whiskers and rakish planter's hat, it confesses that his given name was Jasper.

Certain details, however, rarely do make it onto liquor bottles, and the new Jack Daniel's bottle is no exception. In 1956, Lem Motlow's sons sold the distillery for $20 million, a fact the actual owner tends not to emphasize. On the label of a sour mash whiskey mellowed through sugar maple charcoal in the rolling hills of middle Tennessee, here's a line you won't find:

Proprietor, Brown-Forman Corp. (sales $3.2 billion), Louisville, Ky., U.S.A.

2011

PART THREE

FROM REPORTING TO WRITING

Chapter 1
THE PERFECT VEHICLE

In a rush-hour downpour, a lone taxi in the river of traffic has its roof light lit. If only that shopper out on the street, the one lugging the driftwood side table from Crate & Barrel, knew how to whistle. I've been there, caught in a storm of notes, weighed down by documents, frantically hailing the one vehicle that can bring a story home so I can write it. No amount of research and interviewing will help. That perfect vehicle has to come along.

Seville, I'd read, was a scary place for tourists. Pickpockets worked the avenues, purse snatchers stalked the cathedrals. At stop lights, gangs on scooters smashed car windows, grabbed cameras and roared away. "Avoid Seville at all costs," a diplomat told me. So I went to Seville to look for mugged tourists, and couldn't find any. After hanging around consulates and police stations, I thought: I'll get mugged myself. I put a camera case under my chair at a café. A boy picked it up and put it on my table. "Somebody will take it," he said. I rented a car and left it unlocked with the case on the dashboard. Hours later, the case was still there. I hired an interpreter, a woman. Around and around Seville's worst district we drove, lingering at red lights, her purse on the back shelf. No luck!

Crime statistics and interviews with sociologists wouldn't do. Writing about tourists getting robbed required robbed tourists. Ready to give up and leave town, I was on my way to the checkout desk of the of the Alfonso XIII Hotel when I saw her: Sue Nelson from Wisconsin, arm bandaged and oozing blood. "You don't realize," she said. "It can happen driving. Two guys on a scooter. They broke the window with a rock. They got my purse. Blood all over the place."

Luck! We sat in the hotel restaurant. Sue Nelson ordered gaz-pacho and told me the whole story. She was my taxi home in a downpour.

The diplomat who advised me to avoid Seville belonged to a class of killjoys whose job is to inform reporters that they'll never get the break they need. But for every ten killjoys, there's an angel—like the one I stood next to at Citarella's fish counter on New York's Upper West Side. I'd been scouring the city for a bar that made old people (like me) show proof of age before selling them a drink. It had happened at airports. I thought it was stupid, therefore a story. But of all the gin joints in New York, I couldn't find one to card me. That afternoon, I had been ejected from Fair-way, Citarella's next-door neighbor. Fairway carded all customers at its checkout counter. I was taking notes when a guard, inform-ing me that the Constitution stopped at Fairway's front door, booted me onto Broadway. Defeated, I went into Citarella to buy a piece of fish. A woman in my age range was buying salmon. "Have you ever been carded in a bar?" I asked. She said, "Blockheads, Mexican place on Amsterdam. They don't want anybody to feel discriminated." I walked over to Blockheads, had a margarita, got my story's perfect vehicle, and caught the subway home.

Accidents like these don't happen by accident. They take effort. Where was my ride to a story on people who take pictures of pictures with cell phones? It took me two years to flag down that taxi. In the Metropolitan Museum of Art, I asked picture takers why they were taking pictures of pictures. Useless. It dawned on me that pictures of paintings in art books had to be photographs taken by professionals. I called several, but they all took pictures of pictures in sterile studios. No fun in that. I thought of pro-filing a photographer who took photos of photos. I visited one. His studio was sterility enlarged. Finally, someone told me about Tom Powel, a photographer who got out of his studio and took pictures of pictures wherever they hung. Powel had a job coming up in the unsterilized studio of Marilyn Minter, an artist who took photographs, painted pictures of them, and hired Powel to take photographs of her paintings of her photographs. When we got to Minter's studio, she was picking dog hairs off *Sludge*, her painting of her photo of a high-heeled shoe overlaid with dribbles of goop. Powel took pictures of the painting of the photograph. A *Journal* photographer took pictures of him, and I took pictures of the photographer taking pictures of Powel.

My afternoon at Minter's studio was more than a vehicle for the story—it *was* the story. It reinforces my argument that good stories aren't "about" things, but about things happening to things. I could have written an article "about" America's fixation on prizes, too, a condition that had annoyed me since I won my "Future Scientist of America" award in 1963. But I flagged down a perfect vehicle instead, and won an all-expense-paid trip to Las Vegas.

. . . .

The Awards Awards

LAS VEGAS

Millions of award-winning Americans couldn't have won what they won without the support of all the men and women behind the scenes who engrave the plaques and build the trophies. That's why the Awards and Recognition Association presents awards to the year's best awards at its annual awards gala.

It's the awards awards.

From a ballroom stage on a post-Oscar evening, association president Guy Barone looked out at a few hundred gowned and tuxedoed recognition technicians and told them that the names of 2011's winners would be announced as soon as they finished dessert.

"Are you nervous?" he teased.

"Am I nervous!" whispered Chris Viverata, looking out of place at his table in a checkered sport coat. Viverata, 47 years old, took over Gold Star Trophies, in Baton Rouge, La., from his father. He has worked in the storefront shop since he was 10, but it wasn't until this year that he felt ready to enter one of his awards for an award.

"As you get old, you realize there's more important things than money," he said. Now a spumante bottle he decorated for the organizers of a Mardi Gras float was up for "Best Sandblasting."

"I'm proud of that trophy," said Viverata. "I'd love to win. I hope I do win."

Seated next to him was Lori Champagne, 48, of Champagne Recognition in Carlsbad, Calif., his main sandblasting rival. Her entry was a glass bingo award made to look like a bingo hopper.

What makes Champagne want to win awards for her awards? She looked at her salad for a moment and said, "Personal ego."

Somebody had to lose, of course, which is why lots of people hate awards. Alfie Kohn, author of *Punished by Rewards*, says awards "confuse excellence with victory." Others say they confuse victory with just showing up. Tim Kasser, a Knox College psychology professor, says, "Awards only exist to direct behavior."

To which the awards industry responds: What else is new?

"We haven't found a saturation level for awards," says David Sturt of O.C. Tanner, a Salt Lake City "appreciatology" company. It ships 3.2 million corporate awards a year and advises managers on handing them out, as in: "Be genuine and adopt a celebratory tone."

"People feel underappreciated," Sturt says. "They hang onto their trophies, those little units of success in their lives."

O.C. Tanner is a $400 million star in the $20 billion-a-year galaxy of appreciation. It isn't all about trophies anymore: It's about iPads and spa weekends that America's winners pick out of catalogs. But to 10,000 awards retailers—with $2 billion in sales—there's still no contest between a waffle iron, say, and a gold-plated cup.

The awards association's executive director, Louise Ristau, addressed the issue this way: "A knife set doesn't say, 'You got this because you've been with the company for 20 years.' What says that is a plaque that you keep and look at your whole life."

It was a day before the gala, and Ristau was on the floor of her annual trade show, where 370 suppliers of trophy tools and trophy parts were showing crowds of retailers their newest ideas.

Booths brimmed with statuettes of cheerleaders, weightlifters, quarterbacks and batters. Granite blocks and crystal plinths lined the aisles. Some sample inscriptions: "Most Valuable Vocalist," "Installer of the Year," "Most Improved VIP Reservationist."

R.S. Owens, a high-end manufacturer in Chicago, had an Oscar on a shelf in its booth, labeled "Made in USA." Most appreciation components, however, are Chinese, like the Shanghai-made crystal golf balls at Topmost World's display.

"In China, nobody is recognized for hard work," said Topmost's salesman, Bruce Wang. "It's the norm to work hard. Over here, if you work hard, you get a trophy. Whole different mentality."

The awards in contention for the awards awards were set out anonymously on a narrow table against a wall. Visitors patrolled its length, marking ballots and dropping them into a box.

For best engraving, Champagne entered a plaque made for a priest who was leaving his Minnesota parish. It was a silver-and-red plastic cutout of a locomotive, with Jesus in the cab window. For most creative, she entered a working kaleidoscope (as yet without a recipient) supported by a gavel and a Winged Victory.

For sandblasting, Champagne's bingo hopper was up against Viverata's spumante bottle. She was at the table checking it out when he came along and picked it up to give her a better look.

"Is it hand painted?" she asked. He said it was. "Are all the pearls inlaid?" she asked. They were. "What made you do something so insane?" asked Champagne. Viverata replied: "I wanted to do something nobody else ever did."

The next evening, after the ice-cream cake, the winners were announced. Champagne's locomotive won; so did her kaleidoscope. Viverata's name was called for "Best Recognition Package," a set of plaques and medals he made for Louisiana's high schools. And then, for Best Sandblasting, his name was called again.

Up on stage, Viverata and Champagne got in line with the other victors—Best Trophy, Best Plaque—and returned to the table with two clear-acrylic obelisks apiece, supplied by Awards4U in Tallahassee, Fla. They were the winningest awards-retailers of the year.

"You don't have to be a big shot to win big," Viverata said, accepting pats on the back. President Guy Barone came over and shook his hand.

The gala went on until all the awards awards were awarded. (Jen Burger took Best Customer Service Representative and Myron Funk made it into the Hall of Fame). When it was over, Champagne, who had won 25 acrylic obelisks in 16 years, went back to her hotel room with her mother, who always attends.

After the first win of his life, Viverata wanted to celebrate. He headed for the Paris Casino to "get some booze and do some gambling." He played blackjack and lost $200.

2012

Chapter 2
GET OUT OF THE OFFICE

"Is that the fire-eating escape artist? I'm so glad you answered your phone. I'm a reporter. I'd like to write a story about you."

"Terrific! How about next Tuesday? I'm much too busy eating fire and escaping this week to take time out for an interview."

It's understandable. A fire-eating escape artist knows how to eat fire and escape, not how to report a story for the raw material that will go into the writing of it. If I showed up with a notebook instead of a film crew, there's no way he could guess that I was out to shoot mind movies. But the pictures that readers see in their minds when they lose themselves in prose invigorate the stories I like most to read and try to write. I don't begin to report a story without some idea of the pictures I'll need to tell it. Talking heads bore me as much in print as they do on screen.

"In the short run, I'm not going to be very helpful," Ken Lopez said when I called to suggest a story about his job. He was a broker who sorted through the junk authors amass (their archives) and then sold the junk to libraries for a lot of money. "I've got to leave town tomorrow for Phoenix to pick up an archive and drive it back," he said. Driving at least part of the way with him, in a Penske truck with a load of old boxes, was the mind movie I needed. Lopez got the picture. So did Dan Palmer, at New Jersey's Beneficial Insect Rearing Laboratory. His lab was hatching beetles to eat purple loosestrife, an invasive species. I asked: Do you have a customer in need of these beetles who's having trouble getting them? "That's the situation we have now," Palmer said.

Wonderful! I hung around the lab for a day, while his assistants strained to hatch an urgent order. My opening line: "It's crunch time at the beetle factory."

Vital as it is to pry people out of their offices to watch them do what they do, there's also a personal bonus: It gets me the hell out of my own office. Lots of reporters achieve greatness by working the phones. I'm too twitchy.

Enough material for a story without watchable action usually piles up in a few days of reading at my desk and making calls. For a dry analysis of Russian tanker traffic in the Bosporus under the Treaty of Montreux, I could have stuck to my desk. I went for a wet analysis, and sailed through the strait on a tanker. Someone once gave me a report on the hashish trade in Holland and Morocco. A wire-service reporter might have handled it in an hour. I visited a hash seller in Amsterdam. For symmetry, I had to visit a Moroccan *kif* grower. My first contact, in Tangier, was a crook; I switched hotels to escape him. I tracked down an honest ex-political prisoner who led me to a man whose cousin raised *kif* in the mountains and insisted on meeting us at three o'clock in the morning. We drove for five hours, evading police checkpoints, "on a ruined, rutted road," my notes read, "deep in mud, hairpin turns, drop-offs into blackness. Cowled peasant takes wheel in a steep descent along river, dark shapes of mountains around us, to a cold, concrete house." We left two hours later, evading checkpoints again. The interview took up 395 words in the story I wrote. Without that scene, wire copy would have covered the ground, but that *kif* grower was no talking head.

Some interesting people do work at desks and don't go anywhere. One way to avoid sitting across the desk from them is to get behind it with them. A colorless man worked in a windowless room at the Department of Commerce, selling a news website produced by the CIA. I sat beside him as he scrolled through the site, his desk radio playing quietly; my prose gained a picture. PR guy Todd Brabender worked out of a basement in Lawrence, Kansas. He represented the Fish 'n Flush toilet fish tank and other necessities, but had no Kansas clients. I flew out to see him. All he did was yak on the phone. I asked him to let me listen in. He did; my story gained a second character, and a conversation. A woman, alone in suburban New Jersey, was telling me about her persecuted family in southern Russia when an idea came to me: Let's call them up. I recorded the conversation. When I got home, Jonathan Platt, a scholar of Russian literature (and my son-in-law), translated it. I had my scene:

> *Feruza Mamedova put through a phone call to her uncle Asnar in Krasnodar. "If you had a chance to come to America, would you take it?" she shouted down the line.*
> *Asnar Mamedov shouted back: "Of course!" He is 43, jobless, and tries to live by selling fruit and vegetables in the market.*
> *"How are things now?" his niece asked.*
> *"They're strangling us," said Mamedov. "They take our produce and throw it on the ground. They take people to jail just for selling. It never stops. I would be happy to go to America!"*

Going along for the ride—on the water, in the air, or on the road—means never knowing what will happen until it does. I learned that early, on a flight with Wayne Sperling, a ferry pilot ("aviator sunglasses, Errol Flynn mustache, cigarette dangling from his lip") who was delivering a single-engine American Traveler from the Grumman factory in Cleveland to a crop-dusting company in Managua, Nicaragua. The Traveler had one instrument, a compass. "Wayne figures our ground speed by timing the plane's passage across the mile-square section lines that make mid-America look like a vast expanse of green-brown graph paper," I wrote. "He figures the wind's direction by watching the shadows of small clouds creep across the fields." Sliding between thunderstorms, "the Traveler is bouncing like a peanut in a boxcar when suddenly the engine coughs and dies. Wayne's eyes widen as he quickly snaps several switches and, after a few terrifying seconds, the engine kicks in again." One of the gas tanks had gone dry.

That story ran more than 40 years ago, but the pictures on the page can't fade. I took a train from Paris to Moscow, and a freighter from Singapore to Sarawak, but for out-of-office experiences, sitting next to somebody driving to the supermarket will do. It's the journey, not the destination, I've heard. On the other hand, on the day Marian Dobrowolski invited me to go along with him on a drive to the Guzow Vegetable Experiment Station, the destination was good, too.

. . . .

Polish Potatoes

GUZOW, POLAND

In the staff dining room of the Guzow Vegetable Experiment Station, Marian Dobrowolski watches, expressionless, as the waitress crosses the bare tiles and sets before him a platter of french-fried potatoes.

The potatoes are deep brown, thick cut and of irregular lengths and shapes. Dobrowolski frowns. Seated to his left, Elzbieta Lenkiewicz bites her lip.

Dobrowolski salts. He lifts a single french fry from the platter and holds it to the light. He rotates it. He breaks it in two and follows the rising steam.

Then he puts the potato into his mouth. He holds it there for a long moment. He tilts his head and thinks. Seated opposite, Jan Masternak leans forward, hands clasped prayerfully under his chin.

"H'mm," says Dobrowolski.

This is the most important moment in the entire crisis-ridden history of the McDonald's Polish potato project. McDonald's Corp. wants to grow potatoes here; it wants to serve them in its restaurants in Western Europe. The Poles want to grow them. But can they accept the immutable world-wide anti-deviationist standards of the golden french fry? Can McDonald's impose its system on Poland?

That is what Dobrowolski has come to find out. He was born in Poland 66 years ago. But since 1956 he has lived in the U.S., and for 18 years his office has been on Ronald Lane in Oak Brook, Ill. He is the man from McDonald's.

On a gray morning in Warsaw, when Dobrowolski climbs into a car for his excursion to Guzow, he wears a blazer with a Golden Arches pin in the lapel. His tie has a Golden Arches motif. He has a Golden Arches ring on his finger.

"He is very loyal to his company," says Jan Masternak, joining him in the back seat. "He loves it."

As a representative of Interpegro, Poland's agricultural trading company, Masternak is also loyal. His tie has the Interpegro logo. For six years, he has toiled together with Dobrowolski in the potato struggle.

"Polish people tell me, 'You crazy Masternak. Stop it. What are you doing? Why do you cooperate with American people?' I say, 'Slowly, slowly. We will see what will be.'"

"Listen to me," Dobrowolski says. "Some people don't see the benefits. But in life you must always have challenges. These potatoes are important—important to McDonald's."

Riding down a country highway, past horse carts and along fields dotted with crows, Dobrowolski fills in the background.

The Poles made the first move. In 1978, they revealed a desire to give communism its first taste of special sauce. They were talking restaurant. "A tremendous possibility," Dobrowolski says. "We have millions of people here to feed with hamburgers."

Talks began. Papers were drafted and redrafted, an announcement readied, a reception planned. It was August of 1980, the month the Solidarity free trade union came into being. The Poles sent McDonald's a telex: reception canceled, project suspended.

But "I didn't want to give up," says Dobrowolski. "Maybe, I thought, Polish farmers could grow something McDonald's could use."

Potatoes. McDonald's needs potatoes. Polish farmers grow potatoes. They grow 36 million tons of potatoes a year. And Polish people eat potatoes: dumplings, cutlets, pierogi, pancakes. In a year, they eat 330 pounds of potatoes apiece. Poland has a potato institute, a potato festival. The town of Monki has a potato monument—a huge concrete potato.

Could McDonald's use Polish potatoes?

No. Dobrowolski ran tests. Polish potatoes, he found, don't have what it takes to make golden french fries. They get soggy. They don't slice up in rectilinear tidiness. Only one potato truly does. It is called a Russet Burbank and it comes mainly from Idaho.

McDonald's has never shipped Russets to Europe from America. It would cost too much, and the European Community wouldn't let them in anyway. At the moment, McDonald's settles for less-than-perfect potatoes in its restaurants around Europe. But what would stop it from raising Russets in Poland? If the EC wouldn't take them raw, they could be cut, cooked and frozen first—most likely at a McDonald's-blessed plant in Turkey.

To begin with, though, McDonald's had to teach Polish potato farmers how to grow them. Thus began what Dobrowolski calls "the fiascoes."

"The potato has been grown in Poland for four, five hundred years," he says. "Polish farmers think they know all about potatoes, and nobody's going to teach them. Then comes this American and says do it this way, do it that way."

Polish farmers plant potatoes in narrow rows; Russets have to be planted in wide rows. Russets have to be weeded; Poles don't weed. Russets are susceptible to black blight. If they get too wet and then get too dry, they explode. Russets have to be pampered.

"After the farmers found out this was a demanding potato, they refused to grow it," Dobrowolski says.

"We tried Lublin," says Masternak. "We tried Bialystok."

But in five years, five crops failed to make the McDonald's grade. "We produced nothing for export," says Dobrowolski as the car turns into Guzow Vegetable Experiment Station. Forsaken by the farmers, he has cast his lot with the scientists.

Elzbieta Lenkiewicz stands in the drive as the car pulls up. She wears hoop earrings and white rubber boots. She runs the place.

"We have planted 15 acres," Lenkiewicz says, squeezing into the back seat for a short ride to her potato patch. "We are excited." She rubs her thumb and forefinger together. "The most important thing is money, money, money."

The car stops at the edge of the field. Dobrowolski alights, puts on a pair of galoshes, and walks out onto the soft, dark earth.

A truck stands in the middle distance. Around it, a few dozen young people in jeans and quilted vests load the crop into plastic crates. "We have sprayed against black blight," Lenkiewicz says. Dobrowolski nods and walks on. Near the truck, he stoops to pick up a potato. He runs a finger over its skin and drops it.

"The rows are proper!" calls Masternak, running up.

Dobrowolski gets out his pocket knife and cuts a tuber in two. "This is normal," he says, and returns to the car.

In a while, the scent of deep-frying Russet Burbanks fills the dining room of the Vegetable Experiment Station. Lenkiewicz and her guests sit. Waitresses serve the main dish: ground beef with onions.

"A hamburger," Masternak ventures.

"You might say," replies Dobrowolski. And minutes later, with a french fry in his mouth, he says:

"H'mm. This is not a McDonald's french fry. Absolutely not. It's an inexperienced way of making french fries. But we should not make an issue of it. The potato is OK."

Lenkiewicz beams. Masternak seizes the bottle of vodka on the table, pours everyone a glass, and stands for a toast.

"To McDonald's and the good french fries," he shouts. "To the golden orchards!"

"Arches," says Dobrowolski, standing himself and raising his glass. "To Poland." Then he takes the McDonald's shield from his lapel and pins it to Lenkiewicz's sweater.

"I'm touched," she says, blushing.

The man from McDonald's kisses her hand.

1986

Chapter 3
GETTING THEM TALKING

On-the-street interviews are best not conducted on the street. A few blocks north of Times Square, at four o'clock on a July morning in 1971, a streetwalker expanded on that for me in terms concerning my manhood, and hit me with her handbag. More recently, I have tried to get the point across to chuggers—charity muggers—who stand in mid-sidewalk with clipboards attempting to engage people on their way to the subway in discussions about the threat to the striped newt.

Adolescent fear of talking to strangers (i.e., girls) stayed with me a long time. Though being a reporter is a passable cover for shyness, sidewalk pickups rack my nerves. Strangers won't talk and walk at the same time. Elevator riders carry countdown clocks. So I patrol places where people stay put: park benches, ballparks, bar stools, parking lots, hotel lobbies, movie lines, bus stops.

Here's what I don't say for openers: "Excuse me, sir, I see you're waiting for the bus to Canarsie. Would you care to talk about mammoth tusks?" No, for mammoth interviews I go to the ticket line at the Natural History Museum. "Hey! Are you waiting to get into the mammoth exhibit? Me, too! I'm a newspaper reporter. I'm doing a story about mammoth tusks." The stranger on the museum line then says something about mammoths, and I say, "Wow! What an amazing thought. I've got to write that down!" Out comes the notebook. I don't put it back in my pocket until everybody on the museum line tells me what they think about mammoth tusks.

Settled in and comfortable, people love nothing more than to talk about themselves. It's therapeutic. Psychologists have a

50-minute hour, but I listened to Mike Twigg for five hours and filled 43 notebook pages. Twigg was a slip-house foreman in England's potteries who had been out of work for two years. In his two-up-two-down row house, he sat on the couch beside his gas fire, smoking, sipping tea, and reviewing a life of work, unemployment and regret.

Twigg said, "It's a lack of confidence problem. I'm going stale. I have funny spells. I feel as if I'm dying. I put it down to being idle." He said, "Something's got to come up. I like to go to work, you see. Look at my hands. They're like a baby's, they are." And he said, "Don't write me off. For God's sake, don't write me off!"

When I closed my notebook and got up to leave, he followed and stood in the doorway. He asked me about a "check." Would he be getting a bit more? In Mike Twigg's mind, I had metamorphosed from a reporter to a caseworker for the Department of Health and Social Services. Mike, I told him, I'm not from the DHSS. I have an American accent. I'm an American journalist. Remember? Oh, yes, Mike remembered. Not to worry, he said. He had enjoyed the chance to talk.

Hardball isn't my interviewing game. I've listened to reporters on the phone, firing questions to brush people back. My pitches are meatballs. Peter Vido, a New Brunswick homesteader with one light bulb and a website about scythes, replied to my emailed interview request with, "All journalists managed to put words in my mouth that I had never spoken..." But one night, Vido called me. By then, I had read his essays and could speak the language of bush blades, peening, and bent snaths. "I think the scythe ought to become a common tool again," he said. "I think it will." I told him that I also believed scythes were good, and that my story could be good for scythes.

I did believe it—when I said it. I believed Darlene Sherrill, in her hut in Grenada, when she told me that fluoridation was a plot to dispose of industrial waste. I believed Jim Stevenson, in his Chevy on a Galveston beach, when he told me he'd shot a cat to save a piping plover. The wiles of interviewers have been dissected and debated, but I was back at my desk, studying tooth decay and rare birds, before I made up my mind that Sherrill was wrong and

Stevenson was right. When people who I want to talk to insist on knowing in advance what my story will say, this is my reply: How can I know before we talk?

My first meatball lobs in like this: "Tell me a little about yourself. Are you from Paducah originally?" It leads to a long warm-up and loosens the vocal muscles. The notes from my phone interview with Frank Tims, a booster for Cold War veterans, run 3,473 words, three of which made my story: "Maybe five million." I drove around Tampa for hours with the admiring son of the antitax campaigner (and namesake of the county moral-courage award) who'd died owing $300 million in taxes before the son told me, "My dad tried everything he could to get the right people in office. He was a power broker, big time."

Delightful utterances often fill the moments before interviews begin or just after they end. Phew, that's over with, people think, now we can unwrap our wit. After a conversation with a British port shipper whose forebears had been expatriates in Portugal for 300 years, we retired to the drawing room for a glass of port with his wife. The gentleman mentioned that he had served in the Scots Guards, and his wife said: "One is entirely prepared to *die* for one's country. One isn't prepared to *live* in it." Unguarded flashes of brilliance prove that formal interviews make people say the dullest things. I tune my receiver to shreds of speech: The "H'mm" of the man from McDonald's as he holds a Polish french fry in his mouth; the coarse fisherman's wife, who says, "Do you hear something dripping? He's got bloodworm in the bathtub," and dashes up the stairs; Ronny Beberman, lugging cases of seltzer into an apartment house while the psychoanalyst on the sidewalk yells, "How much is a..."

Scenes contain dialogue (ask any screenwriter) and dialogue creates scenes. Dialogue happens when people talk to each other. At the Rakovica Motor Works in Belgrade to interview one union man, I was shown into a room with a long table. Six union men sat around it. I tore a page from my notebook, drew a circle for the table and squares for the chairs. As each man spelled his name, I gave his chair a number and added his name to a numbered list. I said I was interested in the factory, and for an hour they smoked, drank tea and debated among themselves. I got my dialogue, no questions asked.

Boarding-house meals, Masonic Hall meetings, ballroom-dancing workouts, comedy-club tryouts—anyplace where people (myself excluded) trade words generates dialogue and, with luck, something to witness. Accidental encounters rate highest, like the one between the Florida bug-splat analyst and the carwash manager who was sure the frenetically copulating love-bug was concocted in a laboratory by mad entomologists at the University of Florida.

On occasion, I have made these encounters happen. Renato Pachetti oversaw a program endorsed by the Italian government to certify the authenticity of Italian food in New York. I took Pachetti to an Olive Garden, then proposed going to an authentic Italian restaurant of his choosing. But Pachetti ate at home; his wife was too good a cook. His New York hangout was Shun Lee Palace, where the cuisine was haute-Chinese. I got a dialogue-provoking idea: Ask a gourmet from China to join us there to judge Shun Lee's authenticity. I dug up an expatriate, Zhang Yiguo. At lunch, Pachetti ordered his favorite Chinese dish: shrimp in a sauce of Grand Marnier and cream—inauthentic in the extreme. Zhang loved it, leaving Pachetti to marvel at authentic Chinese flexibility, and my story with a happy ending.

Did I cook up a phony incident? Maybe, but don't cable-news channels engineer debates every time they seat antagonists in their studios? Did I go wrong in Kentucky when I set the scene for a clash of tea-party ideologies? Call me. We'll discuss it over a cuppa.

. . . .

A Tea Party

LEXINGTON, KENTUCKY

There are two tea-party movements in America. One favors low taxes, small government and patriotic feeling. The other favors fine china, orange pekoe and cordial chitchat.

The two have coexisted uneasily since Dec. 16, 1773, when antitax demonstrators dumped 342 chests of quite drinkable tea into Boston Harbor. Lately, tea dumpers have touched off a raucous revival. But tea sippers, enjoying a genteel revival of their own, aren't showing the dumpers much sympathy.

"I'm promoting tea parties—just not that kind of tea party," says Bruce Richardson, who lives in Perryville, a village 45 miles southwest of here. For a living, he imports tea, publishes books about tea and teaches tea-brewing and tea-party proprieties.

Richardson wishes that tea-party politics were more polite, and also that tea could shake its rebellious associations.

"Tea is the communal cup of the world," Richardson says. Yet he has just brought out a book called *Tea & Etiquette* in which tea-expert James Norwood Pratt suggests that the incident in Boston 236 years ago gave Americans "a prenatal disinclination for tea."

Chic as it now may be, tea connoisseurship has been slow to charm the masses. The market for the kind of tea that sells for $4 an ounce has quadrupled in the past decade. Average Americans, though, still put away nine pounds of coffee a year, against seven ounces of tea—most of it iced, bottled, bagged or instant.

Traveling the country for fine-tea seminars, Richardson carries his own loose tea, pot and electric kettle. In restaurants, he is rarely served tea the way he likes it, and rarely misses a chance to offer a brewing lesson.

Nothing ruffles him more than lukewarm water served in a cup with a tea bag on the side. That's how Mica Sims usually serves hot tea at Bar None, a place she and her husband run here in Lexington.

When she hears of Richardson's criticism, she says, "Bring him up here. Tell him to bring some of his tea." Sims is a tea-party promoter herself—the other kind of tea party.

"People are talking, hey, no more taxes, no more spending, pay attention, let's do something," she was saying one Tuesday evening, as a few dozen tea-party veterans pushed tables into a row in her dining area for a political get-together.

She was holding a plastic bottle labeled "Talking Rain Twist Organic Mandarin White Tea." "I thought it was water," said Sims.

She is 25 years old, and a Kentucky Tea Party luminary. Last January, "watching politics" while caring for her year-old daughter at home, she started a blog.

On tax day in April, she organized two tea-party protests and has since been offered her own radio talk show. Meanwhile, she opened the sports bar. It has all the usual attractions—videogames, framed basketball shirts—but no alcohol.

Seated across from Sims, David Adams was fiddling with a BlackBerry and drinking water. Adams manages the U.S. Senate campaign of Republican conservative Rand Paul, the son of Rep. Ron Paul (R., Texas), and has no taste for tea. "I'm out there throwing it overboard," he said. "We Americans are different from the English," said Paul Hunt, drinking coffee. "It all started in 1773. Us against Earl Grey."

A waiter did set a mug of hot black tea in front of Gatewood Galbraith, Kentucky's well-known contrarian libertarian. Asked how it was prepared, the waiter said, "Out of a bottle."

Tea-party activists do imbibe the stuff. They also dump it on politicians. A local radio host, Leland Conway, collected 14,000 tea bags from listeners and delivered them in July to Gov. Steve Beshear, a Democrat. "That's a lot of tea," he says. "That stimulated the tea economy."

At home in Perryville, Richardson was shocked. "I don't think their hearts are in it," he said. "If they were serious, they wouldn't be using cheap tea bags. They'd be using loose tea. Anybody can buy cheap tea bags for a protest."

He and his wife, Shelley, who are both 56, were studying music at a Baptist seminary when they met. Richardson was a choirmaster for 22 years until he came to feel that his church had moved too far right for his taste. The couple bought an old, porticoed mansion, fastidiously restored it, and opened it to the public as a temple of afternoon tea.

"The message is serenity," Richardson said as water in a kettle came to a boil in his kitchen. He spooned Tippy Assam into a pot, brought pot to kettle (not kettle to pot) and let the tea steep.

"Coffee is grab and go," Shelley Richardson said, holding out a cup as her husband poured. "Tea takes time." Pouring for himself, he said, "A lot of Americans have no idea how to even start making tea. You need to calm down. Think. Tea makes you less dogmatic."

It was a rainy Wednesday, and Richardson had to drive to Lexington to sign copies of his etiquette book at a mall. Taking up the invitation from Sims for some instruction in the art of brewing, he stopped in at Bar None for a tea party.

"I'm on board with you," she said, greeting him. "People want something warm and comforting." All smiles, she led him to a table and said, "I'll get what we have," when he asked to see her tea selection. She returned with a few bottles and a basket of bags: Sweet Dreams, Mint Medley...

Richardson took out a container of green Hyson that he packages under the label, "Tea Thrown Into Boston Harbor." Sims said she knew it wasn't the "exact" tea, and asked how to brew it.

"In a pot," said Richardson. She had none. A waiter brought water in cups. Richardson filled "roll-your-own" tea bags and showed Sims his steeping technique. Jiggling was unwise, he told her, and squeezing forbidden. "I understand," she said. "Not elegant."

They raised their cups, and the chat drifted from babies and jobs to tea-party politics. "I wish we could be more inclusive," Sims said. Richardson acknowledged that President Obama may have breached diplomatic protocol when he shook hands and bowed to the emperor of Japan at the same time. He added: "You and I can both agree that we can sit down over a cup of tea and walk away appreciating each other's passions."

Escorting him to the door, the tea party over, Sims said something about the importance of Kentucky's coal industry, and Richardson said something about his fear of global warming. Sims stopped and said, "Oh! You just lost me!"

"What? You think there's a conspiracy?" he said.

"Global warming's a farce," said Sims. She folded her arms and said goodbye to Richardson with a strained smile.

Late for his book signing, he hurried across the street to his car. "This tea-party thing isn't doing tea any good," Richardson said before driving away. "It's a conspiracy of the coffee people. That's my opinion, and I'm sticking to it."

2009

Chapter 4
PROFILES OF THE UNKNOWN

If Lady Gaga, Scarlett Johansson, and Prince Charles called and asked me to write their life stories, I'd beg off, even though life stories are the most engaging stories to write. Starting out, I flirted with the near-to-famous: Pete Sheehy, the New York Yankees locker room attendant (I saw Yogi Berra naked, but was too nervous to ask him a question); Bob Drumheller, a set-decorator buying books with "Death" in the title for *Annie Hall* (Woody Allen was clothed, but I didn't speak to him, either). In New Delhi, I was waiting to board a direct flight to Bhopal and its gas disaster when Mother Teresa, who sat nearby, looked up at me and said, "Are you going to Bhopal?" The world's third-most famous person, after Abraham Lincoln and Marilyn Monroe, was asking me a question and all I could think to say was, "Well, yes. It's a direct flight."

Celebrities make me anxious. Their gatekeepers have gatekeepers. It's hard to get to see them because other reporters are always pushing to see them, too. They want to control what's written about them, and they're stingy with their time. I can't call Jeff Bezos or Ali Hoseini-Khamenei and say I'm coming around to hang out for two or three days. But I can hang out with the man in Savannah who wrote the book about toenail fungus.

Profiles of talkative, unimportant people who feel ignored and have lots of time require minimal intervention; they write themselves. Once located, someone who fills the bill invites me home for a chat lasting, oh, seven hours. I touch the tiller when needed to keep the life story on chronological course. Then we go someplace: job, family, church, meeting, school, gym, fishing hole. I drop in a few numbers, some background, a little news, and that's that.

The standard profile covers a broad story on a narrow scale. It stars a person in a pickle who represents everybody in the same pickle. It begins with a sad anecdote followed by: "Mr. Gherkin is not alone." I am not alone in hating that line; only "Welcome to Pickle World" would be worse. Immigration is a pickle barrel, but I guddled in it for immigrants representative in weird ways: the mail-order bride married to the wrong man; the lesbian science-fiction writer admitted to the U.S. "in the national interest."

Aimless stories "about" *things* gain direction when they're about *lives.* Beyond the pickle barrel, I look for lives that represent rarities. A story about pinball-machine repair took shape around the life of Mike Hooker, pinball-machine repairman. One about elephant toenails (during my foot phase) told elephant-keeper Willie Theison's life story while witnessing him giving an elephant a pedicure. Terry Kester fit my ideal for anonymity: A sculptor, he "fabricated" the masterworks of Jeff Koons at a workshop in California; when he was done, I watched another unknown sign the product with the master's name. But I was stuck: I had to ask Koons, via his PR sentries, to comment on Kester's skills. Koons took up space in my story, carping that the fabrication company charged him too much. He couldn't comment on Kester's skills because he didn't know Kester from Kublai Khan.

People too singular for the police to profile make writing profiles a joy. They represent nothing more than fate's meanderings and their own strangeness. One, and only one, Hollywood gag writer moved to Nebraska to sell gongs. One, and only one, former sewage-plant secretary, living with eight ferrets in a flyspeck Colorado town, ran a shorthand-translation service. "I hated wastewater," she said, "but I loved shorthand. It made me feel special."

Don't we all long to feel special, to be celebrated as a *the? The* lawyer? *The* saxophonist? *The* gag-writing gong guy? If world fame is beyond us, why not achieve it in one pub? Kevin Ashurst, the fisherman and maggot farmer, was famous at the Royal Oak for catching small fish in England's Bridgewater canal. "Once you had success," he said one morning, sprinkling chicken heads into a box of dead fish, "you can't let it stop. It isn't the money. It's prestige."

Frustration inflames passion, the hot sauce of life stories, but passion doesn't always produce quotations. My interviews with

Joseph Sabato, a seat-belt proponent in New Hampshire (a state without a seat-belt law), felt like my interviews with Nicola Barovic, a civil-rights lawyer in Serbia (a country without civil rights). Both were shy dissidents, suppressing anger in order to work inside systems they hoped to overthrow. Sabato, an emergency-room doctor, was standoffish when I contacted him by phone. I didn't get a sound-nibble. His detractors fed me a snoot full. "If somebody fails to wear a seat belt, it affects that person," a state legislator told me. "We have laws that stop you from hurting other people. Laws that protect you from hurting yourself are what I'm against."

When Sabato invited me to his ER, I knew that his profile, short on quotations, would need a car crash. I waited twelve hours. A man driving without a seat belt flipped his van on I-93. Behind him, strapped into a baby seat, was his five-year old daughter. The impact threw the man out of his seat into the back of the van. On the way, he kicked his daughter in the head. That settled it: New Hampshire's law didn't stop a driver from hurting other people. Father and daughter survived. I called the father a few days later, and he recounted his movements leading up to the accident. As I wrote it, the story swung in scenes between the van's progress and Sabato's dull day, until the two threads converged in the ER. When the man was leaving with his child, Sabato handed him a seat-belt pamphlet. I didn't need a quote.

On the spectrum of profile writing—from celebrity tell-all, to victim exposé, to oddball frolic—there's a sweet spot where empathy meets absurdity. The tone, neither condescending nor earnest, strikes a note between weightiness and levity. I like that sound. I never got closer than I did when R. Wayne Griffiths unbuckled his belt.

· · · · · · · · · · · · · · · · · ·

Foreskin Restoration

CONCORD, CALIFORNIA

For more than a century, in the belief that nature can be improved upon, Americans have circumcised their baby boys. Today, the value of circumcision as a health measure is in doubt in some quarters at a time when face lifts, tummy tucks and breast implants have lost their ability to shock us.

Should it come as any surprise, then, that some men would try to regain what circumcision took away?

"If you're willing to walk around with a pin through your tongue," says R. Wayne Griffiths, one of the principal founders of the foreskin-restoration movement, "this is not absurd at all."

It is Sunday morning, and Griffiths is driving to church. His car's license plate reads "NORM.ORG," website of the National Organization of Restoring Men, the fraternity he formed in 1989. Griffiths is 67 years old and works at a local sanitation district. He has white hair, a brush mustache, a voice like a creaky gate, and three matched pens in his shirt pocket. He's a Mormon.

At church, he greets the bishop and takes a pew with his sister and brother-in-law. He joins in the opening hymn: "As I search the holy scriptures, may thy mercy be revealed. Soothe my troubled heart and spirit; may my unseen wounds be healed." He closes his eyes and prays. During a baby blessing, when a mother sheds a tear, he leans over and whispers, "Sometimes you get emotional with children."

Griffiths was married for 30 years before he got divorced. He has had six children; he has 21 grandchildren. That might be reason enough to get emotional about them, and about their unseen wounds. On the way home from church, driving past Pixi Land amusement park, he says, "Do you realize that the first sexual experience you ever had was also the worst trauma you've ever experienced? Maybe that went to the back of your mind and stayed there, just maybe."

He parks outside a complex of tree-shaded apartments; his own is on the second floor, an American flag flying from its balcony. Inside, file boxes fill a small front room. Family snapshots cover the top of an upright piano. Framed above the couch hang four artful pictures of naked couples. The men in the pictures are "intact"—uncircumcised. Taking his *Book of Mormon* from a shelf, Griffiths reads: "Wherefore, little children are whole, for they are not capable of committing sin; wherefore...the law of circumcision is done away in me."

Circumcision, as Griffiths sees it, falls morally into the same category as abortion: Don't unless you must. Nothing beyond the fringe in that. Jews circumcise their boys to signify a covenant with God; Mormons don't, nor do many other Christians. In the U.S., circumcision may be one of the most commonly performed surgeries, but in other countries, far from it. And although many American doctors still insist it reduces infections and a rare form of cancer, the practice is on the decline. The American Academy of Pediatrics no longer deems circumcision of all baby boys a medical necessity.

That said, grown-up boys who try to undo their own circumcisions might well be deemed beyond the fringe. Yet, in its way, foreskin restoration is pure Americana. In his book on circumcision, David Gollaher calls it "the kind of enterprise that draws together far-flung individuals who share a narrow preoccupation." They also share an overarching American belief that anyone can right any wrong.

Wayne Griffiths is living proof. Religion didn't save him from an unkind cut, so he healed himself, adapting methods of epidermal expansion to his anatomical circumstances: With surgical tape and weights, he stretched what he had left. Pacing himself, it took years. Along the way, he has helped thousands attempt the same, and put up with a quantity of ridicule. Griffiths' penile personal portraits have appeared in Benetton's magazine (next to a facelift device and an artificial ear) as well as the *British Journal of Sexual Medicine*.

"Finally, a year or so ago," he says, "I was there." He rises from his couch, and proudly unbuckles his belt.

Thirteen centuries before the birth of Jesus, Egypt had already been circumcising its boys for millennia. Tribes in Africa, the Americas, Australia and Indonesia had, too. For Jews, circumcision was an act of faith, and perhaps a badge of affiliation. Islam saw it as a means of purification. Freud called it a castration substitute. In his studies, Dr. Gollaher found "no theory" to fit "the myriad facts."

America lent circumcision its reputation for preventing disease. Beginning in the 1870s, it was touted as a cure for ailments from hernia to imbecility. Before antibiotics, doctors presented it to new parents as vital to cleanliness and a guard against syphilis. By 1985, despite huge medical advances, 85 percent of baby boys in America had their foreskins cut; 60 percent still do.

Mormonism didn't stop the U.S. Army from circumcising Wayne Griffiths' father, nor a San Francisco doctor from circumcising the father's newborn son. At age 12, Griffiths vividly remembers, he went to a fathers-and-sons banquet in a church hall. One father, whose sons were intact, talked of circumcision and "how we shouldn't do it," he recalls. "From that time on, I had a wonderment in my mind of what it would be like to be intact."

Not that he dwelled on it. Life was moving quickly: junior college, four years in the Navy, a sociology degree from Brigham Young University, a year as a San Quentin guard, back to school for a masters degree in criminology, four years in the Air Force, a masters in education, to Oregon for the Teachers Corps, and to Georgia as an assistant sociology professor at Armstrong State University.

At 21, in the Navy, he married. In 1956, his wife gave birth to twin boys, one stillborn. Was the other to be circumcised?

"They brought the child to my wife," Griffiths says. "I went out and walked in front of the hospital, thinking: Why am I doing this to him? But I did do it—out of fear the hospital would call me some kind of pervert. I was in the military. I didn't want to jeopardize my children or my marriage by doing something heinous."

With the birth of another boy three years later, he made the same choice. "In the 1950s, you didn't tell doctors not to do something. The power was theirs. You didn't buck it."

In 1971, his brother Keith went into business as a construction consultant and asked him to come home to join in. Two years later, Keith and Griffiths' 17-year-old son, Brett, died in the crash of a Piper Cub. Griffiths' marriage soon died, too. By 1981, he was alone in Concord, working freelance, seeing a therapist. "I felt diminished," he says. "You might say I felt emasculated."

Then he watched a talk show. Phil Donahue, that day in 1987, had as his guests a syndicated radio doctor, Dean Edell, and a nurse named Marilyn Milos, both early and impassioned "intactivists."

With them was a man who had tried to have a new foreskin surgically attached. "It was the first time I saw my inner thoughts expressed by someone else," says Griffiths. He called Milos, who referred him to an engineer who was experimenting with nonsurgical foreskin restoration, using tape. Griffiths went a step further. He phoned Bearing Engineering in Emeryville, Calif., purchased a set of stainless-steel bearings and welded them into a two-inch barbell. Deploying tape and the bearings in a manner best described as inspired, he achieved ideal tension for tissue expansion. It worked. The patent is pending.

"To feel whole again, that was the motive," Griffiths says. "I wanted to be covered, and I am."

The accuracy of this claim, as Wayne Griffiths pulls up his trousers and buckles his belt, is hereby confirmed.

In the 1980s, the grass-roots challenge to circumcision gained ground. Opponents compared it with genital mutilation of girls in other cultures. In the midst of his restorative toils, Griffiths went to anticircumcision events. At one, he met Tim Hammond, who turned out to be absorbed in the same solitary pursuit. They agreed to start a support group, and the foreskin-restoration movement was born.

To announce a first meeting, in February of 1990, the two took out ads in San Francisco's alternative press; if guys are squeamish about discussing their privates in public, they thought, gay guys might be less so. Two dozen men showed up that first time. Then 60. Meetings moved from apartments to a church. The gay-straight mix of the participants soon mirrored that of males in general.

In 1992, Jim Bigelow, a psychologist who had also seen the Donahue show, published a book called *The Joy of Uncircumcising*. It has sold 18,000 copies. While Hammond resumed the circumcision fight, Griffiths built NORM into a network, with 27 U.S. chapters and five overseas. The Web, at last count, had 16 foreskin-restoration sites.

A fervor for human rights didn't drive that response. Sex did. The foreskin is ingrained with nerves, like any erogenous zone. In the past, some justified clipping it to suppress sexuality. Griffiths and his friends say restoration heightens sensitivity, yet a number of them were circumcised later in life and know those nerves never grow back. Deep down, Griffiths believes, men seek him out for reasons less physical than psychological, and maybe a little political.

"They come for personal reasons, and then they get enlightened about the broader issue," he says. When he takes off his hard hat and comes home after a day inspecting sewerage projects, Griffiths often finds 100 emails on his computer. "Many are angry at doctors and parents. I tell them, if you start restoration, maybe you can do something with that anger, something constructive."

Marilyn Milos, who has led circumcision protests for years, has this to say about Wayne Griffiths and his foreskin restorers: "They are men willing to declare: We've been wounded. It's affected our sexuality and our minds, and we're doing something about it. Wayne is willing to lead that movement with the gentleness of a father." She adds, "I applaud their courage. I mean, wearing weights on the end of their penises—this isn't lobbying, is it?"

Another Sunday. Griffiths has skipped church to put in an appearance at NORM's chapter in Los Angeles. Gary Harryman, who sells home sites in Topanga Canyon, picks him up at the airport. Harryman has been restoring for a few years. They drive to Culver City, discussing raccoon traps, and park outside a building where support groups meet. Today's calendar also lists Survivors of Child Abuse, Anger Release, and Co-Dependents Anonymous.

A room of couches and soft chairs has filled with 25 men from their late teens to early 70s. Harryman presents the guest of honor: "This is our *grand-père*," he says.

"Men all over want to know what they can do to restore," Griffiths tells them. "We're happy to help." Going around the room, the attendees recite their first names and occupations: locksmith, hairdresser, dentist, machinist, set designer.

"I've been restoring for three years, thanks in good part to Wayne," says Vincent. Bruce says, "I've been restoring for 28 months. I called you, Wayne. I remember our whole conversation." And Bill: "I've been at it for two months. This is the first program of personal growth where I've actually seen some personal growth!"

Everyone laughs, and the meeting settles down for two hours of foreskin-stretching mechanics, aided by charts and plastic models. A loud banging intrudes from somewhere. It sounds like construction. No one seems distracted. Griffiths lectures on about Meissner's corpuscles and somatosensory receptors.

He says: "You can restore if you want, but you can also educate others not to circumcise their boys. All of us should do whatever feels comfortable. I'm not trying to get you to do anything wild."

As the meeting closes, Griffiths shakes hands and then heads for the airport. The men stick around, discussing foreskin-restoration gear the way some guys discuss fishing tackle. One of them, Richard Zerla, circulates an album of his personal penile portraits.

"That banging next door, you hear it?" he says as the others flip through his album. "It's the anger-release group. They beat on pillows! You can't imagine what people get up to on this earth."

2000

Chapter 5
GOING PLACES

When the profile I'm writing is about one person, the two of us have got to sit still together for a few hours. When the profile is of one place, I've got to keep moving for a few days.

London's Summer Olympics gave me an excuse to drive my Buick upstate to run laps around Lake Placid, a New York town that has played cold-weather games all year round since it hosted the Winter Olympics in 1932. I got there on a Monday night and ate dinner at Nonna Fina, where the waiter said, "In the summer, winter sports aren't as affected by the lack of snow." Tuesday, I met the bobsled manager, toured the track, peeked at the U.S. luge team's training ramp, walked through the stables at a horse show, checked out the speed-skating oval, inspected a pile of fake snow in front of the 1932 ice rink, and sat inside the rink while a Turkish-Ukrainian couple skated around. Wednesday, I went back to the luge ramp to meet the team, attended a ski-jump contest, saw freestyle skiers flipping into a swimming pool, and drove 16 miles to get to Santa's Workshop at North Pole, N.Y., before it closed. Thursday, I met the crew that gave tourists bobsled rides (on concrete), talked to tourists as they lined up for a ride, took a ride myself (41 seconds) and talked to tourists when their rides were over. That afternoon, I drove to Recycle Circle (formerly Dump Road) to watch little lugers roll down a hill on wheeled sleds, and drove to the Olympic Museum to see the video, "The Switzerland of America." Then I drove back to Brooklyn.

On my way to profile a place, I usually have an idea of why I'm going, not much more. Flying into Bali—the Asian hotbox Nehru called "the morning of the world"—I didn't know tourists got it mixed up with Bali-Ha'i, the mythical Polynesian paradise from "South Pacific." I discovered that when the man sitting next to me on the airplane jabbed me in the chest and said, "Temples, temples. I'm not interested in temples. Pubs, not temples." My story's scenes shuttled between Bali Hindu trance dancers and stoned Australian bar hoppers. A trip to mid-1990s Russia, by contrast, was an assignment from New York with a stated objective: Find out if freedom makes Russians happy. I was able list the building blocks I needed before my plane landed: intellectuals, workers, priests, farmers, students, pensioners.

On a map of Russia, I drew concentric circles around Moscow and began my reporting at the dead center of the human-rights movement—Yelena Bonner's dining-room table. With a folklorist and an interpreter, I worked my way outward by train to Kaluga, a city where the hotel clerk refused us rooms because we didn't have "special permission" to be there, a scene in itself. After checking off stops on my list in Kaluga—university, seminary, turbine plant—we took a bus to a farm, then hitched to a village of wooden cottages in a birch forest. An old lady vacated her bed for me; she slept on top of her stove. The story was part political analysis, part travelogue, and each stop on the route brought me closer to a conclusion I hadn't planned: Freedom didn't make Russians happy. It was as true in the mid-1990s as it is in the mid-2010s.

Unexceptional places, like ordinary people, can represent a crowd. I spent two days in a Polish bus factory for "a glimpse of the agony that lies ahead for the remains of the Soviet Union." I traveled through Java for an ecological profile: Hungry peasants climbed mountains to cut firewood; deforestation caused floods; floods washed soil from rice land below, forcing hungrier peasants to climb higher mountains to cut more firewood. My editors didn't care about Java; they cared about a Third World food crisis. "Java's experience," I wrote, "is a chilling reminder that a world food crisis is still with us." How did I justify a week in a boringly suburbanized Indonesian mining camp on the island of Sulawesi? With this: "The phenomena occur with geological predictability near major oil and mineral deposits in countries where you can't drink the water."

Like one-of-a-kind people, it's the one-of-a-kind places that make inimitable profiles. Trieste was the imperial port of the Austro-Hungarian Empire, when there *was* an Austro-Hungarian Empire. After World War I, it became "a great hub of inactivity," so I went there. The Monastic Republic of Mt. Athos, an Aegean peninsula autonomous since the seventh century, was a land "subject to miracles," according to a warning on its entry hall's wall. I went there, and spent a night in the hut of a hermit from Long Island who cooked me a spaghetti dinner. A cattle station in the middle of Australia was "a little bigger than Israel, a little smaller than Burundi, about the size of El Salvador." I went there, and to a Chinese shopping mall in Las Vegas where tree-ear fungus outsold Cheez Whiz.

In America, phony oddities like Las Vegas make real oddities, like Chinese shopping malls, harder to distinguish from the surrounding sameness. Even the odder American places usually need some kind of controvery to rate a profile, like the one I managed to do on Delaware Bay, where watermen in wind-driven dredges were arguing with defenders of the red knot, an endangered bird, over the right to catch horseshoe crabs. But home or abroad, my plan for profiling places is the same: Develop a thesis, witness things to prove it, move around and stick around. To lend life to a horse-drawn theory on the nature of European society, I stuck around for a while in Sirvozelo.

. . . .

Behind The Mountains

SIRVOZELO, PORTUGAL

The old man has had a stroke, and he hacks as if he has tuberculosis. But he fumbles with his tobacco, rolls a cigarette and lights it with a twig from the fire.

At home in early evening, he sits with his wife on a bench against the stone wall of their biggest room. A log burns on the concrete floor at their feet. Smoke fills the air and drifts up a flue in the low ceiling. In a kettle hanging above the fire, gruel for the pigs bubbles away; the pigs live in the cellar below.

"I wasn't born here," the old woman says. She has no teeth. A black scarf covers her head. "He was born here. I was born in another house."

They are the parents of Manuel Afonso, who is still out in the fields. Manuel's wife, a powerful woman named Soledade Goncalves, takes a fat sausage from a jar in the larder on this, the eve of her 45th birthday, and serves it by the fire with crusty corn bread and tumblers of red wine.

"I make it all," she says, moving to a long table across the room to break up lettuce for the dinner salad. "None of this is industrial."

Nor is anything in Sirvozelo. Yet this is Europe. The village lies at the base of a granite range that stands between northwestern Spain and Portugal's northern interior, a region called Trás-os-Montes, "behind the mountains." If tourists passed through, which they rarely do, they'd call Sirvozelo picturesque, like many another village from Ireland to Attica where the buildings are old, the people dress quaintly and patches of pasture and farm quilt the countryside.

Less picturesque is Sirvozelo's poverty. This is one of Europe's Appalachias. The "Old World" of style and affluence doesn't come near here. Its boundaries form an imperfect oval that starts in Helsinki, passes through northern England, sweeps south to take in Barcelona, crosses Italy below Rome and circles back to Finland. Inside the oval, a few people grow a lot of food and horses run at racetracks. Beyond it, a lot of people grow a little food and horses haul carts.

Sixty million people on Europe's fringe earn under two-thirds of Western Europe's average income; northern Portugal's peasants earn a tenth of it. For a century, the ambitious escaped to America and to Europe's wealthy core, leaving the unadventurous behind. A quarter of Portugal's work force once lived abroad, but Europe's long industrial decline has driven many home, to places like Sirvozelo, and walled the escape route off.

"When my grandfather died," Manuel Afonso is saying on the morning of his wife's birthday, "this property was split."

He is 50, small and dark, with a cloth cap tilted down over his forehead against the sun. Standing under a grape arbor where the rocky road to Sirvozelo narrows to a cow path as it enters the village, he looks over a stone wall into a shallow bowl of bottomland.

Ditches and vines subdivide the land into irregular rectangles for a quarter mile, until granite and gorse intervene. On a section in the center, a woman tends a few sheep while an old man rakes manure from a wooden-wheeled ox cart.

"I was given that," Afonso says, pointing past his 82-year-old uncle to a plowed strip. "It has potatoes. And I was given this"—a grassy stretch along the road. "Altogether, I have nine pieces." And how many acres? "I have no idea."

Barely bigger than Maine, Portugal has 840,000 farms. Four-fifths of them have a half-dozen plots and cover fewer than 10 acres. The country imports half its food, half its farmers are 55 or older, and almost half are illiterate. They work in their fields until it is too dark to see, and grow just enough to feed themselves.

Before the road to Sirvozelo turns to dirt, it crosses a dam. Built in the 1950s to power Portugal's cities, the dam flooded the village's best land and didn't supply it with electricity until 1978. The hills beyond the dam are pocked by symbols of the returning migrants' success: elaborate chalets with high-peaked snow roofs as useless in this climate as the savings they have swallowed. These, too, have bypassed Sirvozelo; none of its migrants have come back.

Twelve families used to live in this clutter of stone houses. Now seven do—35 people. The plink of mallet on chisel sounding across the fields in midmorning signals the valley's one industry. Stonecutters chop granite loaves from the hills and slice them by hand into fenceposts. One stonecutter lives in Sirvozelo. Two other villagers have paying jobs. Manuel Afonso tends an adjoining national park to help support his parents, wife, three sons and a hired hand, Domingos da Cunha. Driving an ox cart top-heavy with firewood, da Cunha stops on his way to a storage crib behind the village chapel.

He hasn't washed in a while and has some trouble understanding questions. He was born in a nearby village, Afonso explains, but inherited no land. "I have too many relatives," da Cunha says.

Afonso gives him room and board and $23 a month. Other villagers mill corn, bake bread, spin wool. Nothing is for sale. When a need for cash arises, some will help smuggle cattle over the mountains to Spain, but dealers with fast trucks have intruded on that trade. The alternative is to dip into capital.

"I sell a cow or a calf," says Josa Principe, pausing as he leads his small herd along Sirvozelo's principal path. He is 53, and has a bad-looking cyst on his wrist. He holds his staff with two hands and leans on it. "I get a little, spend a little."

A younger woman, his cousin, comes up behind.

"We were born here and we're going to die here," she says.

"I work only in the fields," Principe goes on. "My family eats what I grow. I have a six-year-old son, but he's mentally deficient. I have a three-year-old son, too, also mentally deficient. My five-month-old son is healthy."

"Here," says the woman, "you work until you drop dead."

In distant cities, planners and politicians mix technocratic tonics for Sirvozelo's complaints. But their handiest remedy, redistribution of land, applies more readily to flat country, where the poor till fields owned by the rich. Even there, however, land reform doesn't necessarily work.

Italy tried it. After World War II, the government seized a million acres and diced them into 70,000 plots. Two classes of farmer came out of it: successful capitalists, and peasants stuck on the worst land. When Italy boomed in the 1960s, many abandoned their plots and poured north; the rest stayed to grow old on state handouts. Portugal tried land reform, too. After its 1974 revolution, peasants laid claim to three million acres in the Alentejo, the southern plain of cork forests and olive groves, turning estates into collective farms. But as the revolution mellowed, owners reclaimed the best land, leaving the collectives in debt on rocky ground.

For upland villages like Sirvozelo, planners and politicians have few such nostrums. Older farmers are encouraged to retire early, so younger men, induced by grants, will stay on the land. But no grants go to men with no training from farms that make no profit. Some planners want farmers to sell out and let their plots be melded into tracts of sensible size. Farmers resist; owning land has meanings that transcend economic sense. Other planners want farmers to pool their efforts—buy a tractor and share it, for instance, or consolidate herds on common pasture. What does Manuel Afonso say to that?

"With a tractor, the trouble would begin when you came to use it." He pulls at his cap, stuffs his hands into his pockets, and joins Josa Principe standing in the path. "One person would want it when another also wanted it."

"Everyone would do things his own way," Principe says. "That's what we're like here."

"Putting cows together could be difficult," says Afonso.

"Some families might not work as hard as the others."

"But they would still have a right to the same profit."

Principe shifts his staff. "We'd only have arguments," he says. "It would work better in a village with more discipline."

When development theory was young, it seemed as if industry might save the rural poor. Italy dumped billions of dollars into its south. The economy grew, but the poor stayed poor. Industry no longer holds promise for Europe's boondocks. Not even agriculture does. Planners have come to speak instead of handicrafts and "boutique" foods as the backward farmer's best hope. As cheap, inferior feta cheese from Denmark takes over the Greek market, they want poor Greeks to sell good, expensive feta to gourmet shops in Copenhagen. In the Afonsos' cottage on Soledade Goncalves's birthday night, the gourmet-cheese idea comes across as fanciful. Her sons still choose the traditional cure: They intend to get out.

The family sits around the long table across from the fire as Goncalves dishes out kale soup. (Like most Portuguese women, she kept her maiden name.) Reserving the tumblers for their guests, they drink wine from bowls. Da Cunha, the hired hand, gets no spoon; he slurps his soup with a fork.

"One, two, three, yes," says the eldest son, in English. "My name is Carlos." He is 20, dressed in jeans and a pullover. For two years, he lived illegally in Paris with his aunt, a concierge, but couldn't get work. Home again, he got lucky: He will marry a young Portuguese woman whose parents live in Florida. The couple will move to Miami.

With a two-pronged fork, Goncalves lifts a cured ham from a pot on the gas burner and carries it to the table.

"We make enough for ourselves to eat," she says of the ham. "We have no one to sell it to, no one to order it."

"We would need a proper channel to retail them," Carlos says in his own language. "The only people who might do that here are people like me, of my generation. The older ones, they're not inclined to do anything different."

Afonso eyes his son silently.

"It's not that I never thought about it," says Carlos. "I have. I'd stay if I could. But you can't make a living. It's subsistence. I want more than that."

Goncalves clears the table and serves brandy; her birthday goes unmentioned. Carlos reaches over to the sideboard and turns on the old television. "Blackboard Jungle" is on, with subtitles. "That's just what I'm gonna do, big shot," Glenn Ford is saying.

Under the table, the dog crunches on a bone. Afonso nods sleepily. "Is there no way," says Glenn Ford, "to make these kids understand?" The old people usher out their guests and go to bed, leaving Carlos to watch the movie on his own.

1985

Chapter 6
DUALITY

The London bureau chief handed me a press release printed on heavy stock with a gold logo. A rich American had bought an expensive sailboat and was expensively refitting it to win the Whitbread Round the World Race. He was available for interviews. A feeling arose in my stomach possibly akin to organ rejection. I did not want to profile the man whose "winning philosophy" and "pioneer spirit" was ballyhooed in this release. To survive it, I found an antidote—a near-broke old sea dog with a bare-bones boat who thought he could win the race himself. I profiled the two of them at the same time.

Double profiles intensify contrasts: night and day, black and white, sweet and sour. Set side-by-side, contrasting personalities can define each other. So can two far-apart places. Jumping from person to person, from place to place, brings out the sadness or the dumbness in things without compelling me—heaven forfend—to express a personal opinion. And profiles doomed to monotony by themselves can sing as a duets. Nusret Çolpan, an artist I met in Istanbul, painted 20th-century oil rigs in the style of 16th-century Turkish miniatures. He was a worthily solid subject for the arts page. For the front page, I paired him with Cemil Karababa, a Turkish "maximalist" who once painted a seven-story-tall, 6,000-square foot portrait of Dwight D. Eisenhower bearing the legend: "Hello, Ike!" Çoplan, in defense of smallness, said: "A miniature can be very small or very big. It depends on how far away you are when you look at it."

Plastic surgery came to the Czech Republic. That was new. I hung around the Medical Cosmetics Institute in Prague and talked to Czechs getting tummy tucks and breast implants. Then

I went to a sanatorium in Jachymov and took a bath in radioactive water. That was old. I gave the new and the old equal space in a story emblematic of the Czech passage from quirky communism to quirky capitalism, with no need for a quote from a sociologist. From childhood through my daughter's wedding in 2002, I ate at Gage & Tollner, a restaurant on Fulton Street in Brooklyn that had been serving oysters—Baltimore broiled, Chicago broiled, milk broiled, cream broiled, celery-cream broiled and broiled on toast— since 1892. Its dining room—facing mirrors on burgundy-velvet walls—was declared a city landmark in 1975. Almost four decades later, I walked past Gage & Tollner and saw that it had turned into a junk-jewelry store. The walls were bright pink! In my old-new story on Gage & Tollner, the contrast came from my memory's archive.

When people emigrate and immigrate, profiles of two people can double as profiles of two places. West Germany, in the 1980s, was goading its Turks to go back where they came from. I found a jobless Turk in Berlin. He'd thought of moving to Mersin, his Turkish home town, but worried he wouldn't fit in. He had a friend who had moved back already, so I flew to Mersin and interviewed the friend. My story raised the question: What becomes of Turks who do go back where they came from? One returnee's life story hinted at an answer. On my own way back where I came from, fifteen years later, I detoured to Macedonia to find winners of the U.S. visa lottery for a "Coming to America" story. I met a young woman who spoke no English; a couple with a baby; and two classical musicians. After my repatriation, I met them again in Detroit and Pittsburgh: two continents, three cities, three months and six people, counting the baby. I wrote 3,000 words. My editor, Ken Wells, told me to make it longer, an order I gladly followed. The story ran 4,000 words. It opened in America with new arrivals in new homes; presented the lottery's basics; flashed back to Macedonia for life stories and the packing of suitcases; filled in the lottery's history; and circled on to America to be with the Macedonians while they settled in.

Double profiles blend smoothly with the fundamental maxim: Get the other side. In Karlovy Vary, a Czech spa in the Sudetenland,

I profiled two houses: One was stolen by the Germans from a Jewish family before the war. After the war, the other house was stolen from a German family by the Czechs. The Jews were getting their house back. The Germans weren't. Impolitic as the parallel may have seemed, my story gave two sides and took neither.

Competition is also the meat and potatoes of duality and, in my experience, often involves eating. A McDonald's opened in Singapore opposite Min Ho, a Chinese stall. "Here, in direct confrontation, are two great philosophies of fast food," I wrote, shuttling between the beeps of McDonald's "fish-fillet-cooking computer" and Min Ho's "frying, crashing and screaming." Hungry again, I swung from tubs of rigatoni at Mother Kelley's, on Long Island, to Spartan pizzas at Pizza the Action, in London, using a two-restaurant strategy to ask why Europeans see "huge portions as another weird facet of American retro-freakishness, like pink motels and gigantic neon signs."

Like every Yank, I'd seen the daily ad in the *International Herald Tribune* for Harry's Bar at 5 Rue Daunou: "sank roo doe noo." I was having a drink at the Harry's in Trieste when I first heard that the Harry's in Venice and the Paris Harry's were fighting over which Harry's had a rightful claim to being called the original Harry's Bar. The Venice Harry's invented the Bellini. The Paris Harry's invented the Bloody Mary. After eight years confined to beer and vodka in Eastern Europe's grayness, it was time to investigate.

. . . .

Harry Harry

VENICE

Harry Cipriani, owner of Harry's Bar on the Grand Canal, recently published a cookbook. His first sentence: "There's only one Harry's Bar."

If not for the Harry's Bar in Hong Kong and the one in Florence, that would be correct, as long as you didn't count the Harry's in Singapore, the three in London, the one in Shanghai or the two in Mexico, and left out the Harry's in Barcelona and Geneva, while ignoring the Harry's at sea on the MS *Europa* and the rumored Harry's on the Thai island of Koh Samui.

There are no Harry's Bars in the U.S., either, aside from New York's five and Philadelphia's four, the ones in New Orleans and Los Angeles, and 20-odd others, excluding Harry's Oyster Bar & American Grill in Oklahoma City, which has changed its name to Jake's.

So that settles it. There is one Harry's Bar—except for the original Harry's New York Bar at 5 Rue Danou in Paris.

"There's only one Harry's," repeats Duncan MacElhone. "That's where it gets maddening." As the cocktail crowd thins on Rue Daunou, he sits in a back corner of his bar swizzling a drink. "There's only one Harry as far as I'm concerned," he says. "That was my grandfather."

"Most of them, they copy this one," Harry Cipriani is saying. On a gray Venice morning, his bar is bright, the marble floor heated gently from below. "These people come and say, 'Harry, how are you?' Their attitude is, you should be flattered."

MacElhone and Cipriani have something in common: Neither is a McDonald's. The two are small-business men in a multinational world, and both lay claim to a name bartenders are wild about. After 60 years, they have taken to tussling over it, and to hunting down every Tom, Dick and Harry who opens a Harry's Bar.

"You're dealing with people who have so little imagination they can't name a bar after themselves or their mother-in-law or their dog," MacElhone says.

"About a restaurant," says Cipriani, "what's important is that you remember the name."

Defining what makes Harry a great bar name is the problem. The Venice Harry's has cachet and fine food, the Paris Harry's atmosphere and hot dogs. Some places called Harry's copy Venice, some Paris. Some fall between the stools, and some are owned by somebody else called Harry.

The Harry's in Barbados is a reggae music joint. They play dominoes at the Harry's in Mexico City. The Harry's in

Tuscaloosa, Ala., is owned by 1972 University of Alabama basketball All-America Harry Hammond.

"My name's Peter, Peter Chow," says the owner of the Hong
Kong Harry's on the phone. "Yes, I know. Harry's famous in the
world. Oyster, mussel. Anything you want, we got." Something
crashes in the background. "There's one in Paris?" Chow says. "In
Italy? I got no idea."

To Cipriani, owner of the one-and-only Harry's, his Venice
bar affords a kind of luxury you can sense with your eyes closed.
"Simplicity," he says. "It allows the spirit to develop." He is 61,
partial to bright ties, and the deftest of hosts. His two airy rooms
seat just 85. The gray-marble bar seats five. On the wall hangs a
photo of lower Manhattan in the 1930s.

A near-duplicate of it hangs on Rue Daunou, not far from
the boxing glove dangling above the bar. "This is a cocktail bar,"
MacElhone says. He is 40, a former banker in a sports coat. "It's
about drinks and the way people live in them."

The two bars couldn't be less alike, but MacElhone believes
both spring from the same Harry. In 1911, as he tells it, an
ex-jockey crated up a mahogany-paneled bar in New York, shipped
it to Paris and opened the bar. Harry MacElhone, a Scot, came
along to shake cocktails and took over in 1923.

"Harry'd go to Venice," his grandson says. "He'd stay at a hotel
where there was one Giuseppe Cipriani, who told Harry he wanted
to open a trattoria. Harry said that wasn't as good as opening a bar.
So they opened a bar. It was called Harry's."

But Harry Cipriani says his father, Giuseppe, never knew
Harry MacElhone. In 1929, he says, Giuseppe met a Bosto-
nian, Harry Pickering, who was out of cash. Giuseppe paid his
way home. Two years later, when Pickering repaid the debt,
Giuseppe opened a bar and named it Harry's. When his son
was born, Giuseppe named him after the bar. "My father didn't
think of the Harry's in Paris," says Harry Cipriani. "It wasn't
so famous."

According to Cipriani, Harry Pickering died in Monaco.
According to MacElhone, he didn't exist. After World War II, he
maintains, his grandfather revisited Venice and found that Harry's

Bar was a restaurant. "He had a major run-in with the Ciprianis," says his grandson, "and we've had a run-in ever since."

Whether Harry met Giuseppe or not, their legacy is a muddle. They gained renown for fixing meals and mixing drinks, not for practicing trademark law. Neither thought of untangling their reputations—so their names escaped them.

Florence struck first. Enrico Marlotti opened a knockoff of the Venice Harry's there in 1953. Florence spawned a Rome Harry's and a Los Angeles Harry's, which once put out a mock movie poster with the line, "Based on the original by Enrico Marlotti."

Then came London: a private club where the bar is pink marble, and men must wear dark suits. "It was just a name that sounded rather good," says Gavin Rankin, who helps manage it.

But the choice of name for Harry's Bar in London wasn't quite a coincidence. Here's why: In 1958, Giuseppe Cipriani opened a hotel in Venice, Hotel Cipriani. The hotel has changed hands, and the current owner is Orient Express Hotels Inc. of New York, which also owns 49 percent of the London Harry's.

Having annexed his first name, Orient Express is now after Cipriani's last one. In the 1980s, Cipriani opened a restaurant in New York. He called it by his full name: Harry Cipriani. So Orient Express is suing him. It says people booking rooms at Hotel Cipriani get mixed up.

"It's complicated," Cipriani admits. And the fight for his last name is just the half of it. He says, "We also have a little problem with MacElhone."

After years on the ropes, the MacElhones began sparring with Harry's bars in the 1970s. They put five under license: two German, two Swiss and one at sea. They closed Harry's in Portugal and Austria. Duncan MacElhone's invitation to the grand opening of a Harry's in Toronto, he says, quickly led to its "grand closing."

But no global trademark code supports him. MacElhone shut a Cannes Harry's only to have it reopen in Monte Carlo. Spain denied him the Harry's name in Barcelona, then gave it to a clone. Once, he went after Harry Helmsley, but since Helmsley is a Harry with bars in New York, he was judged fit to own a Harry's New York Bar.

That leaves the original namesake: Harry's in Venice.

Cipriani puts out a line of pasta. The label said Harry's Bar until MacElhone had a shipment of it seized in Germany. Cipriani also bottles his Bellini cocktail. The caps say Harry's Bar, so when a shipment arrived in France, MacElhone had it seized, too.

This led Cipriani to do what he had never done: He traveled to Paris a few months ago and set foot in another Harry's Bar. MacElhone was willing to talk, on one condition.

"Harry is a gentleman extraordinaire," he says. "But I won't let him go one inch sideways in not recognizing that my grandfather helped his father open up."

Cipriani went home, without an agreement, to nurse his identity crisis. He has done a "Do you know me?" American Express ad, and finished a novel about a surreal Harry's that opens in Beirut. When celebrities come to his bar, as they do, he still chats amiably, even if he is too distracted to know exactly who they are.

"I'm good with faces," Harry Cipriani says often. "I'm no good with names."

1994

PART FOUR
WRITING

Chapter 1
OPENERS

This is a chapter of instructions for starting stories. Ah, go on, read it anyway.

In 1979, Eric Morgenthaler, a *Wall Street Journal* reporter, got away with a lede like that. (The term is *lede*, to distinguish it from *lead*—gray stuff once used to stamp words onto white stuff made from trees.) "This is the story of the western world's 27th-largest steel producer," Morgenthaler wrote. "Oh, read it anyway." Luxembourg's money-losing steel mill was renting out workers to other companies instead of firing them. I don't know how many people remember the story, but, oh, I remember the lede.

Here's another idea for a lede: "This is a story about pencils. What's the point?" I haven't used it because I don't have a story to write with a point about pencils. Once, I knew my lede before I went looking for a story to accompany it: "Down is up." If down (the feathers) weren't up, that lede would have been pointless, too. On the metals beat one day, I filed: "The price of lead went up. The price of lead went down. The price of lead stayed the same." My story recorded each up and down. But my lead lede paled before *Journal* editor Mike Gartner's immortal, "This morning we will discuss carrots." In the story that morning, carrots were discussed.

This is the point: A lede should lead directly to the story underneath it. Its purpose, whether it concerns lead, small steel mills, or carrots, is to charm readers into reading paragraph two. Dozens of other stories encircle every story in a newspaper, every newspaper is encircled by magazines and books, and they're all engulfed by the Internet's torrent of clickbait. When an eye lands on a lede that reads like the first page of a novel, in my opinion, the eye loses patience. But Twitter isn't entirely to blame, and here's proof: "Copy readers in the old days used to insist that all the facts in the story be bunched together in the opening paragraph. This never made for a very moving chronicle, but at least you got the idea of what was going on." Robert Benchley wrote that—in 1925—warning of a menace to American journalism: The "pretty belief" that "every reporter is potentially master of the short story...."

A reporter's best stuff, it's said, belongs in the lede. "At night, the rats come out," was the best stuff I had after lying for six hours on a plywood table in a refugee camp off the coast of Malaysia while rats skittered around on the rafters above my face. The story's subject was America's grilling of Vietnamese boat people before taking them in, not my rodent-induced sleep deprivation, but that lede guaranteed a readership for paragraph two, so I went with it. I began my story about everything that may or may not be Turkish with: "You can get Turkish coffee in Turkey again." The reflex I wanted was, "Turkish coffee doesn't come from Turkey? Whaddya mean?" I began one about Robert J.M. Rickard, an archivist of unexplained events, with: "Things happen. For instance: In 1980, a shower of peas fell on Trevor Williams in Dan-y-Byrne, Wales." Readers went on to paragraph two, I hope, asking themselves where those peas came from. To get them asking questions about Greek bananas, I asked the questions myself:

Are there no bananas in Olympia?
Yes.
Are there no bananas in Thebes? Yes. In Corinth? Yes. In
    Sparta, Marathon, Delphi? Yes, yes, yes.
Are there no bananas on Crete?
That depends on your definition of banana...

In Benchley's day, even a person's address—typically the perpetrator's—still went into the lede of many a news story. If that's too much for late-breaking bulletins like mine, bunched-up facts aren't. This lede telegraphed the dope on a perp set to stand trial for cat murder:

*Before he pulled the trigger, before the car chase, before the cops
ran him down and threw him in jail, Jim Stevenson had a calm
look at the Texas penal code, and judged that it would permit
radical measures in defense of a piping plover.*

That took care of the cat killer's basics, and dangled enough
bait for a curious reader to bite. So did: "Upside down, underwater and moving backward, Natalie Coughlin swims faster than
almost anybody who isn't a fish." And: "Sometimes a cigar is just a
cigar—unless the Food and Drug Administration and a congres-
sional committee think it might be a cigarette." And: "No, plastic
slipcovers aren't making a comeback. They never went away."

Editors who notice that story after story starts the same way
sometimes issue blanket bans: No anecdotal ledes, no historical
ledes. Up to a point, I agree. I don't love ledes that coyly refer
to a "he," a "she," or an "it" without divulging their identities. I
tire of ledes that describe at length how a thing used to be before
announcing in paragraph four that the thing has just changed. Like
all reporters, however, I'm an exception, and I will die defending
the historical lede I put on my profile of Brunei after I found Capt.
Rodney Mundy's 1846 journal in the Bandar Seri Begawan public
library.

Stories, I've heard, shouldn't begin with jokes. My
Paris-to-Moscow train story began with a joke: A train from Paris
to Moscow stops in Warsaw; a Parisian looks out and thinks, "This
must be Moscow." A train from Moscow to Paris stops in Warsaw;
a Muscovite looks out and thinks, "This must be Paris." The story
went on to test that punch line's pertinence in the age of "openness." Weird datelines (PUKE, Albania, for example) should not
be the basis for a lede, I've also been told. "ONIKURADARAN-
NAI, Papua New Guinea" was the dateline on my Bible-translator
profile. He was the only person on earth who could translate Oni-
kuradarannai into English: "The place of the standing stone." My
lede was his translation of my dateline.

Breaking the rules, or the mold, is a function of relevance and
inventiveness. I began my scoop about Malaysian Chinese sausages
with a parody of investigative journalism ("sausage sources say").

I started my profile of Todd Brabender, the Kansas PR guy, with a parody of his press releases: "Hi, there. Hope you are well. We thought you'd like some information for an interesting feature." But the choice of a playful lede over a straight one can prompt legitimate differences in a newsroom. I can see why my lede for a story about obstructions in the wastewater infrastructure might have been over the top.

Ah, go on, read it anyway.

. . . .

Municipal Heart Attack

NEW YORK

Why wait until the next story about coagulated fat in sewers comes along when you can read this one now?

District Council 37, the municipal employees union, has been putting up posters in the subway lately, praising the "everyday heroes" who work for the City of New York. The posters have pictures of a tree pruner, a museum guard, a dental hygienist. Do the guys who get rid of fat clogs in the sewers rate a picture?

Nah.

"Never got on a poster," George Markovics, who works for the Department of Environmental Protection, shouts above the oceanic roar of his jet-flusher truck. He is standing over a manhole in south Brooklyn, looking down. At the bottom of the hole, where raw sewage should babble along, a smear of sickly gray goop is blocking the pipe. "I like water, you know, sewers—I love it," Markovics yells, positioning his rig near the hole. "We do a lot for the city. We're the best. Hey, watch your back!"

Markovics could qualify as a poster boy for the national sewer-fat crisis. America's sewers are in a bad way. Three-quarters are so bunged up that they cause 40,000 illegal spews a year into open water. Local governments spend $25 billion a year to keep the sewers running. The Water Infrastructure Network, a coalition of the wastewater-aware, warns that it will cost another $20 billion a year to keep them from falling apart.

Roots, corrosion, cave-ins, bottles, broken stick-ball bats, rusty car parts—anything will divert sewage on its way to the treatment plant. But the blockages are almost all wrapped in fat. The perpetrator is fried food. Fueled by fast food and an influx of immigrant cooks, America's appetite for eating out has bloated the output of viscous goop called restaurant grease to three billion pounds a year. Old grease once ended up in the cauldrons of the rendering industry, but for reasons ranging from Malaysia's palm-oil boom to a crackdown on New York's garbage Mafia, more goop than ever is going into the sewer. How it gets there—by pipe? by bucket?—is a matter of culinary mystery and governmental mystification.

But once the goop arrives, the effect is clearer than mud: Grease and sewage don't mix. Don Montelli stands over a manhole on another Brooklyn corner—a "notorious grease spot," he says, in front of a Chinese take-out. Montelli, a high-tech sewer worker, holds a video screen attached to a robot camera down below. "What you're looking at right now," Montelli explains, "is grease down the sewer."

With colonoscopic clarity, the camera shows a pipe with a drippy coating of fat. Fat won't pollute; it won't corrode or explode. It accretes. Sewer rats love sewer fat; high protein builds their sex drive. Solids stick in fat. Slowly, the pipes occlude. Sewage backs up into basements—or worse, the fat hardens, and a chunk breaks off and rides the pipe until it jams the machinery of a floodgate. To use a more digestible metaphor, that causes a municipal heart attack.

Fat infarctions have struck Honolulu, Columbus, Ohio, and Lake Placid, N.Y. A grease clot in Cobb County, Ga., set off a 600,000-gallon sewage surge into the Chattahoochee River. The U.S. Environmental Protection Agency has sued Los Angeles for allowing 2,000 overflows in five years; it blamed 41 percent of them on fat.

New York's sewers run 6,437 miles. Waste water and storm water mix in 70 percent of the system. When it rains hard, treatment plants can't cope. The mess gushes into rivers and bays. On dry days, the floodgates stay closed, except when grease gums up the works. With 21,000 places serving food, New York gets 5,000 fat-based backups a year. Its environmental protectors have fingered greasy-spoon districts as suspects, not just Coney Island and Chinatown, but the area around Carnegie Hall. New York's greasiest sewers lie in the section of the borough of Queens called Flushing.

Flushing is solidly Asian and restaurant-intense. Bouquet of deep-fryer wafts over hole-in-the-wall stalls abloom with signage. So much fat gets flushed in Flushing that it blocks the sewers 50 times a year. Three times a year, it locks the floodgates and lets sewage flush into Flushing River.

"We are subjected to the stench of sewer dirt to the degree that we are throwing up. This is not to laugh!" So said Julia Harrison, to laughs, at a city sewer-fat hearing. Harrison is Flushing's City Council member. "Restaurant people have been preached to, given literature, and still plead ignorance," she said. "It's not ignorance. It's up yours!" "And down ours!" came a shout from the audience.

New York requires "grease-generating establishments" to have grease traps. Greasy water flows through grease traps and slows, allowing the grease to rise. The water drains into the sewer and the grease stays. Grease traps fit under kitchen floors. In small restaurants, they must be emptied by hand. Nobody likes to empty a grease trap. Often, nobody does. When a trap fills with grease, greasy water races right through it. A Chinese kitchen with four wok stations needs a 5,000-gallon trap or it may as well have no trap at all. Lots of places, Chinese and otherwise, don't.

A New York "Grease Outreach" campaign uncovered a 73 percent rate of grease-trap abuse. The fine is $1,000 a day, but the sewers are still full of fat. The city has only six grease inspectors and only one trap-grease recycler. "We thought this was the future," says Livio Forte of A&L Recycling. It wasn't. Trap grease is watery—expensive to boil down. In a month, A&L collects only 15,000 gallons of it.

So where does the grease go? Grease-trap grease is only a drop in the can. Much more restaurant grease wells up in deep fryers. You can't pour gallons of fryer grease down a kitchen drain. The real issue is: What happens to the deep fat?

The city's trap inspectors aren't sure. "Talk to people in the business," one suggests. A place to start is Darling International Inc., a rendering company whose website says, "We are the grease team. We love it. We dream grease. Its color. Its...you know... greasiness." Neil Katchen of Darling's eastern region says, "The value on this product is low. The cost of processing is high." Katchen is talking yellow grease. After french-fry particulates are centrifuged out of deep-fryer grease, yellow grease results. Yellow grease has uses in animal feed, paint, face powder and adhesive tape. Now some renderers are burning it as biofuel.

Yellow grease is a commodity, up against Brazilian soy oil and Southeast Asian palm oil, cocoa butter, Borneo tallow, meadowfoam oil and beeswax. Global oil-and-fat output has tripled since 1960. With this grease glut sending prices downward, high-cost old fryer fat can't compete. So a grease pumper like Darling won't collect fryer grease in New York. Darling gets it from scavengers willing to wrestle five-gallon jugs and 50-gallon drums out of cellars and back alleys.

"My family came here from Europe and got into grease because grease was good business," says Bob Sirocco, one of the grandchildren. His company is called American Byproducts. The grandfather paid for old fat; the grandson charges to haul it away. "We don't charge enough," Sirocco says. But his customers are in revolt. They aren't required to pay for grease collection, so why should they? "They just, ah, do with the grease whatever they do with it," says Sirocco. "It's something I don't pursue."

This is where the Mafia comes in. The trick to grease disposal, some restaurant people say, is to freeze it in plastic jugs and chuck the jugs into the garbage. Problem one: In summer, it melts all over the sidewalk. Problem two: In 1996, Mayor Rudolph Giuliani broke the private cartels that fixed prices on restaurant-garbage pickups. "One of the things they did," the mayor said at the time, "was to beat people up, bust their kneecaps and kill them." The city asked national haulers to take over garbage routes and clapped a lid on prices. That took care of the Mafia, but not the grease. Profitable garbage is light and fluffy. Grease is heavy and sloppy.

With prices capped and profits slim, private haulers won't take grease-soaked garbage.

"No, absolutely not," says Bill Johnson at Waste Services of New York, a company with restaurant routes all around Flushing. "Grease is something we do not want to see in our trucks."

So? Where does it go?

"They dump it in the sewer at 1 o'clock in the morning," John Lagomarsino of J&R Rendering says. He's Bob Sirocco's cousin and a fellow grease man. "Look in the sewers," Lagomarsino recommends. "You see grease trails going into them. I mean, this is primeval."

In Lower Manhattan, a garbage collector drops a can and says, "Here, I'll show you." He walks to a corner sewer and points in. "See. That's grease." The basin is plugged solid. Lots of Flushing's are, too. One, on a restaurant-thick street, is so full even its grate is gunked up, and simple to sample: Sewer grease is gritty yet supple, sticky yet smooth, with hints of putty and beach tar.

"To me," George Markovics is yelling across the open manhole in south Brooklyn, "it's almost a concrete substance."

Markovics has lowered his flusher hose into the manhole. He maneuvers its nozzle into the sewer pipe, hits a lever and guns the water pressure. The nozzle rockets into the blockage. Sewage boils out. Filthy hunks of fat ride the rapids. "Know what this is from?" Markovics says as the torrent eases to an ooze. "This is from good cooking. Good cooking—know what I mean? Whenever I see grease, that's what I think of. Good cooking and good food."

2001

Chapter 2
NUTS

"Very coarse. Delightful," said the manager of the water-buffalo abattoir in Australia's Northern Territory, describing a fellow he thought I ought to meet. I'd driven 100 miles out of Darwin looking for a buffalo catcher to write about. Delightfully coarse was a good recommendation, so I drove on to Wildman River Station and found Josh Brooker. Brooker wore a sleeveless undershirt, dungaree shorts, a stained cowboy hat and no shoes. He had one eye and didn't bother with a patch. Brooker chased buffalo through a swamp in an old Toyota Land Cruiser with a hay bale for a front seat. I sat next to him. His son stood in a cage on the bumper, flipping a lasso over the horns of fleeing bulls. Brooker rammed his Toyota into trees and sideswiped termite castles, showering us with muck and hairy caterpillars. The story I sent to New York was, I thought, coarsely delightful.

Then came a note from a copy editor: Why are we writing about Brooker? Where does he fit in? Aren't there other buffalo catchers in Australia? Is Brooker the *best* buffalo catcher in Australia?

The story needed a nut graf. A nut can be a paragraph, a few paragraphs, or a few words. It's the kernel that places a story in context, explains why it's timely and relevant. It's where the "Why do we care?" question gets answered. So why should anyone care about a lout like Josh Brooker? Australia did have better buffalo catchers, with big crews and helicopters. Any one of them would have made better nut material, but I'll bet they weren't delightfully coarse. I raked my notebook for anything vaguely nutlike, and sent this:

> *Brooker isn't the best buffalo catcher in Australia. "I ain't no*
> *glamour boy," he says. "I ain't the best of nuthin'."*

I added a line about the best buffalo catchers, stated that the Brooker method was at variance with theirs, and cut to the chase in that old Toyota. It worked, and lent credence to my personal nut-graf theory: Like a baby's pacifier, the nut is a reassuring presence, larded with stunning journalese and proof to readers of a frivolous story's redeeming importance. Nuts can achieve heights of clunkiness, as in this one I committed about the Florida bug-splat analyst:

> *In his way, Dr. Hostetler is playing a part in a national move-*
> *ment to promote natural habitats....If humans follow his ex-*
> *ample in learning to recognize bugs by their splats, he reasons,*
> *they'll get to like bugs better.*

A nut graf, I've been told, must be balanced by a "to-be-sure graf" to temper the nut's reassuring assertions. Here is my to-be-sure graf about nut grafs: To be sure, nut grafs have journalistic uses. Knowing that editors will demand one, I hunt for it. The mental strain focuses my reporting. The moment I hit the nut, bells clang. I know I have what I'll need to distill a story's essence into a paragraph that will make it publishable.

But once I know what that paragraph is, the last thing I want to do is write it. This is where the stories I like part company with the news. A paragraph distilling what a reader needs to know (fireman rescues cat from tree) comes first in a news story; readers who want to know more keep reading. But when placed lower, in news features, a nut graf that seems to tell readers all they need to know invites them to quit. When a news feature begins with a long anecdote (cat sees bird, climbs tree, gets stuck) I skip down to the nut (fireman rescues cat), read that, and quit there. Why would anyone—besides firemen and tree surgeons—continue reading a cat-in-tree feature story when they've been told in the nut graf how it will end?

I've never made peace with nuts, but I've agreed to a cease-fire. Instead of seeing a nut as a reason to write a story, I see it as an excuse. The polite term for excuse is "news peg." Since everything changes all the time, everything always has a timely peg. Good change gets happy pegs, bad change sad pegs. A boom in sales of used books was not, I admit, an ideal peg for a story on the love notes and lewd pictures that people inadvertently leave in used books when they sell them, but it got the story published. Sometimes, I also admit, readers can't tell if a peg is an excuse for a story, or if a story is an excuse for the peg. I waited ages after moving from London to New York to write about America's tea-making ignorance. Then the tea party came along. Tea was my story. Politics was my peg. Honest.

News pegs need only graze my underlying subject, just enough to nudge it toward currency. A slushy New York winter was my excuse for the story on galoshes that I'd wanted to do ever since I learned that the Soviet Union had deployed the ABM-1 Galosh. When Indonesia's volcano and Haiti's earthquake led the news, I had cause to check out the Florida sinkhole situation. The London Olympics gave me an excuse to ride the summer bobsled at Lake Placid. I wanted to ride the bobsled not because it was news, but because it was scary and fun.

A newsy nut graf has a hidden danger: It may fool readers into thinking that the news is the story. My solution is to close the nut on a note of expectation, not a thud of finality. I got curious in 2010 to know why I couldn't pump my own gas in New Jersey, but the self-pumping ban had gone into effect in 1949; I rounded up a few station owners who wanted to lift the ban, allowing me to write a nut raising that unlikely possibility. On occasion, I've wedged in my real source of fascination ahead of the nut, as in my profile of Tom Powel, the photographer who took hyper-accurate pictures of other people's pictures. My theme came directly after the lede: "He's a star in an occupation that stands out for self-effacement." The nut graf's thud came next: "While news photographers have lost business to Flickr's amateur crowd, photographers of pictures are in big demand."

To be sure, a nut can be more than an excuse for a story, or a sop to journalism's platitudes. It can be sufficiently wonderful to grow into the story itself. Searching for a nut graf to let me write about the hazards of slicing bagels, I didn't set out to document the clash of bagel-slicing technologies, or to apply computer-assisted reporting to bagel-related injuries. But what I got was stunningly nutty—a sharply sprawling dramatic new development (for bagels). Why should we care? Don't ask. Read.

. . . .

Bagel Slicing

NORTHAMPTON, MASSACHUSETTS

"On a Sunday morning, not entirely awake, I decided it was a good day for a bagel," Howard Rose said. "It turned out not to be a good day for handling a knife."

Rose, an audio engineer, was at the Bruegger's bagel place in this New England town, recalling how he joined the ever-expanding ranks of BRI victims. A BRI is a bagel-related injury.

After slicing a finger instead of the bagel (a Band-Aid took care of it), he signed up with another crowd: those who attempt to build bagel-control devices. "I made a bagel vise from two chunks of wood," said Rose. "The prototype was OK. I never followed up."

That's why he dines where "someone else cuts the bagel." But just a flight up from the Bruegger's, unknown to Rose, is the office of a man who did follow up. He's Rick Ricard, a carpenter of French-Canadian descent and inventor of the Bagel Guillotine.

"My guillotine isn't associated with death," Ricard said one afternoon as he dropped a bagel into a holder, positioned a viciously pointed plastic-encased blade above it, and shoved firmly downward, slicing the bagel humanely in half.

The Bagel Guillotine, introduced 15 years ago, sells steadily at 80,000 a year. By Ricard's calculation, that makes it history's most successful bagel-control device. He says, "We achieved a paradigm shift in bagel cutting." He sees no need for new bagel slicers. And yet people keep inventing them—people like Dennis Moss and his son Michael. As long as the BRI menace persists, they believe, bagel-safety technology is open to improvement.

On a recent evening, Dr. Moss, a 66-year-old radiologist, was at home in Rochester, N.Y., watching his son saw through a bagel with their latest innovation: a slender knife fitted inside a molded-plastic guard. They call it the Brooklyn Bagel Slicer.

"My dad and I have a mission," said Michael Moss, who is 36. Said Dr. Moss, "If we keep anybody out of the emergency room it saves health-care dollars." His son said, "Dad's against unnecessary procedures." They call bagel injuries "an epidemiological scourge."

In 2008, according to an analysis of fingers cut by knives as reported in the government's National Electronic Injury Surveillance System, 1,979 people appeared in ERs with a BRI. Chicken-related injuries (3,463) led the category, but recorded bagel injuries were otherwise exceeded only by potato, apple and onion injuries.

Bagels, in fact, were implicated in more finger cuts than pumpkins (1,195) or cheese (1,236). Fewer than 100 incidents in 2008 involved turnips; ditto for wedding cakes.

(Of course, many BRI victims skip ERs and go to urgent-care offices. Or they stay home and eat breakfast anyway.)

When bagels were on a roll in the 1990s, moving beyond the urban enclaves where they first landed from Eastern Europe, some attributed the BRI problem to untrained slicers in white-bread regions. Untrue, say bagel-control experts. Every American now eats an average of 11.06 bagels a year at home, according to the market-research group NPD. But the crux of the issue is bagel authenticity.

As Maria Balinska tells it in her book, *The Bagel*, fear of bagel-injury litigation led Lender's to sell its frozen bagels pre-sliced, even before they hit the Midwest in the 1970s. Today, bagels at Wal-Mart or Dunkin' Donuts are steamed before baking. They may be round and have a hole, but they're fluffily sliceable.

Jim Dodge, the guillotine's sales manager, says, "We don't sell to Wal-Mart. That customer doesn't need us."

Real bagels are boiled, then baked. It makes them chewy on the inside and hazardously slippery on the outside.

Dr. Richard Nelson, head of emergency medicine at Ohio State University Medical Center, calls the traumatic consequences "pretty common."

"Once you pierce that crust," he says, "you're into the bread and suddenly that knife is moving real fast."

Yet many buyers of authentic bagels—sold mostly at small bakeries and chains like Bruegger's—seem unaware of the BRI threat. They keep slicing with naked knives. Nor does there seem to be any immunity among those who share the bagel's Jewish genes.

Andrea Shapiro was a 12-year-old on Long Island when she cut a bagel and her thumb. She had surgery and 100 stitches. Now Shapiro is a 45-year-old Manhattan real-estate lawyer, and a couple of weeks ago she did it again. "I was able to stop the bleeding this time," she says. "I got complacent."

Knife wielders often stand bagels upright and cut downward. Carolyn Susman, a blogger in Florida, did it that way; her gash needed a tetanus shot. "I never learned proper slicing form," Susman says. Marshall Hoffman thought he had: One night, hungry, he laid a bagel flat on a cutting board and sliced horizontally. As the Virginia public-relations man recalls, "The ER nurse took one look and said, 'You were cutting a bagel, right?'"

Each of these BRI victims owned a bagel holder. Shapiro's was "packed away." Susman lost hers. Hoffman's was too small for his bagel. But to the father of the Bagel Guillotine, every one of those devices was a bagel-control failure by definition.

In his office above the Bruegger's, Ricard had laid out a retrospective exhibit of other inventors' bagel-slicing ingenuity: bagel grippers and squeezers; bagel cradles, clamshells and clamps; and a bagel "trap" that looked like a table saw. None worked without a separate knife.

"Whenever you put a knife in a person's hand, it's an issue," Ricard said. "People don't know how to use knives." It was this insight, which came to him while he was chopping wood 15 years ago, that led to the guillotine's self-contained blade.

The breakthrough gave rise to a new era in bagel-safety—and a multitude of competing contraptions, most of which have flopped. Ricard has collected a bunch—from the "Bagel Wizard" with three handles for two hands, to a Ginsu slicer that resembles a slot machine. All operate on the principle that pushing an unreachable blade into a bagel beats sawing a bagel in half.

Now comes the Moss family and the Brooklyn Bagel Slicer.

Offered one to try out on a bagel, Ricard studied it for a moment and waved it away. "This thing is going to let you cut towards your hand—exactly how not to do it," he said. "This is designed by a doctor?"

Yes, and a doctor's son, whose bagel-slicing theory is: People follow their instincts no matter what they're told, so they may as well have a way to do it safely.

"Our slicer lets you saw," Michael Moss said at noontime on another day. "It's a linear action, what you naturally want to do."

He was in line at Balsam Bagels, near downtown Rochester, where the Brooklyn Bagel Slicer was undergoing trials. Behind the counter, Taryn Muscarulla, 19, took his order: plain, lightly toasted.

She cradled the bagel in her left hand, seized the slicer with her right and sawed fast, directly at her palm. The plastic guard stopped the blade an inch short of it. She flipped the slicer over, finished the cut with a deft upward stroke and said, "Ta-dum!"

Looking pleased, Moss asked Muscarulla for a schmeer of cream cheese and smoked whitefish. Then he sat down and ate lunch.

2009

Chapter 3
ORGANIZING PRINCIPLES

In its old New York office, above a downtown Woolworth's, the *Journal* had three "writing rooms." Small and windowless, each had a typewriter and a bare desk. Reporters ready to write carried their raw material into a room and stacked it on the desk: books, notebooks, clippings, releases, academic papers, official documents, scribbles on matchbooks. I remember looking at my stack and feeling sick. Where to begin? If I had a lede in mind, I'd type it. Then I needed a fact, a quote, a statistic. It was in the stack. Somewhere. I'd dig for it, wasting time, blowing my cool, losing my mind. Faced, at last, with stacks of stacks for a UN conference on sea pollution (one issue was whether the lobster is a fish), I took a pen, wrote a number on the title page of each turgid document, and made a numbered list of them on a separate piece of paper. Thus began my life as an indexer.

Every reporter has a system. One fellow I knew walked the newsroom, mumbling, before he sat down to bash out a complete story in 30 explosive minutes. Another never glanced at his notes while writing; later, he flipped through them for quotations to insert. Me, I make lists. In my National 1 Subject, the notebook that opens like a regular book, I take notes on the right-hand page only. I number the pages and list each interview in a table of contents on the cover. Later, I underline the quotes, facts and descriptions that look good enough to use in my story. On the left-hand page, I assign a label to each underlined item, by category: "history," "background," "opponents." I also underline my typed notes from phone interviews, leaving space in the left-hand margin for the labels. And I underline my stacks of documents, moving (or typing) the underlined passages to a single text file, labeling each of those passages, too.

What does this accomplish? One, it cuts those stacks down to a small pile. Two, it lets me make an index. On a yellow pad, I write a category's name. Underneath it, I list the items that belong in that category. A category for my Grape-Nuts story was "shredder," the evil device that tears apart loaves of bread. Under it, I made this list: "how it works," "bombs," "bake and destroy," "death moan." Next to each item on the list, I wrote the number of the page in my notebook where I could immediately find it. As related items accumulate, they coalesce into potential paragraphs. The act of reading, underlining, labeling and listing reveals connections, patterns and meanings that I haven't seen before. The only job left is to put the paragraphs in order. That's an outline.

Something I haven't mentioned: creativity. Underlining, labeling and listing clarifies material. It exposes gaps and overlaps. Indexing ended my hysterical searches for errant factoids and freed me to focus on the less mechanical business of telling stories by finding my muse. It took me three years to learn the *Wall Street Journal* formula: lede, nut, quote, to-be-sure, history, and so on. Once I got the formula down pat, I wanted to mess with it. Is that creativity? I'm not sure, but it does have its satisfactions.

An outline's mission is to keep readers reading. The formula's requisite block of components, packed in after the lede, conspires to stop them. When do the preliminaries end? When does the storytelling begin? My ideal is to crush up the block and sprinkle it through the story like a trail of Grape-Nuts in the forest, giving readers reason to read on. Stories all have story lines. Chronologies move along time lines, over hours or years, flashing forward or back. Conflicts and case studies, the grist of newspaper features, progress from argument to argument, from point to point. After searching fruitlessly for S. Larson, the mysterious signee of every Citibank customer letter, the outline of the story I wrote was the timeline of my frustrated reporting. Occasionally, I begin at the beginning. My Paris-Moscow train ride started in Paris and ended in Moscow. But the cross-channel swim I followed started at the end, as the swimmer caught sight of a French beach. The flight I took to Managua from Cleveland in a light plane started in the middle, with Wayne Sperling, the pilot, trying to find the airport in Brownsville, Texas, at sundown.

Old Hopalong Cassidy episodes are my organizational influence, though the outlines I like have also been called "novelistic." Hoppy and the novelists handle transitions beautifully, whether it's the cliffhanger before a commercial break, or the point where a novel's narrator interrupts to fill in a character's childhood traumas.

Outlines take shape as a string of scenes—witnessed moments when something happens. As a scene closes, the narrator (me) steps in to supply perspective. In the Malaysian camp where the rats kept me awake, each scene in my story described the questioning of a different refugee family. Each family's fate was sealed by a different regulation. After each scene, I stepped in with that regulation's dry details. To break up a dense story on a German company's reluctance to market its abortion pill, I dropped in three scenes of three women in the lounge of an Edinburgh infirmary, waiting for the pill to work. It wasn't comic relief, but readers saw and heard real people instead of getting a bunch of statistics, and quotes from talking heads.

Before pulling away from the curb, drivers usually know where they're going. Reporters who sit down to type ought to know where their stories will end. But so much rests on grabbing attention with a lede and nailing it with a nut graf that what remains is often left to drift. A good story is strong all the way through. A good outline is its road map—from lede to kicker. I had the kicker for a story about baseball socks in mind before I made the first phone call: "The socks won." And I knew the lede and the kicker—both—for my story about Brooklyn's campground the instant Cindy Woulf told me where she and her husband were planning to go for the weekend.

. . . .

Camping in Brooklyn

NEW YORK

When New Yorkers get out of town, they often go to a place covered with trees and dirt known as "the country." When out-of-towners come to New York, they usually end up in a hotel—the

Best Western or something. Now there's one destination that can accommodate them all: A campground is growing in Brooklyn.

"I love it here," Beverly Wong was saying toward sunset on an August Friday. "I love going to the theater."

She and her husband, Patrick Neeson, both in their 40s, and their five kids, six through 16, had spent a few days at the Jersey Shore and were towing their tent-camper home to Montreal.

"So my wife says, 'Why don't we go to New York?'" said Neeson, who was busy setting up rafter poles. The best hotel deal he found on the Internet for a gang of seven was $500 a night.

Then this came up: a $20-a-night campsite at the south end of Flatbush Avenue in the borough of Brooklyn. Neeson didn't know it, but the campground had only just opened—on July 4—as the first-ever spot where anybody anytime can rough it legally in New York City.

It's also the only campground for the general public inside any American city's limits that belongs to the National Park Service, the outfit that brings you peaks, lakes, canyons, geysers and glaciers, from the Everglades in Florida to the Gates of the Arctic in Alaska.

"My 14-year-old said, 'Where's the campground?'" said Wong, the Montrealer. "We're used to, you know, sand and grass. This is, uh, you know..."

"An airstrip," said Neeson.

Well, yes. They were camped at Floyd Bennett Field, a disused airport on Jamaica Bay, 15 miles from Times Square. An expanse of concrete stretched out before them to a distant shore. A chain-link fence behind them collected plastic bags in a stiff wind.

A sign on the fence named their RV site: "Amelia Earhart #42." She flew out of here once. So did "Wrong Way" Corrigan, who swore he was going west but ended up in Ireland. Floyd Bennett was famous for flying to the North Pole, though it later came out that he never actually got there. He was living in Brooklyn when he died in 1928.

The Navy used the field in World War II, and the Coast Guard moved in until 1971, when Gateway National Recreation Area was born. Floyd Bennett was no Yellowstone. It fell to ruin. People came to fish, fly model planes, watch birds in the weeds.

The idea for a public campground came up in 1983, and the Park Service didn't get to building it until this year: 41 sites in the bushes between runways, and six on the tarmac for recreational vehicles. Picnic tables, fire rings, grills and mosquito magnets set the federal budget back $63,000.

"I'm a big dreamer here," says Linda Canzanelli, Gateway's superintendent, who envisions 90 campsites on the field in a couple of years as part of President Barack Obama's new "America's Great Outdoors" initiative, aimed at city types who spend too time much indoors.

"The smell of burnt marshmallows," Canzanelli says. "Ghost stories around the campfire. Sunlight on the tent in the morning."

Brooklyn's got it all now. In Yellowstone, where the price of gas rules, July's overnight stays sank to 430,000 from 696,000 a year ago. At Floyd Bennett, reachable by bus and subway, overnights took off—from zero to 1,300.

What the old airfield lacks in variety of wildlife, it makes up for in low-cost life of the human variety.

One Saturday afternoon, hot and humid, a family of Japanese expatriates from Westchester County lugged coolers past an orange barrier to a clearing in the bushes.

Another family, of Colombians, was unpacking suitcases, playing a radio, and eating croissants out of a plastic tub. A young man walked by them with a queen-size air mattress on his head. "Apartment camping," he said.

Kaziah Hall sat at a picnic table, sewing a tail on a kite. He makes kites for a living in Virginia. He was in New York to deliver one. Usually, he and his wife sleep in their SUV in the rest area off Exit 12 on the New Jersey Turnpike. He says Floyd Bennett is prettier.

"The national parks," said Hall. "A model for the world." A Brooklyn friend, Robert Brown, was taking pictures. "Why travel to a place that looks like this when you got this right here?" he said. Hall told him that all his food was in the car to keep it away from the raccoons. Brown said, "That's nature, man."

The Park Service shares Floyd Bennett with a police helicopter base and a training center for garbage-truck drivers. It classifies the campground as primitive. There's no electricity. The outhouses are supplied by a company called "Rent A Throne." There's a junked stainless-steel sink on a taxiway, but no running water.

"This is pretty natural, even with the concrete, which, mind you, I don't like," Scott Woulf was saying.

He sat in the shade of his camper at Amelia Earhart #47. His wife, Cindy, was grilling chicken. "I have some beautiful sunrise pictures," she said. "We only called the cops once, when somebody set fire to a trash can out there."

The Woulfs are the deans of Brooklyn camping, with the computer skills to extend their Park Service reservation beyond the 12-day limit. In June, they drove their Ford Taurus to New York from their home in Neenah, Wis., bought a used camper upstate, and pulled both of them into Floyd Bennett Field early in July.

They haven't left yet.

Woulf, an out-of-work member of the Carpenters Union, found a job in Manhattan. Cindy drives him to the subway, shops for food ("a lot of kosher") and has dressed up the picnic table with a clam-shell collection and a pot of pink pansies.

"We've been into the city, like tourists," Cindy said. She paused as a police helicopter came in low overhead. "But we don't particularly care for the crowds."

So on the Friday evening when the family of Montrealers rolled into camp (and quickly drove off for dinner in Chinatown and a trip to Times Square) the Woulfs were packing their overnight bags.

By sunset, they were on Flatbush Avenue in their Ford, getting out of town for a weekend in the country.

2011

Chapter 4
KEEP IT SHORT

Strunk & White give the best advice for writing short: "Omit needless words." But which ones? Deciding takes time. To appropriate a line from A.J. Liebling: I can write shorter than anybody who can write faster. Writing short is like packing and repacking a small bag for a three-week trip, and has the same advantage: no excess baggage.

It can become obsessive. Retyping paragraphs to expunge widow lines in manuscripts will have no effect on published pages. It is sick. However, unlike other writerly habits—such as getting drunk and throwing up in a trash basket—it does omit needless words. I'm no lover of newsroom edicts that freeze story lengths. They handcuff editors the way mandatory sentences handcuff judges. Stories, like crimes, deserve to be appraised by their individual demerits. Limits on length can also confine stories to simple ideas covering less time or territory. But I confess: Length limits rein in my weakness for elliptical outlines and irrelevant discursions. A shorter story does have a better shot at holding a reader's attention in today's world, especially when its subject isn't adorable sleeping animals.

Longer stories don't have to deal with heavy subjects. Sewer fat, foreskin restoration and global chatter were among my longest. Then again, short stories needn't be all fluff. Some readers might have been less entranced than I was with the revival of railroad barges in New York harbor, or the impact of potash mining on the crust of the Bonneville Salt Flats. I dealt with each in 1,200 words, enough of them fluffy, I hope, to keep a few readers attentive.

A secret to short writing is long reporting. The closer I get to mastering a subject, the better I am at separating what's worth saying about it from what's not, and at compacting techno-speak into plain words. Take these three sentences from my Salt Flats story:

"Checking the old measurements, the geologists found errors. They recalibrated the old figures and matched them with their own new ones. It turned out that the flats hadn't changed in 16 years."

I indexed the facts and figures for those sentences under, "Shrinkage claims and earlier mistakes." The heading has ten items listed under it, and 17 references to documents and interviews. It took me hours to amass, understand and excavate that geological heap. The sentences took about ten minutes to write. Like sex and Chinese cooking, writing short requires a great deal of preparation, but it's quickly over.

Understatement conserves words. If editors banned superlatives, they'd save the forests and protect the gigabyte. Yet superlatives are spiraling out of control. The ramping up of "going forward" must be reversed. The modern *Wall Street Journal's* founding editor, Barney Kilgore, said in a memo that if he saw "upcoming" in the paper, he'd be downcoming and somebody would be outgoing. In the "going forward" era, he'd be coming downward and somebody would be going outward. Puns? Expunge them. Birdwatchers don't flock, coffee doesn't perk things up, the police aren't cop-outs. Unfunny stories aren't funnified by puns, not even brilliant ones—*meow culpa*—about cats. Lavish descriptions of sunsets, auto parts and wallpaper might help set scenes, but unless an object acts, or is acted upon, I leave it offstage. Mawkishness wastes words. When I write the heartrending saga of the motherless dolphin whose tail is reattached by a nine-year-old paraplegic surgeon found living alone in a roach-infested room, I will make it mawk free.

Handing in long stories invites editors to shorten them. It's a trap I've fallen into when seduced by inapt facts. In Savannah to meet the man who wrote the book on toenail fungus, I needed an expert to pass judgment on his cure. A druggist directed me to a locally famous podiatrist. He was locally famous because he had lost his feet tripping over a power line. I spent two spellbound hours at home with the footless foot doctor who had given up podiatry, it turned out, to write epic novels of the Old South. He had forgotten everything about toenails and declined to evaluate the fungus cure.

But I was in love, and devoted 130 words to the podiatrist in my story. In New York, a *Journal* copy editor amputated them.

Self-amputation is less painful. Copy editors used to chop from the bottom, assuming the last paragraph to be least important. Others removed internal growths, such as scenes and dialogue. I'd rather perform the surgery on myself, and the *Journal's* editors have let me. I don't chop. I weed. One midnight, in Prague, New York called to tell me that 2,600 of my 3,400 words on nuclear smuggling would run the next day. Which words? My choice. I felt weirdly free. Dozens of small decisions I had avoided while writing were suddenly upon me. I weeded with joy. Nineteen years later, at deadline on the night before my last story as a full-timer was to appear in the paper, I got a note saying that a total of 1,189 words was 170 words too long. I had 20 minutes to weed them out. What a way to go.

Do stories get better when they get shorter? On my first trip to Albania, I flew in without a visa, was admitted by mistake, stayed in a hotel crawling with spies, ate goat stew every night, witnessed some chaos and concluded that the tragically crazy place was worth 3,000 words. The *Journal's* European edition printed them. My New York editors demurred. They asked for a 1,200 word weeding. I cut out: the sludge in Albanian orange drink; waifs in rags begging for gum; the arrival of the first Walkman; the legalization of beards. "The nights are black in Tirana," I wrote. "Caped policemen stand in dark doorways and crouch in corners." That went. Readers in Albania (if any) might have preferred the longer version, but the short one looks fine to me.

. . . .

Albania Short

TIRANA

"Microwave oven? I have heard of this," Ylli Hyka says. "It is in a song by Dire Straits. 'We got to move this refrigerator, we got to move this microwave oven ...' By the way, what is a microwave oven?"

Hyka and his friend Frederik Seiti, 22-year-old university students, are in the campus coffee bar taking an unscientific test to see just how out of it Albanians really are.

They know all about Madonna, next to nothing about AIDS. "What happens to you?" asks Seiti. Fax machines? No idea. American Express? "A newspaper," Hyka guesses. Handed a credit card, he fingers it, holds it to the light. "Lottery ticket? Playing card?"

An attempt is made to explain. "You mean it is valuable?" Seiti says excitedly, but his friend is crestfallen. "Sorry," he says, handing back the card. "We do not belong to the world."

Albania, 55 miles from the heel of Italy's boot, has been out of this world for 46 years. Its absolute ruler, Enver Hoxha, took Stalinism to extremes Stalin didn't contemplate. Slighted by insults to his hero, he broke with the Yugoslavs, the Soviets, the Chinese. Since 1978, this country of 3.3 million hasn't had a single friend.

While its youth peeked at the West through the keyhole of rock music and others heard of events in their region on the Voice of America, the revolutions in Eastern Europe passed Albania by. After Hoxha's death in 1985, his heir, Ramiz Alia, tried to sugar the Stalinist pill. But last December, revolution arrived here anyway.

It started on a Saturday night. The lights had gone out in the university's cold, leaky dormitories and students gathered to protest. In a state that hadn't tolerated a whisper of dissent, thousands were soon keeping vigil on campus. Three days later, Alia caved in and agreed to bring Albania back from the land of Nod.

Multiparty elections were set for the end of March, political prisoners are being freed every day, and the churches and mosques of history's first atheist state have opened to worshipers again after 24 years. But the students stayed angry. Late last month, their supporters stormed Tirana's main square, demanding that Hoxha's name be removed from the university, and tore down the dictator's statue.

Though Alia relented, the turmoil continues, leaving at least four dead and raising possibilities ranging from military takeover to civil war.

For the third time in eight months, thousands are fleeing the country. This time they have headed by sea to Italy, where the Italians can't seem to decide whether to welcome them or send them home. Albania's president, meanwhile, has taken charge of the government, named a new prime minister and imposed a partial state of emergency. Yet three tense weeks remain before the election intended to cap a year of uneasy reawakening in Europe's last fortress of totalitarian communism.

The dribble of Westerners who make it here has increased to a trickle. Albanians who find a working phone can direct dial overseas now, without permission. At the Hotel Dajti, where foreigners stay and students rarely stray, an American Express card imprinter has appeared at the front desk. A man from Tirana, it is said, has gone to Italy to bring back a private car; until this month, owning one was prohibited.

The possibilities seem limitless, but don't let it fool you. This is still Graham Greene country.

A "businessman" flies in from Rome and spends five days in the Dajti lobby, shaking hands. Another Italian says to an acquaintance, "Do you read Italian?" flashes an official-looking card, and whispers: "Intelligence. Very delicate situation."

In a jittery culture shaped by the blood feud, Communists fear revenge, democrats a coup.

"Somebody is planning bloody days for Albania," Sali Berisha says one morning. He and other leaders of the new Democratic Party confer anxiously at their headquarters. Dr. Berisha, a cardiologist, is calmer by evening. The coup hasn't happened on this day. But nothing is a certainty here. Rumor rules.

Word travels the country during one week that South Africa needs labor. Its Rome embassy will pay the passage of all comers. Four ferries will pick them up Saturday in the Adriatic port of Durres, Durazzo to the Italians. In the Dajti on Saturday of that week, the man from Italian intelligence hisses, "Durazzo. Bang. Bang."

It takes hours to hire a taxi. Trailing troop trucks, it arrives in Durres at dusk. Riot police guard the port gates. Shattered bricks cover Enver Hoxha Boulevard. Embers glow where the tomes of the nation's hero have been burned, watched by knots of deceived young men.

"We heard four boats would come," one says. "Only one did. The police stood in the way. People threw rocks. The police fired."

Another: "The boulevard was full of people. Everyone wanted to get on." A third: "I wanted to go. I ran. Of course it was no use." Later, the police say two rioters were shot. The ferry was the regular service to Trieste, but the rumors wouldn't let up and now thousands of young Albanians have commandeered boats at Durres and sailed to Italy. While chaotic scenes play out in Italian ports, Albanian troops are striking hard to stop the exodus; some reports say ten more people were killed in Durres over the weekend.

Back at the Dajti, Dr. Berisha speculates that a "third force" is at work in the country. But to an outsider, the most active third force here is Albania's removal from reality.

Albanians say they descend directly from the ancient Illyrians, though they seem to have taken side trips into other races. Illyria battled Rome for centuries, split in two when Christianity did, then battled Slavs, Bulgars, Normans and Neopolitans until the Turks came in 1423 and stayed for 489 years.

Even after Albania won independence in 1912, a German prince ran it. In World War I, Serbia, Montenegro, Austria-Hungary, Bulgaria, Italy, France and Greece invaded it. In 1939, after the brief reign of a tribal chief who crowned himself King Zog, Italy conquered it.

You begin to see why Enver Hoxha didn't trust foreigners.

Under his rule, Albania closed in on itself. Even the religion ban, with a wary glance at the Vatican, had less to do with ideology than xenophobia. "When winds blow cold, you button up your coat," says Deputy Foreign Minister Muhamet Kapllani, at the Dajti for an interview. "History has been bitter toward the Albanians. Perhaps that hasn't been very comprehensible to the rest of the world."

Not until Christmas Day 1989 did Enver Hoxha's heir see that he could hide from history no more. Two weeks earlier, speaking of "processes" in Eastern Europe, Ramiz Alia had said: "The events taking place over there have nothing to do with us." Then Nicolae Ceausescu was put to death in Romania, and Alia became a picture of human kindness. He relaxed on religion, let everyone have a passport and by Christmas 1990 was finally prodded into multiparty elections.

Yet the totalitarian fog lies thick. Albanians don't all realize how bad they've had it. And if the jig is indeed up, many Communists don't seem to know it.

At the Enver Hoxha Museum, a marble-clad pyramid lidded by a great red star, the guide who greets a visitor in the atrium wears dark glasses. Asked why, Emirjeta Xhunga starts to cry.

A childhood accident disfigured her eye, she explains. If help was possible abroad, she never found out. "My bad luck," she says, touring the liberator's achievements: draining the swamps, defeating illiteracy. "Hoxha was a great Albanian," she says at the end. "That can never be undone. The facts are as clear as daylight."

They certainly are to the Communist Party. At the Dajti to explain its platform, Fatmir Qumbaro, a central committee political worker, insists it has nurtured human rights. "Otherwise, we couldn't have withstood for one day the threats against national existence." Have Albania's Communists made any mistakes? Qumbaro comes up with one: "We shouldn't have collectivized livestock in 1978."

But the Communists can't fool everyone. They did keep Albania in the dark for 46 years; they didn't kill the instinct for freedom.

Sunday morning in the city of Shkodra: The Roman Catholic Cathedral stands shrouded in stucco, still a sports hall. The Museum of Atheism has closed—and reopened as a branch of the Democratic Party. But nearby, at the end of a dirt alley, a mass is in progress at the Church of the Madonna of the Rosary.

It had been used as a warehouse. Now, it is Albania's first reconsecrated church. The old gilt altar came from the prop room of a movie studio. The Museum of Atheism provided the statues.

While the children's choir sings, the choirmaster stands toward the rear. "I have always continued to be a priest," Father Antoni Nogaj says. "I will serve the people as before."

He has no bibles, no rosaries, no hymnals, but no matter. "We have found excitement for religion in all the people, even the young," he says. He has spent years in prison. So has Father Alex Baqli, leaving church as mass ends. "We have 32 priests who are breathing again," he says.

But many priests died in chains. And for many other Albanians, who languished without the sustenance of a cause or a faith, learning to breathe again will take longer.

Sokol Ngela, 35, sits in a Tirana coffeehouse after a day searching for a place to live. He was born lucky, the son of a member of Enver Hoxha's cabinet. In 1975, his father ran afoul of his master. He was sent to prison and his family banished to internal exile.

At 19, Ngela went to work in a bitumen mine near a village called Selenec. Four years later, in the privacy of his cottage, he uttered a criticism of the dictator. The cottage was bugged. He was arrested and confessed to being an enemy of the state.

The prison camps where he spent the next seven years had no heat, no panes in the windows. He lived through beatings, solitary confinement, and four daily hours of readings from Enver Hoxha's works. In 1986, he was released and sent back to the tar pit. Last March, his exile ended. With no money, he stayed in Selenec, but a short while ago he quit to seek a new life in Tirana.

It is a routine story here. What makes it striking to a stranger is Ngela's reaction on his return home after 16 years:

"Tirana hasn't changed," he says. "When I came back I saw nothing different. Just the Hotel Tirana and the Hoxha Museum. Nothing else. I think all of Albania must have been a prison. All the people of Albania have been in exile."

1991

Chapter 5
DIGITIZING

Technology has affected my writing. I know, I know. Can we discuss something else? Did Medieval monks talk about nothing but technology when moveable type killed the illuminated manuscript? Or did they get on with their true vocation: spreading the good news? Let the bean counters agonize over digitization. Stories are stories. The reporter's job is finding and telling them. And technology, I've learned, can be a terrific help, except when it gets in the way.

Since buying a used Pentax Spotmatic in 1967, I've carried a camera on every outing. *The Wall Street Journal* didn't print photos when I was hired. The best thing about their absence in the paper was the absence of photographers in the newsroom, as Fred Taylor, the managing editor, used to say. I took pictures anyway, and studied them to fill in the color I didn't capture in my notes—Kurdish costumes, pasta machines, residential caves. In the 2000s, photos—color ones, no less—did come to the *Journal*. Videos, too. Though photographers are all delightful people, I'd watched them creeping around underfoot, getting in the way as other reporters tried to work. There was only one way to escape them: shoot myself.

The reward for taking charge of technology is independence, a rarity on newspapers. I acquired a taste for it in Singapore, where I was 14,000 miles from the *Journal's* copy desk. When I arrived, in 1976, my editors communicated by *telegram*. A man on a motorbike delivered them at four in the morning. To reply (when I woke up) I had to drive to the post office. Direct-dial international phones didn't exist. I was blissfully beyond supervision. Yet only a few years later, technology's liberating possibilities hit home.

New York threw me to the journalistic hounds covering the gas disaster in Bhopal. Thousands of Indians had died there when a tank cracked at Union Carbide's pesticide plant. I flew into New Delhi on the same plane as NBC News, and had to wait for its equipment trunks to rumble down the conveyor before my bag appeared. NBC had chartered its own plane to shuttle video tape in and out of Bhopal. All I had was my Olivetti Electra 32. Once in the city, I talked to everyone, including a gang of American ambulance chasers. I couldn't possibly send a long feature on the ancient teletype machine in Bhopal's Post Office. I had to fly back to Delhi to use a hotel telex, occasioning two of my career's greater embarrassments.

One, I got off the plane at the wrong stop. I was in a bus speeding along the tarmac of Gwalior Airport before realizing it. I screamed, the driver braked, I jumped out and galumphed back to the plane just before the door shut. Two, and more to the point, the story I telexed from Delhi 36 hours later gave top billing to those American ambulance chasers. New York's reply: *Sorry. Story unusable.* In a frenzy, I rewrote it, switching themes from punitive damages to death and betrayal. Unknown and unknowable to me, NBC had been giving the ambulance chasers top billing on TV for a week.

Technology quickly exhumed me from isolation. A Toshiba laptop replaced the Olivetti, my keystrokes replaced the Linotype. Instead of searching for telex machines, I searched for clear phone lines. Instead of talking politics, my fellow reporters and I talked baud rates. On the Web, I could read what they were writing. Now my editors were only an email away. The paper that swore off pictures printed hundreds. On every story, I shot myself repeatedly.

It was thrilling to see my own photos on Page One. I treated myself to a micro four-thirds Olympus E-P2. It takes fine pictures in low light, HD videos and, with a microphone shoe, records good sound. Much as it hurts to steal work from real photographers, it's a relief not to have them underfoot. Yet I have anachronistic misgivings about shooting myself, both physical and philosophical.

In an upstate New York dump one winter's day, I was watching falcons chase seagulls off trash heaps. It was sleeting. The falconer, a young woman, had driven to a hilltop and stood with a falcon on her forearm while I interviewed her. I had a notebook in my left hand, an umbrella jammed under my right elbow, and was endeavoring to hold a pen and the camera in my right hand. At the crucial moment when the falconer removed the hood and released the bird, the umbrella slipped and my notebook fell into the mud. The camera got wet and I couldn't find the falcon in the LCD grayness.

Worse, I failed to record a mind movie. Images went straight from the dump and into the camera without passing into my notebook by way of my brain. My pictures stank and the story lost a daub of color.

Is that the future of feature writing? I hope not. I have faith in the primacy of print. Photos and videos can't pick up mumbled asides or peripheral incidents. Cameras and microphones invade the intimacy of interviews. A video camera, I've noticed, has the power to turn schlubby Americans into hucksters who emit sound bites laden with puffery suitable for the lamest of nut grafs. Yet pictures—especially the talkie-movie kind—perform feats beyond words. They have the potential to supplement print without supplanting it. So I have a compromise: With pen and notebook, collect the scenes, the dialogue and all the color a color story demands. Then put it all away and with a new mindset, and a set of the latest digital hardware, take pictures and make videos.

I've tried it. I've even tried it with a videographer. It works, as long as the videographer doesn't show up until after I've toggled my mindset to video. The *Journal's* video of a rail barge docking with a float bridge in New York harbor beat all my writerly attempts to explain the maneuver, as did its video on the mechanics of bagel slicing. In Nebraska, I recorded the sound of a gong that was tuned to the frequency of a dwarf planet near Pluto. No amount of word processing could imitate that tone. Much as I favor the old ways,

I'll admit that my Olympus E-P2 HD was better than my BIC Cristal Easy Glide at explaining how to peen a scythe. For some jobs, only the journalistic equivalent of a WeedWacker will do.

. . . .

Whacking Weeds

With a WeedWacker under his arm, Dan Kowalsky was at work trimming the median strip of U.S. Route 1 in suburban Westport, Conn., when he was asked, above the din: Why not use a scythe?

"You mean that Grim Reaper thing?" he yelled. "Can't get grass nice and short with that thing, nice and perfect."

People who scythe put up with a lot of Grim Reaper cracks. Then again, long-handled, crescent-bladed scythes don't use gas, don't get hot, don't make noise, do make for exercise, and do cut grass.

Which is what Jean-Paul Pauillac, a 55-year-old French chef, was doing a five-minute drive away. "This is my samurai chop," he said in his backyard, swinging a scythe through ankle-deep growth. His neighbors' lawns were cropped like putting greens. "They come to the fence and look," said Pauillac. "Maybe they think I'm cuckoo."

While Americans persist in cutting grass with labor-saving devices, faithful scythers believe their old tool has plenty of life left in it. In the dozens just 10 years ago, U.S. scythe sales are nearing 10,000 a year now, for a kit that costs about $200. Predictably, scythe buyers are small, green farmers; unpredictably, they are also city folk and suburbanites.

At Marugg Co., which has been selling scythes out of Tracy City, Tenn., since 1873, the typical scythe buyer used to be an Amish farmer or a horror-movie prop master, according to Amy Wilson, the current owner. Now, it's "anybody and everybody," she says. "It makes it difficult for advertising, but still..."

"I get emails from people who just want to mow the lawn," says Botan Anderson, a Wisconsin scythe promoter. Carol Bryan, owner of Scythe Supply, in Maine, says: "We have backyarders who say, 'My WeedWacker just threw a rock through the window. I want a…how do you pronounce that thing? A sith?'"

Ruth Callard, 58, a personal trainer, got a scythe (rhymes with writhe) to cut the grass around six apple trees that she and a few neighbors have planted on the I-5 freeway embankment in Seattle. The city let them plant but refused to mow. "It's the budget," says Callard, "so we bought the scythe. The hips do most of the work."

Patrick Crouch, 35, bought his to tend a community garden on central Detroit's "urban prairie." He likes it because it's "totally brutal." As he blogged: "What could be more badass than walking the streets of the Motor City with a scythe slung over one's shoulder?"

In Detroit, maybe, but to cut a wide swath through the Great American Lawn, scythers have longer rows to hoe. Scythes are poetic. ("My long scythe whispered," wrote Robert Frost; not, "My lawn mower whispered.") Yet scythes may be better known now to videogamers as the Dark Knight's favored weapon in "Final Fantasy XIV."

The early-American scythe (a British import) was, in fact, a back-aching tool with a humpy snath (the handle) and heavy blade. It was quickly superseded by mechanical mowers. Scythe sellers still make snaths, but an American hasn't forged a blade since 1958.

Germany's last scythe factory died with communism. Spain and France soon lost theirs. The favored source now is the Schrockenfux factory in Austria, a maker of quality ergonomic blades since 1540.

Schrockenfux produces 200,000 blades a year and sells 60,000 to Iran, having assured sanctions authorities of their peaceful intent. But in developing countries, it battles low-cost scythes from Turkey and Kyrgyzstan. Russia exports scythes, too (and hammers and sickles).

The situation raises a fear for the quality scythe's future. Peter Vido, a homesteader who subsists in New Brunswick, Canada, with one light bulb and a website devoted to scythes, worries that scythe production at Schrockenfux "may just roll over and die."

To keep it alive, he argues, "demand for quality blades in the wealthy countries must increase dramatically." It's happening, but a vital element is absent: qualified scythe instructors.

Duffers can pick up tips on the Web: Never scythe downhill; if you trip you might fall on the blade. Casualties are few, unless you're like British novelist Marcel Theroux. He scythes in the London suburb of Tooting, and committed the error of honing a blade while chatting with a neighbor. "I almost cut my thumb off," he says.

It takes a pro, nevertheless, to teach the perfect stroke. At this point, scythe pros are needles in haystacks—which explains why Kurt Weaver was happy to find Larry Cooper.

Weaver, 52, is a researcher who lives in a brick house in a suburb of Raleigh, N.C., with his wife, Stella, and their son, Oliver, who is nine. They have a front lawn, a back lawn, a driveway basketball hoop, and a garage with a scythe hanging on the wall.

In 2009, Weaver used it a few times to cut roadside grass for compost. "It can wear you out," he said. He has since let his scythe lie fallow, but on hearing that a pro was in town, Weaver said: "A scythe lesson? That'd be great."

Cooper, 54, is a blacksmith from Alabama who set up shop in the Raleigh area to make tools. When his WeedWacker broke in 2006, he got a scythe, studied the moves with an expert and became an expert himself.

"It's all subtleties," he said, rolling up to the Weaver's in his pickup one evening. "How to rotate. Lead with the shoulders. Don't work the arms. If it hurts, you're doing it wrong."

On seeing Weaver in the driveway with his scythe, Cooper told him, "You got a ditch blade there. A grass blade's skinnier."

"You want to demonstrate?" Weaver asked. First, Cooper gave him a lesson in sharpening (it's done by peening—with a hammer and anvil—never by grinding). Then he said, "We'll mow together."

Weaver took a swing at his back lawn. Cooper stopped him: "It's not a slap shot. It's not a hockey stick." He got a grass scythe from his truck and went into a smooth, floor-mopping motion.

"The blade stays on the ground," Cooper said. "Try it." Weaver did, and soon found his rhythm. "It really works," he said. "I can't wait to do the front lawn, see if anybody calls the cops."

To his son, who was standing to one side with an uncomprehending gaze, he said, "You want to learn to do this, Oliver?"

Oliver didn't. His father and Cooper scythed into the twilight. A riding mower droned somewhere up the street. Oliver got out a ball and shot baskets in the driveway until dinnertime.

2012

Chapter 6
FINAL EDIT

Rewrite, as I first understood the term, referred to a row of desks in a newsroom reserved for fast typers who take calls from the field and bash out stories on deadline—the ones who pick up when the reporter in the phone booth yells, "Get me rewrite!" At the *Wall Street Journal*, rewrite means what it says: An editor takes a story that a reporter believes to be a finished product, and writes it all over again. The procedure sharpens and shortens, corrects errors of style and substance, and requires reporters to answer a million questions. Much the same goes on at magazines, and while the *Journal's* daily pursuits have become more urgent, its Page One department often still lives up to its pet name: The Temple of News.

Some reporters don't mind rewrites. They answer questions with long memos, and get on with their next project. My ambition was to write markups—stories that don't need rewrites, only neatening here and there. It makes me feel good. Three years into my *Journal* job, Bill Mathewson, a Page One copy editor, walked up to my desk in a bad mood. I had handed in a story about a kid who'd been lost while hiking on a New Hampshire mountain. With scissors and tape, I'd stuck in a new paragraph. Back then, copy was faxed to the printing plant. If a paragraph was improperly stuck in, black lines would make the fax unreadable. I had stuck in my paragraph the wrong way. "If you're going to write markups," Mathewson said, "you have to do this right."

That was my first compliment for writing markups. John Barnett and Mack Solomon, two editors on Page One, bought me a martini in Hoboken shortly afterward and told me I could write. I had no idea. At a Chinese restaurant on a Friday afternoon,

Don Moffitt said, "By the fifth paragraph, you should say what the story's about. It's English composition." I didn't know. Hints from editors kept dropping at the *Journal*: I learned the difference between *such as* and *like* from Henry Myers; between *since* and *because* from Kathy Christensen; between *this* and *that* from David Sanford. Because of that, I have never since begun a sentence such as this with anything but *that*. Most important, in a newsroom where events of the moment always seem momentous, Mike Gartner and Peter Kann showed me the uses of bemused detachment.

Once I was able to write markups, I believed my stories would go to print untouched by editors. I was mistaken. Mike Marks, who tended my earlier work, asked seventeen questions per thousand words. Dan Kelly asked seven per inch. My bureau chiefs asked questions. So did my foreign editors, chief Page One editors, copydesk editors and final readers. Kelly's fixes, if any, were so unobtrusive I didn't notice them. (He did replace "Idaho" with "Russet Burbank" in my Polish potato story.) Other copy editors could on occasion take a sentence like, "These are the times that try men's souls," and make it: "These days, men's souls are being tried, more and more." One Saturday, after I'd filed a story on Poland's feuding chief rabbis, an editor sent me so many questions I was driven to disrespect the Sabbath: "All my life I work and I slave to write nice articles," I wrote back, "and what do I get? I get questions. Questions, questions, questions. All the time questions. If I get one more question I'm going to *plotz*! Enough already with the questions!"

Editors in receipt of memos like that are apt to approach a reporter's next story in the way lab rats approach a piece of cheese after having nibbled one that delivers an electric shock. It's a form of aversion therapy that I practiced, with mixed results, for few decades. Some lines I once snipped from a *New Yorker* article and kept in my wallet have lent me courage: "You can reach a nice rapport with editors, but sometimes you've got to educate them. They've got to realize that you're not going to take crap any more than they are, or screw up your livelihood by jeopardizing yourself. You're an independent contractor, within your work, and the price of liberty is eternal vigilance." The tactic doesn't win popularity contests. "Like a clever five-year-old, Barry likes to test limits and pitch fits," David Sanford wrote (in jest, I think) to the London bureau for my good-bye roast. I reached a nice rapport with David. A fine writer in his own career, he has fussed over my copy for 32 years. Someone reading our emails might think we can't stand each other; in fact, we've bickered over things dear to us both: what words mean, and how they sound. David cares about accuracy. I hear music. We'd meet in the middle: He'd ask plain questions, I'd insert poetic answers—attaching lists of excuses for doing less than requested. David didn't just edit my copy. He contained my impulses.

After years of questions, questions, questions, I did evolve a superego of sorts. To avoid rewrites, I tried to play inside the *Journal's* creative sandbox. My ideas qualified as news. My stories had nut grafs. My reporting was solid enough, much of the time, to fill holes detected at deadline. I hewed to my allotted space. Impossibly slow, I put in long hours to feign speed. My reward was unimaginable freedom to travel and to write about anything that came to mind for a publication that multiplied my every keystroke two million times.

I didn't want to use the word *you* in this book, but I'll break my rule and use it now: You can't do this (or that) without copy editors. You can't do it without bureau chiefs and interpreters, or neighbors, friends and family. You can't do it, especially, without the people who open their lives to you when all you open is a notebook. Going out and getting the color is like swimming solo across the English Channel. You can't do it alone.

. . . .

Swimming Solo

ON THE ENGLISH CHANNEL

From his boat's cabin Mike Oram can make out the volleyball players on the French coast, less than a mile away. He sticks his head out the port window to let Margaret Broenniman know.

"You can see the land," he shouts. "It's in front of you all the time. See it!"

Broenniman, in the water, doesn't seem to hear. Her ears are plugged with cotton and thickly greased. She doesn't seem to see. Oil films her goggles; her eyes are swollen nearly shut. She has stopped swimming. A jellyfish hovers at her kneecap.

"How far is it?" she says, tilting her head toward the deck.

Oram leaves the cabin, leans out over the gunwale and shouts louder: "Start swimming!"

"Oh God," Broenniman says. "I want to finish."

"Don't worry about it, girl," Oram screams. "Keep going. You can't afford to stop!"

Without a word, Broenniman resumes her crawl.

Solo swimmers don't cross the English Channel alone. Ted May tried it in 1956. He died. Oil slicks, jellyfish, ships, seaweed, garbage, cold water, rough water, the fog, the tide—all lie in wait for swimmers in the channel. So Margaret Broenniman hired Mike Oram to get her across. He does that for a living.

One try in 10 used to succeed. One in five does now. Fit swimmers and smart escorts explain the improvement. But the channel probably is still the most taxing of long-distance swims. In 109 years, only 261 aspirants have matched Capt. Matthew Webb, who swam it first. And the channel still deals in death.

In August, a 36-year-old Sri Lankan, Kumar Anandan, set off on his swim. The weather was fine, his escort seasoned. Four miles out, Anandan broke down and became the first person to die under escort. He was thin. The cold killed him.

Margaret Broenniman was in Massachusetts when it happened. At 21, between her junior and senior years at Smith College, she was training hard for the channel swim. With Maura Fitzpatrick, a classmate who would try crossing at the same time, she had swum the 12-mile Boston Harbor Race, fought the cold currents of the Connecticut River and stroked miles a day in Smith's pool. A friend brought the news of Anandan's death.

"I listened," Broenniman said later. "I didn't react. Then I sat down alone and let myself get scared."

She and Fitzpatrick left for London on a Saturday with Kim Bierwert, their coach at Smith. Mike Oram, whose name they picked last spring from the Channel Swimming Association's list of pilots, had proposed a swim on the next neap tide, when the channel's flow would ease. That gave them a week to settle down. At the National Gallery, sightseeing, Fitzpatrick bought a print entitled *Shipping Becalmed Offshore*; Broenniman bought a Renoir of two women rowing on a placid river. On Tuesday, the swimmers took a train to Dover, checked into a guest house and walked to the beach. The sky was clear, the channel calm.

It was calm again Wednesday, and Oram knew it couldn't last. So he traded a good tide for the best weather. He told his swimmers they would go that night.

The women marshaled their nerve. Then the fog rolled in. It's hard to swim around a supertanker you can't see. Oram told them to wait a day. On Thursday, fog still clung to the cliffs. The women ate potatoes and bread ("carbo-loading," Broenniman calls it) and went to bed early. Oram woke them at 9 o'clock that night to call off the swim again.

The wait is a channel swimmer's first trial. Some have waited months for weather and tide to coincide. Broenniman and Fitzpatrick waited only one day more. Friday, the fog thinned. The neap tide was due at 5 a.m., Saturday. Oram told his swimmers to get ready.

It's Saturday now—4:50 a.m.

"You want to jump in, girls," Oram says.

Aremajay, his 36-foot, 26-year-old sailboat, idles off Shakespeare beach, west of Dover, sail furled, engine fuming in the dark. Alongside rides *Amber*, Dave Whyte's boat. He will escort Fitzpatrick, with her family and Bierwert, the coach, on deck to cheer her on. Oram's wife and Broenniman's family are aboard *Aremajay*. So is Jane Randall, an observer for the Channel Swimming Association. She enforces the rules:

Swimmers must walk into the water and walk out on the other side; they can't use floats or flippers, and not once can they touch the boat or anybody on it.

Oram has filled in his customs form ("Destination: French coast") and collected his fee from Bierwert: 550 pounds—about

$750—for each swimmer. The women have coated their broad-shouldered bodies with a mixture of Vaseline and lanolin, four pounds of it apiece. They have fitted their goggles, pulled on their caps, pinned luminous "light sticks" to their tank suits.

"Off you go, then," Oram says. Fitzpatrick leaps. Broenniman composes herself and dives. They walk up onto the beach and stand together as a local photographer pops his bulbs. Then they walk back into the black water and swim swiftly toward the demon that Mike Oram thought he had escaped: a bank of dense fog.

It encloses the convoy in an intimate pool, lit dimly by the dawn. In *Aremajay*'s cabin, Oram positions himself at the wheel, radio above to his left, radarscope above to his right. *Amber* begins to fall behind as it tracks Fitzpatrick, the slower swimmer—and it doesn't have radar.

A foghorn blasts. Something very big is very close. Oram jumps from the wheel to the scope and back to the wheel. He glances at Broenniman, oblivious off the port bow, hits his own high-pitched horn, and gets Dave Whyte on the radio.

"Dave, keep your eyes open. You've got a vessel abeam."

"Cheers," Dave says.

Foghorns blow from every direction now. "A ferry closing in on us," Oram says, his eyes hidden in the scope's viewer. "A ship astern of us...." He hits the horn, adjusts the throttle and swings to the scope again. "It's going around the front of us, going the wrong way.... He's right smack down our bows...."

Broenniman's mother climbs up from the galley with a mug of soup. "Do you think they know we're here?" she asks.

His beard wild, his belly escaping his shirt, Oram takes a deep breath and lets it out. "You earns your living," he says, addressing the wheel. For a long moment he looks out at his swimmer, then turns to her mother. "They usually miss us," he says.

Mike Oram has been at this three years. He is 37. A mechanic by trade, he has owned a garage and a color-photo lab, bought and rebuilt country cottages, organized fox hunts. "No good having a hobby unless it pays for itself," he likes to say.

Sixteen swimmers have hired him this season. Fifty or so usually try crossing the channel between June and October. In recent years, they have included a deaf-mute boy from India, a 12-year-old girl, a 65-year-old man and an epileptic sponsored by the company that makes his pills. Except for the epileptic, they all made it across.

"Anybody's got to be slightly crazy to get in there," says Jane Randall, the observer, who has been dozing on the skipper's bunk. "Slightly?" Oram says. "They have to be totally mental." He puts the engine into neutral. Time to feed the swimmer.

"I have that soup," says her mother. Oram vetoes it. "Hot lemon squash with dextrose," he insists. "Not much digestion. Keeps the cramps down. Saves time." His wife hands him the brew in a paper cup. He climbs over the rail, leans out, and passes it to Broenniman. She drinks. In 20 seconds, she is swimming.

Her pace, as her father clocks it, holds at 78 strokes a minute. Her speed is a strong two knots. Only 20 miles separate Dover from Cap Gris-Nez, the nub on the French coast closest to England. But a swimmer can cover 40 miles across the channel, fighting the tide.

The flood tide sweeps a swimmer up-channel on the first leg of her crossing and the ebb carries her down on the second. If she has made enough headway when the tide turns, she will nick Cap Gris-Nez on the ebb. Penny Lee Dean, the record holder, did it that way six years ago in seven hours and 40 minutes. But if a swimmer misses the cape, the next flood will turn her around and drive her toward Calais. Crossings like that have taken as long as 20 hours.

The idea is to swim hard until the tide turns while keeping energy in store for the second leg, and maybe, a third. For five hours, Broenniman swims hard—through Coke cans and driftwood and seaweed, and through the fog. *Amber* drops back more, but stays in range of *Aremajay's* radar. Plotting the optimum course, Oram keeps up his frenetic watch for ships. Then, at last, the fog lifts. The sun comes out. And Margaret Broenniman starts to tire.

After her fifth feed, she asks for another in 45 minutes instead of the usual hour. Oram won't have it.

"You're halfway through," he yells at her. "That doesn't mean you can slow down." And he lectures her parents: "They always do that. They get a bit ratty and a bit shouty. They don't stop for a drink. They stop for an excuse. Totally ignore her. Make her fight for it."

He returns to the cabin and checks the radarscope. It registers the French coast.

Soon, Broenniman stops. She wants to be fed. "You're shortening your hour," Oram shouts. "Why?" Broenniman doesn't answer. She just starts swimming. "You've got to know your way around these Americans," Oram says. "They can't hack defeat." But in two hours, he is giving her an early feed himself.

"She's getting cold," he tells her parents, "getting tired, going through a bit of mental anguish." Her pace has slowed. Well onto the ebb tide, Oram has recalculated her course. If she does graze the cape, it will be with minutes to spare before the tide turns.

Broenniman plods on toward the three-mile buoy. The grease on her shoulders has worn off. The sun and salt have turned her back the color of raw hamburger. As the coast appears in the haze, another escort and another swimmer approach from the opposite direction. Margaret Broenniman and Kevin Murphy splash within a few hundred yards of each other and never know it.

"They always give up here," Jane Randall says when Broenniman reaches the buoy; this swimmer keeps crawling. At the next feed, Oram tells her: "Swim well and you'll be on the beach in two hours." Cap Gris-Nez lighthouse soon comes into view. But the tide is pushing her past it.

"This is the hard bit," Oram says. "She's struggling now. If she stops again, she's out."

"How much farther?" Broenniman demands.

"C'mon, fight it!" Oram shouts—and he keeps on shouting until his swimmer is inside the headland.

A windsurfer sails up on the blue bay. A lobsterman circles, standing in his little boat. "*C'est bon,*" he calls. "*Allez!*" On the beach, people stop what they're doing and converge in a cheering crowd.

Oram lets *Aremajay* drift. He toots the horn as his swimmer walks out of the water, 10 hours and 37 minutes after she walked in. Finishing strongly, Maura Fitzpatrick will touch France half an hour later.

Broenniman bends to collect a few pebbles as souvenirs. Then the lobsterman gives her a lift back to the boat, and the volleyball game resumes.

1984

ACKNOWLEDGMENTS

The professors in my school of journalism were the editors and reporters I worked with, and alongside. By turns pushing, pulling, encouraging and demanding, their direct involvement in my work—or often their mere presence within earshot—gave me the kind of education I hope some readers may gain from this book.

Here are a few, in order of appearance: Shelly Binn, John McCandlish Phillips, Ted Fiske, Mike Kaufman, Dave Jones and Arthur Gelb at the *New York Times*. Mike Gartner, Roger Ricklefs, Sonny Kleinfield, Glynn Mapes, Fred Taylor, Bill Clabby, Stew Pinkerton, John Barnett, Mack Solomon, Mike Marks, Dan Kelly, Henry Meyers and Paul Martin at the *Wall Street Journal* in New York. Larry O'Donnell, Seth Lipsky, Neil Ulman, Bob Keatley, Peter Kann and Norm Pearlstine at the *Journal* when I was in Singapore. Paul Steiger, Alan Otten, Phil Revzin, Kathy Christensen, Tony Horwitz, Geraldine Brooks, Roger Thurow, Jim Perry, Larry Ingrassia, Karen House, Jim Stewart, Lee Lescaze and John Bussey at the *Journal* when I was in London. Ken Wells, John Brecher, Bill Grueskin, Mike Miller, Jim Sterba, Jonathan Friedland, Bruce Orwall, Mike Williams, Mike Allen, Gabe Kahn, Lisa Bannon, David Sanford, Carrie Dolan, Chris Rhoads, Josh Prager, Suzanne Sataline, Rebecca Blumenstein, Matt Murray and Alex Martin at the *Journal* when I was back in New York.

Beyond newspapers, my encouragement came early from Corona Machemer, lately from Vauhini Vara, and has kept coming from Mark Kramer. My thanks to Jan Chamier for her kind editing of this book, to Araby Williams for the video version, to Stephen Shepard and Tim Harper at CUNY Journalism Press for making it happen, to Bianca Flowers for helping design www.barrynewmanjournalist.com, and to John Oakes and his crew at OR Books, including Emily Freyer for marketing and distribution, Matthew Schantz for publicity and Courtney Andujar for designing the cover and overseeing production. Finally, my gratitude to Carol, Jon and Emily for their devoted cheerleading and, of course, to my wife, Dinah, for her love, tolerance, and unconditional fact checking.

APPENDIX

Most of the articles in *News to Me* first appeared in the *Wall Street Journal*, sometimes in slightly different form.

PART ONE: IDEAS

1. ESCAPE FROM HISTORY
As for Canada, Finding the Border Is a Bit of a Trick—With Weeds to Be Whacked And Markers to Be Found, It's a 5,525-Mile Problem. July 10, 2007. *The Wall Street Journal*

2. HUH?
Don't Be a Square At the Post Office—There's a Surcharge—Card Makers Feel Boxed In By Rules Favoring Rectangles; Friedman's 'Debacle.' November 15, 2007. *The Wall Street Journal*

3. RELATIVES ARE EVERYTHING
In Movies, to Err Is Human, To Nitpick Is Even More So—A Committed Cadre of Carpers Catches Flubs in Flicks; Rikki Rosen's Watching. March 25, 2010. *The Wall Street Journal*

4. NEIGHBORHOOD WATCH
The Spritz Mystique: Cool Old Bottles, Service With Attitude—Beberman Plies Brooklyn In Last Real Seltzer Truck; Poseurs Need Not Apply. December 17, 2003. *The Wall Street Journal*

5. IT'S ONE THING AFTER ANOTHER
If It's a Russian Rub You Want, Have We Got A Place! If Turning Beet-Red Isn't Your Thing, Don't Forget The Kishke & the Kreplach. May 3, 1974. *The Wall Street Journal*

5. **MISINTERPRETATION**
    Brooklyn Exile Seeks The Swedish Essence Of Pickled Herring—
    Stockholm Lovingly Honors Fish in Myriad Varieties; But Ocean
    Avenue It's Not. January 19, 1984. The Wall Street Journal

6. **ABROAD AT HOME**
    Empire of Light: Immigrant Waves Power the Survival Of Tiny
    Retail Row—'Lampland' Lasts a Century Battling Suburban
    Malls, Joining Global Commerce—On Two City Blocks, 29 Stores.
    August 27, 2002. The Wall Street Journal

7. **GATHERING STRING**
    Global Chatter: World Speaks English, Often None Too Well;
    Results Are Tragicomic—Talking Turkey With Japan, Czechs Can
    Get the Drift; Compu-Jargon Is Vexing—Some Fatal Miscues in
    the Air. March 22, 1995. The Wall Street Journal

8. **GATEKEEPERS**
    Last Call for Lynchburg (Pop. 361) As Jack Daniel's Rejiggers Its
    Label—Proprietor Lem Motlow Had to Go, Too, And There Are
    Some Other Little Fiddles. June 3, 2011. The Wall Street Journal

PART THREE: FROM REPORTING TO WRITING

1. **THE PERFECT VEHICLE**
    Oscar Who? This Time, the Award Goes to...the Maker of the Best
    Award for the Underappreciated—Creators of Offbeat Trophies
    Fete Their Own; Ms. Champagne Goes Up Against Award Fash-
    ioned From Spumante Bottle. March 24, 2012. The Wall Street
    Journal

2. **GET OUT OF THE OFFICE**
    Its Eye on Fries, Poland Pursues Potato Parity—Its Agronomists
    Slowly Learn To Raise a Tuber Worthy Of the Golden Arches. Octo-
    ber 9, 1986. The Wall Street Journal

3. **GETTING THEM TALKING**
    There Are Tea Parties and Tea Parties, And Here the Twain Meet,
    Uneasily—Richardson, Who Knows How to Brew, Visits Ms. Sims,
    Steeped in Politics. December 24, 2009. The Wall Street Journal

4. **PROFILES OF THE UNKNOWN**
    *Lonely Causes—A Matter of Gravity: Restoration Campaign Finds
    Converts; They Often Find Ridicule—'Intactivists' Seek to Undo
    A Long-Practiced Ritual; The Going Is Very Slow—One Man's
    Weighty Solution. December 28, 2000. The Wall Street Journal*

5. **GOING PLACES**
    *The Outsiders: Beyond 'Core' Region Of Europe, Many Lead Lives
    of Abject Poverty—Old World of Wealth, Style Bypasses Millions
    Living On Fringes of Continent—'Work Until You Drop Dead.'
    July 3, 1985. The Wall Street Journal*

6. **DUALITY**
    *The One and Only, Original Harry's Bar: Its Tangled History—
    Venice Has One, as of Course, Does Paris; Beyond That, Copies Are
    Everywhere. February 18, 1994. The Wall Street Journal*

PART FOUR: WRITING

1. **OPENERS**
    *The Sewer-Fat Crisis Stirs a National Stink; Sleuths Probe Flush-
    ing—Illegal Dumping of Fryer Grease Leads to Infarctions; Yikes,
    A Municipal Heart Attack. June 4, 2001. The Wall Street Journal*

2. **NUTS**
    *To Keep the Finger Out of Finger Food, Inventors Seek a Better
    Bagel Cutter—Slips of the Knife, Resulting ER Trips Spawn Battle
    of the Guillotine vs. the Brooklyn Slicer. November 30, 2009. The
    Wall Street Journal*

3. **ORGANIZING PRINCIPLES**
    *A Campground Grows in Brooklyn, Bringing a New York Edge to
    Roughing It—Adventurers Bed Down on Old Airfield, 15 Miles
    From Times Square; 'We're Used to, You Know, Sand and Grass.'
    August 13, 2011. The Wall Street Journal*

4. **KEEP IT SHORT**
    *Albanians Awake, Fitfully, From a Kind Of National Coma—
    They Can Speak to Foreigners And Even Own Cars Now, But Ask:
    What's a Fax? March 11, 1991. The Wall Street Journal*

5. **DIGITIZING**
   Who Needs a WeedWacker When You Can Use a Scythe?—Grim Reaper Jokes Aside, Suburbanites Take Swing at Ancient Mower. June 30, 2012. *The Wall Street Journal*

6. **FINAL EDIT**
   You Need Company If You're Swimming The English Channel—Escort Who Knows Dangers Contributes to the Success Of Margaret Broenniman. September 17, 1984. *The Wall Street Journal*

CUNY Journalism Press

The CUNY Journalism Press is the academic publishing imprint of the CUNY Graduate School of Journalism. Part of the City University of New York, the CUNY Journalism Press publishes both traditional print books and e-books about journalists and journalism. We welcome inquiries about our books and our authors, and we welcome proposals for future books from prospective authors. See more at: www.press.journalism.cuny.edu

The Press was launched in the autumn of 2012 with the mission of publishing serious books about journalism and the news media — history, theory, criticism, craft, memoir and more. The Press is organized, in conjunction with the independent publishing house OR Books, as a new model for publishing — some call it co-publishing — in response to changes in the publishing marketplace and publishing technology. Our aim is to publish books by, for and about journalists that might not otherwise be published in the commercial marketplace.

The CUNY Graduate School of Journalism, widely known for its emphasis on multimedia, interactive and cross-platform reporting and storytelling, offers an intensive three-semester Master of Arts in Journalism curriculum. The school is also known for its innovative training in emerging technology and its Tow-Knight Center for Entrepreneurial Journalism, dedicated to finding new business models. The school is the first in the world to offer an M.A. in Entrepreneurial Journalism, and is planning to add an M.A. in Social Journalism beginning in 2015. See more at www.journalism.cuny.edu

Also Published by CUNY Journalism Press

THE PLEASURES OF BEING OUT OF STEP
NAT HENTOFF'S LIFE IN JOURNALISM, JAZZ AND THE FIRST AMENDMENT
by David L. Lewis
ISBN 978-1-939293-19-0 (paperback)
ISBN 978-1-939293-20-6 (e-book)

GEEKS BEARING GIFTS
IMAGINING NEW FUTURES FOR NEWS
by Jeff Jarvis
ISBN 978-1-939293-73-2 (paperback)
ISBN 978-1-939293-74-9 (e-book)

DISTANT WITNESS
SOCIAL MEDIA, THE ARAB SPRING AND A JOURNALISM REVOLUTION
by Andy Carvin
ISBN 978-1-939293-02-2 (paperback)
ISBN 978-1-939293-03-9 (e-book)

FIGHTING FOR THE PRESS
THE INSIDE STORY OF THE PENTAGON PAPERS AND OTHER BATTLES
by James Goodale
ISBN 978-1-939293-12-1 (hardcover)
ISBN 978-1-939293-08-4 (paperback)
ISBN 978-1-939293-09-1 (e-book)

CITIZENS RISING
INDEPENDENT JOURNALISM AND THE SPREAD OF DEMOCRACY
by David Hoffman
ISBN 978-1-939293-29-9 (paperback)
ISBN 978-1-939293-30-5 (e-book)

THE ILLUSTRATED COURTROOM: 50 YEARS OF COURT ART
by Elizabeth Williams and Sue Russell
ISBN 978-1-939293-52-7 (paperback)
ISBN 978-1-939293-53-4 (e-book)

ABOUT THE AUTHOR

BARRY NEWMAN went to work for the *Wall Street Journal* in 1970 after a few years as a copy boy and news clerk at the *New York Times*. In 43 years at the Journal, he wrote more than 400 features for the front page from more than 65 countries and most states in the USA. He won the Overseas Press Club's award for explanatory journalism and the National Press Club's award for humor writing. His stories have been collected in several books, including *East of the Equator, The Literary Journalists* and *Floating Off the Pag*e.